Literary Taste, Culture and Mass Communication

Volume 14

THE CULTURAL DEBATE PART II

Literary Taste, Culture and Mass Communication

Volume 14

THE CULTURAL DEBATE PART II

edited by

Peter Davison/Rolf Meyersohn/Edward Shils

CHADWYCK-HEALEY CAMBRIDGE
CHADWYCK-HEALEY INC. TEANECK, NJ

Chadwyck-Healey Ltd
20 Newmarket Road
Cambridge CB5 8DT

ISBN 0 85964 049 3

Chadwyck-Healey Inc.
623 Martense Avenue
Teaneck, NJ 07666

Library of Congress Cataloging in Publication Data.
Main entry under title:
Uses of literacy.

   (Literary taste, culture, and mass communication; v. 13-14)
   Includes indexes.
   1. Popular culture – Addresses, essays, lectures.
   2. Mass media – Social aspects – Addresses, essays, lectures.
   I. Series

AC1 . L79 vol. 13-14 [HM101] 301 . 16′ls [081] 77-90622

British Library Cataloguing in Publication Data

Literary taste, culture and mass communication.
   Vol. 14: The cultural debate, part 2.
   1. Arts and society – Addresses, essays, lectures.
   I. Davison, Peter II. Meyersohn, Rolf III. Shils, Edward Benjamin IV. Cultural debate

700 NX180 . S6 77-90623

Printed in Great Britain at the University Press, Cambridge

Contents

Introduction

Cecilia Brady, early in the first chapter of Scott Fitzgerald's *The Last Tycoon*, remarks (and see 13/xvi):

> When I was at Bennington some of the English teachers who pretended an indifference to Hollywood or its products, really *hated* it. Hated it way down deep as a threat to their existence.

Looking back over the volumes of this series, with, fresh in mind, the experience of compiling the index, one cannot but be struck by the appositeness of Cecilia's assessment. The responses of many critics and scholars, literary and sociological, imply or directly point to the threat which mass culture, mass communication, or simply 'the mass', presents to 'existence'. The threat may be described as specifically directed at culture — the cultural, the cultured — and thus only indirectly at the existence of those interpreting events in this manner; but sometimes, as for example, in the work of those who fled Hitler's Germany, the threat to existence itself is more personal, more direct. Inevitably, this experience conditioned their approach to the object of their study. That Horkheimer is looking over his shoulder in his remarks in 'Art and Mass Culture' is plain:

> The only hope remaining is that the deaf ears in Europe imply an opposition to the lies that are being hammered at men from all sides and that men are following their leaders with their eyes tight shut. One day we may learn that in the depths of their hearts, the masses, even in fascist countries, secretly knew the truth and disbelieved the lie . . .
>
> 12/17

It is understandable that Adorno should have written in 'Cultural Criticism and Society':

> Cultural criticism finds itself faced with the final stage of the dialect of culture and barbarism. To write poetry after Auschwitz is barbaric. And this corrodes even the knowledge of why it has become impossible to write poetry today.
>
> 1/122

It did not, however, require the direct experience of the Germany of the 1930s to occasion such a view of the decline of cultural standards. F.R. Leavis, in his Retrospect to *Scrutiny*, compared the Sunday papers of that time (1962) with those of but ten years earlier. He argued that they had 'virtually abandoned . . . all pretence of expecting what can plausibly be called educated attention . . . They see as their freely avowable function today that of being agreeably distracting and time-passing' (13/106-7). The decline since then has continued and it is even more striking if one contrasts, say, *The Daily Mail* of the first decade of this century with what that newspaper now offers. How very, very limited, after a century or so of full-scale education, is the degree of serious attention that is expected of readers of most of the British newspapers. It is that which gives especial bite to Leavis's more damaging claim that 'the culture of the Sunday papers is what tends more and more to prevail at the senior levels in universities' (13/107). This may seem exaggerated — one hopes it is — but I have even now just heard, on a 'serious' radio programme about literature, a senior academic's scholarly credentials described in terms of his writing thousand-word reviews for 'the heavy Sundays' (BBC 4, 11.12.1979). These are not, of course, his true scholarly achievements; they are simply those which strike an 'educated commentator' as particularly impressive.

It will be obvious from the series that a less than one-sided, less despairing view of mass culture is also possible. Edward Shils makes a strong case for a more balanced approach, urging that

> intellectuals should not, out of impossible political zeal or out of furtive indulgence in pleasures which they know to be unworthy of their own traditions, blame these newly-born strata for ruining what is neither yet ruined nor necessarily ruined.
>
> 13/38

Michael Wilding, writing in the Australian journal *Dissent*, took to task what he called the 'amateur-sociologist literary-critics', arguing that 'A commercial elite running the media is no worse than a moralistic elite, or a morally-improving-art elite' (13/176); and Herbert Gans has explained in detail why mass culture in America is a manifestation of that society's pluralism and democracy (1/233-304).

It is not my purpose here to make some attempt to resolve the multitude of arguments on this and every other topic advanced in this series; that is for those for whom the series is intended, each in his or her own way; that, indeed, is the function of the series. Nevertheless, it might be proper to offer one or two comments, if only with diffidence.

It would be easy to dismiss Adorno's approach if only because events have overtaken his rhetoric. Poetry, and much other creative art, has proved possible after Auschwitz. Alan Swingewood discriminates between the approaches of Adorno and Horkheimer, who see capitalist culture leading to 'social and political disintegration exemplified in an anonymous mass culture', and Benjamin, who saw the possibility of a capitalist culture with 'enormous potential for the development of a democratic, collectivist culture'. Although Benjamin may exaggerate certain aspects of his argument, says Swingewood, 'he never attempts to argue that capitalist culture must inevitably achieve the total and passive integration of the masses'. He concludes that

> Capitalist culture is not a totalitarian system, it is not a form of domination exercised from above. The decay of the aura [associated with great aesthetic works] and the mass reproduction of high culture and the trends towards the artistic depiction of

reality in everyday terms are elements of a potentially democratic culture and not the symptoms of cultural stagnation and decline.[1]

This is surely an accurate analysis and certainly one in which I should like to place some confidence. For, whereas I agree with the description of a daily and Sunday press in Britain which decreasingly has a right to claim its reader's serious attention,[2] and that the brighter hopes of universal primary and secondary education, and wider access to tertiary education, have been in some measure unrealised, there is, as the Introduction to volume 9 suggested, much to record on the positive side of the cultural balance sheet (9/viii).

Yet, nagging fears remain. Poetry did survive Auschwitz, but may not Adorno, in the long run, be right?

The premise upon which most literary critical and much sociological cultural analysis is based is that, put very crudely, there is a high art which can and should be made available to all. Failure to support Wesker's Centre 42 or success in the development of good youth orchestras in Britain are then duly entered in the balance sheet of cultural development and a profit or loss declared. Alongside that higher art — or against it, if you will — is a powerful, commercial industry that seeks in the main (to adapt Leavis) to be agreeably distracting and time-passing. Now, whether cultural development can be realised; whether such a powerful form of mass entertainment is destructive or not; whether so much effort should be devoted to promoting and satisfying Ennui For All, are all questions to be asked. These volumes are full of attempts at such analysis. But I am mindful of another way of looking at the issues involved. These were conveniently suggested by the dramatist Trevor Griffiths in an interview with Catherine Itzin and Simon Trussler in 1976.[3] He was asked about his play, *Comedians* (1975), which, it was suggested, was 'an overtly political piece'. 'Yes', he agreed,

[1] Alan Swingewood, *The Myth of Mass Culture* (London 1977), pp.120, 122, 123. This is a lucid, clear-sighted attack on the problem of mass culture. It ranges over a very wide field of literary, sociological, and philosophical approaches from de Tocqueville to the present day. It considers, for example, the work of the Frankfurt School; Shils and Bell; Eliot, Leavis, Hoggart, and Raymond Williams; and such creative writers as Tressell, Greenwood, Grassic Gibbon, Braine, Sillitoe, and Hines. It also has a very useful bibliography.

[2] British television, despite occasional attempts at full-scale studies of current problems, too often only simulates earnestness. Its approach is epitomised by the favourite device used by many interviewers to wind up a discussion. A short interview on a complex topic will end with a demand for a summary conclusion 'in a sentence'. Not only does the interviewer often require more time to frame the question than he allows for an answer (itself sometimes cut short by, 'Sorry, we must leave it there. Sue —'), but too often, one suspects, the broadcasters underestimate the capacity of a mass audience to be interested in a serious current issue.

[3] *Theatre Quarterly,* VI, 22 (1976), 42.

> It's basically about two traditions — the social-democratic and the revolutionary tradition. It's about a tradition in culture that, say, Richard Hoggart represents, which is the persuasive, the rational, the humane tradition — arguing, educating for good, trying to change through education, through example. Set against that, there is a younger tradition, very violent, very angry, very disturbed, that says, 'No, that isn't the way'.

Almost as an afterthought he added, 'The play has been read as being about humour, as a play about comedians. At another level, it is probably that too'.

Could it be that that younger tradition not only rejects the rational, humane tradition, attempting to effect change through education, but is also uninterested in, and barely heeds, the alternative offered of Ennui For All? Could it be that that older tradition is Adorno's 'poetry' and that it cannot, in the long term, survive Auschwitz? If that is so, the centre of discussion now needs to be shifted radically if we are to be able to assess what is happening in societies which have inherited that older tradition. To repeat a line of a quotation from Dr Johnson's *A Journey to the Western Isles of Scotland* already given (5/xiv):

> The true state of every nation is the state of common life. The manners of a people are not to be found in the schools of learning, or the palaces of greatness, where the national character is obscured or obliterated by travel or instruction, by philosophy or vanity . . . .

But perhaps, as some of the studies in Further Reading may suggest, a start has been made.

Finally, although inevitably misprints in such a lengthy series will creep in, one in particular must be mentioned. The Introduction to volume 7 contains on p. viii a very curious sub-heading: 'Civil War'. Quite how this got into the final version escapes me but it does *not* refer to what follows! The two words should simply follow the last word of the preceding paragraph, preceded by a colon and printed in light roman, not bold, type.

PETER DAVISON

Further Reading

This volume and volume 13 form two parts of one subject: *The Cultural Debate.* Much of what would be appropriate for Further Reading is given in volume 13. Alan Swingewood's *The Myth of Mass Culture* (London 1977) makes a fitting appearance in this final list, however, and reference to it has already been made in the Introduction. F.R. Leavis and *Scrutiny* have frequently been a point of reference throughout the series. Leavis's literary criticism has recently been studied by R.P. Bilan *(The Literary Criticism of F.R. Leavis,* Cambridge 1979), and, belatedly, a full-scale study of *Scrutiny* has now been published: *The Moment of 'Scrutiny'* (Francis Mulhern, New Left Books, 1979), treating its subject from a Marxist point of view. A useful collection of essays under the title *Culture and Crisis in Britain in the Thirties,* ed. Jon Clark, Margot Heinemann, David Margolies, and Carole Snee, was also published in 1979. This touches on a number of matters discussed in these volumes, especially volume 11. The twelve essays include considerations of Leavis and *Scrutiny;* Auden, MacNeice, Cornford; *The Left Review;* the Left Book Club; theatre, literature and the cinema, making particular reference to Agitprop and Unity Theatre; and 'Film-making and the Working Class', which gives some account of the influence of *Kino News.*

Among the work done on aspects of what Trevor Griffiths calls 'the younger tradition' (see Introduction), attention might be drawn to what has been published by the Centre for Contemporary Cultural Studies at the University of Birmingham, England. In addition to books emanating from the Centre's staff and graduate students in this field, a number of relevant articles have appeared in the Centre's journal, *Cultural Studies,* and the Centre has also issued some fifty Occasional Papers in stencilled form. There is sometimes a measure of overlap between the stencilled papers and the journal and both should be consulted. Thus, Dick Hebdige's 'Reggae, Rasta and Rudies' in *Cultural Studies* 7/8 (summer 1975) is an extract from his thesis, from which the full-length section on this topic, together with other papers, forms Occasional Papers 20, 21, 24 and 25.

The double issue of *Cultural Studies,* nos. 7/8, is entitled *Resistance through Rituals* and is devoted to post-war youth subculture. Among the score of subjects discussed are Subcultures, Cultures and Class; Doing Nothing; Girls and Subcultures; the Politics of Youth Culture; and four articles on Teds, Mods, Skinheads, and Communes. The criticism levelled by Geoffrey Marshall at the language used in some of the Centre's work (see

Introduction to volume 6, p. xv) does not, in the main apply. Some of the descriptive accounts are illuminatingly illustrated with transcripts of recorded dialogues. There are also several informative tables — the chronologies of Counter-Culture 1965-75 (pp. 58-59) and of Education 1945-75 (pp. 240-41), for example.

Issue 2 (spring 1972) has a Bibliography of Rock by Bryn Jones; this includes sections on Aspects of Subculture and Political Aspects.

Stanley Cohen contributes a particularly good article to the spring 1974 issue (no. 5): 'Breaking Out, Smashing Up and the Social Context of Aspiration'. Drawing on Paul Goodman's *Growing Up Absurd* (1956) — 'still the best book on the subject', Cohen remarks (p. 47) — Cohen concludes with Goodman that far from there being misunderstanding between adults and disenchanted youth, there has *not* been a failure of communication. Perhaps the social message has been communicated all too clearly and has been found unacceptable. It is hard for adults to realize this, even when they are told it in articulate, literate and politically sophisticated terms; it is harder still if they are told in a muffled and angry way (p. 60). One or two titles might usefully be noted in addition to those given earlier. Peter Selz contributes the chapter on 'Art and Politics: The Artist and the Social Order' in Herschel B. Chipp's *Theories of Modern Art: A Source Book by Artists and Critics* (University of California Press, 1968), pp. 456-500, with selected and annotated bibliography, pp. 646-48. Colin Seymour-Ure's *The Political Impact of the Mass Media* was published in 1974. This is in two parts. The first is concerned with political communication and the effects of mass media; the second is a series of case studies ranging from *'The Times* and the appeasement of Hitler' to *'Private Eye:* the politics of the Fool'.

George Watson's *Politics and Literature in Modern Britain* (London 1977) includes among its ten papers a critique of The New Left; short essays on George Orwell and D.H. Lawrence; a longer discussion of Matthew Arnold's social criticism; reflections on the literary world of the thirties from the point of view of affiliations to the Left and the Right (complete with a list of what the author lightheartedly calls the 'opposing teams'); accounts of the Literature of Fascism (and see Alexander Henderson's 'The Function of Literature under National-Socialism' in volume 5), Race and the Socialists, and The Myth of Catastrophe.

Finally, whilst these volumes were in production, Anthony Smith's *The Politics of Information: Problems of Policy in Modern Media* (London 1978) was published and the *Co-Evolution Quarterly* devoted a special issue to the media (1978).

PETER DAVISON

Literary Taste, Culture and Mass Communication

Veblen's Attack on Culture
Theodor Adorno

from

Prisms by Theodor Adorno, trans. Samuel and Shierry Weber,
Neville Spearman, London, 1967.

Veblen's *Theory of the Leisure Class* became famous for its doctrine of conspicuous consumption, according to which the consumption of goods, from the very early 'predatory' stage of history to the present, has served not so much to satisfy men's true needs or to provide what Veblen chooses to call the 'fullness of life' as to maintain social prestige—status. With respect to aesthetics, the conclusions Veblen derives from his critique of consumption as mere ostentation are very close to those of functionalism, which Adolf Loos formulated at about the same time. Where the practical is concerned they resemble those of technocracy. But although these are the elements in Veblen's sociology which were historically effective, they do not adequately describe the objective impulses of his thought, which are directed against the barbaric character of culture. Again and again, from the first sentence of his work, the expression 'barbarian culture' appears, immobile, like a ritual mask. He uses the term to refer specifically to one phase of history, an unusually broad one to be sure, extending from the archaic hunter and warrior to the feudal lord and the absolute monarch, a phase whose boundary with the capitalist period is purposely left unclear. In innumerable places, however, it is unmistakably his intention to denounce the modern as barbaric precisely where it most emphatically raises the claim to culture. According to Veblen the very features which seem to prove that modernity has escaped the principle of unvarnished necessity and become humane are relics of historical epochs long past. For him emancipation from the realm of utility is nothing but the index of a purposelessness arising from the fact that cultural 'institutions' and anthropological characteristics do not change simultaneously and in harmony with the means of production but rather lag behind them and at times come into open contradiction with them. If one follows the direction of Veblen's thoughts instead of concentrating on his formulations, which waver between the vitriolic and the cautious, one arrives at the conception that those characteristics of culture in which greed, the search for personal advantage, and confinement in mere immediacy appear to have been overcome are nothing but residues of objectively obsolete forms of greed, personal ambition, and bad immediacy. They originate in the need to prove that crude practical considerations have been dispensed with, to prove, in particular, that one can spend one's time on the useless in order to improve one's position in the social hierarchy, increase one's social honour, and, finally, strengthen one's power over others. Culture turns against utility for the sake of a mediated utility. It is marked by the life-lie. In tracking down this lie Veblen displays a persistence not unlike that of his contemporary, Freud, in his investigation of the 'dregs of the world of phenomena'. Under Veblen's gloomy gaze, lawn and walking-stick, umpire and domestic animal become revealing allegories of the barbarism of culture.

It was as much this method as the contents of his teaching that led people to defame Veblen as a crazy and destructive outsider. As a professor in Chicago he even created an academic scandal which ended in his dismissal. At the same time, however, his theories have been assimilated. Today they find wide official recognition, and, like Freud's, his striking terminology has penetrated into journalism. One sees here the objective tendency to disarm a tiresome opponent by giving him a warm reception. Veblen's thought, however, is not completely out of harmony with such a reception; he is less an outsider than he seems at first sight. In pursuing his intellectual genealogy one would need to name three sources. The first and most important is American pragmatism. Veblen belongs to the older, Darwinistically inclined tradition in it. 'The life of man in society,' the central chapter of his main work begins, 'just like the life of other species, is a struggle for existence, and therefore it is a process of selective adaptation. The evolution of social structure has been a process of natural selection of institutions. The progress which has been made and is being made in human institutions and in human character may be set down, broadly, to a natural selection of the fittest habits of thought and to a process of enforced adaptation of individuals to an environment which has progressively changed with the growth of the community and with the changing institutions under which men have lived.' The concept of adaptation or adjustment is central. Man is subjected to life as to the experimental conditions set down by some unknown laboratory director, and he is expected to adjust to the natural and historical conditions imposed upon him in such a way that he has a chance to survive. The truth of thought is judged according to whether or not it serves this adaptation and contributes to the survival of the species. Veblen's critique always begins at points where this adaptation is incomplete. He is well aware of the difficulties the doctrine of adaptation encounters in the social realm; he knows that the conditions to which men must adapt are themselves a product of society, that there is an interaction between the internal and the external, and that adaptation may work to reinforce reified conditions. This insight forces him to refine and modify his doctrine continually, but he rarely reaches the point of questioning the absolute necessity of adjustment itself. Progress is adaptation and nothing else. Veblen stubbornly refuses to see that the inner constitution of this concept and its dignity could be qualitatively different in the case of conscious beings than they are in the blind world of nature. The harmony of this fundamental position with the intellectual climate in which Veblen found himself greatly facilitated the reception of his heresies.

The specific content of his adjustment theory, however, has a second source in an older variety of positivism, the school of St. Simon, Comte, and Spencer. The world to which, according to Veblen, men are supposed to adjust is that of industrial technology With St. Simon and Comte, Veblen proclaims its supremacy. For his progress means, concretely, the adaptation of the forms of consciousness and of 'life', that is, the sphere of economic consumption, to those of industrial technology. The means to this adjustment is science. Veblen conceives of it as the universal application of the principle of causality, in opposition to vestigial animism. Causal thinking is for him the triumph of objective, quantitative relations, patterned after industrial production, over personalistic and anthropomorphic conceptions. Above all, the notion of teleology is strictly excluded. The conception of history as slow and irregular but inherently continuous progress in adjusting to the world and demystifying it corresponds to a classificatory theory of stages not unlike Comte's. In this context Veblen occasionally gives indications that he expects the coming phase to witness the abolition of private property. This points to Marx as his third source. Veblen's attitude towards Marxism is controversial. The object of his critique is not the political economy of bourgeois society seen in terms of its foundations but the uneconomic life of that society. His continual recourse to psychology and 'habits of thought' to explain economic facts is incompatible with the Marxian theory of objective value. Nevertheless, Veblen incorporated as many of the secondary theories of Marxism into his basically pragmatic position as he could. Specific categories like conspicuous waste and reversion also originate there. The notion of a kind of consumption which exists not for its own sake but as a reflection of the social qualities of exchange-objects is related to the Marxian theory of commodity fetishism. The thesis of reversion, the compulsive regression to obsolete forms of consciousness under the pressure of economic conditions, is at least indebted to Marx. In Veblen, as in Dewey, the attempt to grasp the process of human adjustment, which is conceived pragmatically, produces dialectical motifs. His thinking is an amalgam of positivism and historical materialism.

Such a formula, however, offers relatively little insight into the heart of Veblen's theory. What is crucial is the force which drives these motifs together in his theory. Veblen's basic experience may be characterized as that of pseudo-uniqueness. As the mass production and centrally organized distribution of goods which are all basically similar advances, and as the technological and economic framework of life increasingly excludes the individuation of the here and now based on hand-production, the appearance of the here and now, that which cannot be replaced by countless other objects, becomes an imposture. It is as if in claiming to be something special and unique—and this claim must be constantly exaggerated in the interest of sales—each object were mocking a condition in which all men are subjugated to an order whose principle is more of the same. Veblen cannot bear this mockery. Bitterly, he insists that the world present itself in that abstract sameness of its objects which is predetermined by the underlying economic conditions. When Veblen argues for a rational organization of consumption, he is actually demanding nothing less than that mass production, for which the purchaser is from the outset an object of calculation, reveal its true colours in the sphere of consumption. Now that such phrases as 'deliciously different' and 'quaint' have become standard formulas in advertising, Veblen's insight is obvious. He was the first, however, to reach it spontaneously. He recognized the pseudo-individuality of things long before technology had snuffed out real individuality. He saw sham uniqueness in the intrinsic inconsistency of the objects themselves, in the contradiction between their form and their function. At the risk of exaggerating, one could say that the kitsch of the nineteenth century, in the form of ostentation,[1] appeared to him as the image of future tyranny. He saw a side of kitsch which escaped aesthetic critics but which helps explain the shockingly catastrophic expression which so many nineteenth-century buildings and interiors have assumed today—the look of oppression.

[1] Its economic basis should be precisely determined. That kind of presentation might well stem from the necessity to depict oneself as a good risk with a high credit rating. This necessity could reflect the scarcity of capital during periods of expansion.

In Veblen's eyes the ornamentation becomes menacing as it becomes increasingly similar to old models of repression. Nowhere does he indicate this more strikingly than in a discussion of the buildings which house charitable institutions: 'Certain funds, for instance, may have been set apart as a foundation for a foundling asylum or a retreat for invalids. The diversion of expenditure to honorific waste in such cases is not uncommon enough to cause surprises or even to raise a smile. An appreciable share of the funds is spent in the construction of an edifice faced with some aesthetically objectionable but expensive stone, covered with grotesque and incongruous details, and designed, in its battlemented walls and turrets and its massive portals and strategic approaches, to suggest certain barbaric methods of warfare.' Veblen uses this emphasis on the threatening aspects of magnificence and ornamentation to support his philosophy of history. For his belief in progress, the images of aggressive barbarism which he saw in nineteenth-century kitsch, and particularly in the decorative efforts of the years after 1870, represented relics of past epochs or indications of the regression of those who were not producing anything, those exempt from participation in the industrial labour-process. But the things Veblen calls archaic characteristics are at the same time indications of the dawning horror. His sad innervation disavows his optimistic outlook. The form human history took for him anticipated its most terrible phase. The shock he experienced in seeing the fortress-like foundlings' home became an historical force in the Columbus House, the National Socialists' neo-functional torture chamber. Veblen hypostasizes total domination. For him all culture becomes the distorted image of naked horror. His fascination with the impending doom explains and justifies the injustice he does culture. Culture, which today has assumed the character of advertising, was never anything for Veblen but advertising, a display of power, loot, and profit. With splendid misanthropy he ignores everything that goes beyond this. The mote in his eye becomes a means of perceiving the bloody traces of injustice even in images of happiness. In the name of the right to unlimited disposition over human history, the metropolis of the nineteenth century assembled a deceptive collection of pillars from Attic temples, Gothic cathedrals, and the arrogant palaces of Italian city-states. Veblen pays it back; for him the real temples, palaces, and cathedrals are already as false as the imitations. World history is the world's fair. Veblen explains culture in terms of kitsch, not vice-versa. His generalization of a situation in which culture is consumed by advertising has been concisely formulated by Stuart Class: 'People above the line of bare subsistence, in this age and all earlier ages, do not use surplus, which society has given them, primarily for useful purposes.' By 'all earlier ages' is meant everything unlike the business culture of the most recent age—the belief in the real power of ritual practices, the impulse of sexuality and its symbolism (sexuality is not mentioned once in the entire *Theory of the Leisure Class*), the compulsion to artistic expression, all yearning to escape the enslavement to utility. Against his will, the pragmatist, mortal enemy of teleological speculation, proceeds according to the scheme of a satanic teleology. His ingenious intelligence does not shrink from using the crudest rationalism to expose the universal domination of the fetish over the ostensible realm of freedom. Under his attack the concretion which imposes unity on the monotony of that which is nature-bound is perverted to a mass-produced article which falsely claims to be concrete.

Veblen's evil eye is fertile. It strikes phenomena which are overlooked or deemed harmless when one does not linger over them but merely dispenses with them from above as nothing more than the façade of society. One of these phenomena is sports. Veblen bluntly characterized every kind of sport, from children's contest and college gymnastics to the grand athletic pageants which subsequently blossomed in the dictatorships of both varieties, as outbursts of violence, oppression, and the predatory spirit. 'These manifestations of the predatory temperament are all to be classed under the head of exploit. They are partly simple and unreflected expressions of an attitude of emulative ferocity, partly activities deliberately entered upon with a view to gaining repute for prowess. Sports of all kinds are of the same general character.' According to Veblen, the passion for sports is of a regressive nature: 'The ground of an addiction to sports is an archaic spiritual constitution.' But nothing is more modern than this archaism; athletic events were the models for totalitarian mass rallies. As tolerated excesses, they combine cruelty and aggression with an authoritarian moment, the disciplined observance of the rules—legality, as in the pogroms of Nazi Germany and the people's republics. Veblen senses the affinity between the excesses of athletics and the manipulating elite: 'If a person so endowed with a proclivity for exploits is in a position to guide the development of habits in the adolescent members of the community, the influence which he exerts in the direction of conservation and reversion to prowess may be very considerable. This is the significance, for instance, of the fostering care latterly bestowed by many clergymen and other pillars of society upon "boys brigades" and similar pseudo-military organizations.' His insight extends even further. He recognizes sports as pseudo-activity, as the channelling

of energies which could otherwise become dangerous, as the endow-
ing of meaningless activity with a specious seriousness and significance. The less one suffers from economic constraint, the more one
feels impelled to create the semblance of serious, socially reputable
and nevertheless non-profit activity. At the same time, however,
sports suits the aggressive and practical predatory spirit. It provides
a common denominator for the conflicting desires to act purpose-
fully and to waste time. But it thus becomes fraudulent, make-
believe. Veblen's analyses, of course, should be expanded. For
sports includes not merely the drive to do violence to others but
also the wish to be attacked oneself and suffer. Only Veblen's
rationalist psychology prevents him from seeing the masochistic
moment in sports. It is this which makes sports not so much a relic
of a previous form of society as perhaps an initial adjustment to its
menacing new form—as opposed to Veblen's complaint that the
'institutions' have remained behind the industrial spirit, which, of
course, he limits to technology. Modern sports, one will perhaps
say, seek to restore to the body some of the functions of which the
machine has deprived it. But they do so only in order to train men
all the more inexorably to serve the machine. Hence sports belong
to the realm of unfreedom, no matter where they are organized.

Another complex in Veblen's critique of culture, one which seems
less topical, is the so-called woman question. Because the final
emancipation of women was so self-evident to socialist programmes,
there seems for a long time to have been no need to think through
the concrete position of women. Since Shaw the woman question
has been regarded as comical in bourgeois literature. Strindberg
perverted it to the question of men, just as Hitler shifted the
emphasis from the emancipation of the Jews to the emancipation
from the Jews. The impossibility of liberating women under the
present conditions is attributed not to the conditions but to the
advocates of freedom, and the frailty of emancipatory ideals, which
brings them close to neurosis, is confused with their realization. The
open-minded office girl who is satisfied with the world as long as
she can go to the movies with her date has supplanted Nora and
Hedda, and if she knew about them she would reproach them in
chic phrases for being unrealistic. Her counterpart is the man who
makes use of his erotic freedom only to take his partner coldly and
joylessly in her obtuse compliance and then show his gratitude by
deriding her all the more cynically. Veblen, who has much in common with Ibsen, is perhaps the last thinker of note who does not
avoid the woman question. As a late apologist of the feminist movement he has absorbed the experiences of Strindberg. For Veblen

woman becomes as a social phenomenon what she is for herself psychologically—a wound. He perceives her patriarchal humiliation. He compares her position, which he includes among the relics from the period of the hunter and the warrior, to that of the servant. Free time and luxury are allotted her only to strengthen the status of the master. This implies two contradictory consequences. Taking some liberties with Veblen's text, one might state them as follows: on the one hand, precisely by virtue of her debased situation as 'slave' and object of ostentation, the woman is in a certain sense exempted from 'practical life'. She is, or at least still was in Veblen's time, less exposed to economic competition than the man. In certain social strata and in certain epochs she was protected from the necessity of developing those qualities which Veblen describes under the general heading of the predatory spirit. By virtue of her distance from the process of production she retains certain traits which characterize the human being who is not yet entirely in the grasp of society. Thus women belonging to the upper social strata seem most ready to turn their backs on their class. Opposed to this, however, is a counter-tendency the most prominent symptom of which Veblen designates as the conservatism of woman. She rarely takes part as subject in historical development. The state of dependence to which she is confined mutilates her. This counterbalances the opportunity offered her by her exclusion from economic competition. Measured against the man's sphere of intellectual interests, even that of those men absorbed in the barbarism of business, most women find themselves in a mental state which Veblen does not hesitate to term imbecilic. Following this line of thought, one might reach the conclusion that women have escaped the sphere of production only to be absorbed all the more entirely by the sphere of consumption, to be captivated by the immediacy of the commodity world no less than men are transfixed by the immediacy of profit. Women mirror the injustice masculine society has inflicted on them—they become increasingly like commodities. Veblen's insight indicates a change in the utopia of emancipation. Hope cannot aim at making the mutilated social character of women identical to the mutilated social character of men; rather, its goal must be a state in which the face of the grieving woman disappears simultaneously with that of the bustling, capable man, a state in which all that survives the disgrace of the difference between the sexes is the happiness that difference makes possible.

Veblen, to be sure, did not draw these consequences. Despite his vague talk about the 'fulness of life', his image of society is based not on the ideal of happiness but on that of work. Happiness enters his field of vision only as the fulfilment of the 'work instinct', his supreme anthropological category. He is a puritan *malgré lui-même*. While he never tires of attacking taboos, his criticism stops at the sacredness of work. His critique has something of the paternal platitude which asserts that culture is not sufficiently proud of its own work but instead takes excessive pride in being excluded from work, in leisure. As its guilty conscience, he confronts society with its own principle of utility and proves to it that according to this principle culture is both a waste and a swindle, so irrational that it raises doubts about the rationality of the whole system. Veblen has something of the bourgeois who takes the admonition to be thrifty with grim seriousness. Thus all of culture becomes for him the meaningless ostentatious display typical of the bankrupt. Through his single-minded persistence in this one theme he un-masks the absurdity of a social process which can survive only by making 'false calculations' at every step and constructing labyrinths of deception and illusion. But Veblen had to pay for his method. He idolizes the sphere of production. His theory implies a distinction like that between predatory and productive capital in bourgeois economics. He distinguishes between two categories of modern economic 'institutions: pecuniary and industrial'. He divides human occupations accordingly, and the modes of behaviour which sup-posedly correspond to these occupations as well: 'So far as men's habits of thought are shaped by the competitive process of acquisi-tion and tenure; so far as their economic functions are comprised within the range of ownership of wealth as conceived in terms of exchange value, and its management and financiering through a permutation of values; so far their experience in economic life favours the survival and accentuation of the predatory temperament and habits of thought.' By failing to grasp the social process as a totality, Veblen arrives at a distinction between productive and non-productive functions. His primary target in making this distinction is the irrational mechanisms of distribution, as is evident in his talk of 'that class of persons and that range of duties in the economic process which have to do with the ownership of enterprises engaged in competitive industry; especially those fundamental lines of eco-nomic management which are classed as financiering operations. To these may be added the greater part of mercantile operations.' Only in the light of this distinction does it become clear what Veblen's objection to the leisure class really is. It is not so much the pressure it exerts on the others as the fact that there is not enough pressure on it to satisfy his puritanical work ethos. He be-grudges it its chance to escape, grotesque though that chance is.

The fact that the economically independent are not yet wholly within the grip of the necessities of life seems archaic to him: 'An archaic habit of mind persists because no effectual economic pressure constrains this class to an adaptation of its habits of thought to the changing situation'—an adaptation, it should be noted, that Veblen constantly advocates. The countermotif, it is true, leisure as the precondition of humanity, is not alien to him. But here an atheoretical, pluralistic scheme of thought prevails. Leisure and waste are granted their rights, but only 'aesthetically'; as economist Veblen will have nothing to do with them. One should not overlook the contempt for the aesthetic implied in such a division. The question of what 'economic' means for Veblen becomes thereby all the more imperative. The problem is not the extent to which Veblen's writings can be included in the discipline of economics but rather the meaning of his own conception of economics. The economic in Veblen remains implicitly defined as the 'profitable'. His talk of economics converges with that of the businessman who rejects an unnecessary expense as uneconomical. The concepts of the useful and the useless presupposed in such thinking are not subjected to analysis. Veblen demonstrates that society functions uneconomically in terms of its own criteria. This is both much and little; much, because he thus glaringly illuminates the unreason of reason, little, because he fails to grasp the interdependence of the useful and the useless. He leaves the question of the useless to heteronomous categories produced by the intellectual division of labour and makes himself a cultural efficiency expert whose vote can be vetoed by his aesthetic colleagues. He fails to see in the opposition of jurisdictions itself an expression of the fetishistic division of labour. While as economist he is all too sovereign in his treatment of culture, cutting it from the budget as waste, he is secretly resigned to its existence outside the budgetary sphere. He fails to see that its legitimacy or illegitimacy can be decided only through insight into society as a totality, not from the departmental perspective of the questioner. Thus a moment of buffoonery is inherent in his critique of culture.

Veblen would like to make a clean slate, to wipe away the rubble of culture and get to the bottom of things. But the search for 'residues' regularly falls prey to blindness. As the reflection of truth, appearances are dialectical; to reject all appearance is to fall completely under its sway, since truth is abandoned with the rubble without which it cannot appear. Veblen, however, refuses to see the impulses behind all that against which his basic experience rebels. In the posthumously published papers of Frank

Wedekind is the remark that kitsch is the Gothic or the Baroque of our age. Veblen did not seriously grapple with the historical necessity of kitsch Wedekind has in mind. To Veblen the phony castle is simply anachronistic. He does not understand the distinctly modern character of regression. The deceptive images of uniqueness in an era of mass production are only vestiges for him, not responses to highly industrialized mechanization which betray something of its essence. The world of these images, which Veblen unmasks as that of conspicuous consumption, is a synthetic, 'imaginary' world. It represents the futile but compulsive attempt to avoid the loss of experience involved in modern modes of production and escape the domination of abstract equivalence through self-made concretion. Men prefer to deceive themselves with illusions of the concrete rather than abandon the hope which clings to it. Commodity fetishes are not merely the projection of opaque human relations onto the world of things. They are also the chimerical deities which originate in the primacy of the exchange process but nevertheless represent something not entirely absorbed in it. Veblen's thinking recoils before this antinomy, which, however, is precisely what makes kitsch a style. Kitsch does not designate simply a misuse of work. The fact that the synthetic images depict regressions to the distant past only testifies to its inaccessibility. The most advanced art has conceived images which bring together the level of technical possibilities and the human demand for the concrete, but they have been ill received by society. Perhaps it is permissible to formulate the relationship between progress—'modernity'—and regression—'archaism'—in the form of a thesis. In a society in which the development and the stifling of energies are inexorable consequences of the same principle, each technical advance signifies at the same time a regression.[2] Veblen's talk of the 'barbarian normal' reveals a suspicion of this. Barbarism is normal because it does not consist in mere rudiments but is steadily

[2] Freud's psychological theory, which makes regression the product of a censorship exercised by the ego—the subject of all 'progress'—contains something of this fact, except that regression cannot be determined solely in terms of 'man' and his psyche, the object of all previous history, but must rather be seen as emanating from the actual social process, from the non-conscious subject whose naturalness comes to light in the fact that for every creation it pays the price of annihilation. The ambiguity of 'sublimation' is the psychological symbol of the ambiguity of social progress, just as the Freudian principle of economy, which designates the constant balancing of credit and debit in the psychological household, denotes not a primary and unalterable anthropological condition but rather the perpetual invariance of everything that has happened up to the present.

reproduced along with and in direct proportion to man's domination of nature. Veblen took this equivalence too lightly. He saw the temporal disparity between the castle and the railway station but did not grasp this disparity as a historical law. The station masks itself as a castle, but the mask is its truth. Only when the technical world of things becomes the direct servant of domination is it capable of throwing aside such masks. Only in the totalitarian terror-states does it appear as what it really is.

In overlooking the compulsive element in modern archaism and thinking it possible to root out synthetic images as mere illusions, Veblen also abdicates before the social *quaestio iuris* of luxury and waste, which as world reformer he would prefer to extirpate like a growth. Luxury has a dual character. Veblen concentrates his spotlight on one side of it: that part of the social product which does not benefit human needs and contribute to human happiness but instead is squandered in order to preserve an obsolete system. The other side of luxury is the use of parts of the social product which serve not the reproduction of expended labour, directly or indirectly, but of man in so far as he is not entirely under the sway of the utility principle. Although Veblen does not explicitly distinguish between these two moments of luxury, it is unquestionably his intention to do away with the first as 'conspicuous consumption' and to save the second in the name of the 'fullness of life'. In the crudeness of this intention, however, lies the weakness of his theory. *Faux frais* and happiness cannot be isolated in luxury today. They comprise the inherently mediated identity of luxury. Although happiness exists only when men have momentarily eluded the process of a pernicious 'societalization', the concrete form of their happiness always contains in itself the general condition of society, the negative.[3] Proust's novel might be interpreted as the attempt to develop this contradiction. Thus erotic happiness relates

[3] Veblen's inability to articulate the dialectic of luxury is most strikingly evident in his conception of the beautiful. He tries to purge the beautiful of pomp and ostentation. He thereby deprives it of every concrete social determination and reverts to a pre-Hegelian standpoint on beauty, a purely formal concept oriented on measurable natural categories. His discussion of beauty is very abstract because there is nothing beautiful in which the immanent moment of injustice can be eliminated. To be consistent, Veblen would have to advocate the abolition of art. His pluralism, which adds to the economic principle of thrift the aesthetic one of non-illusion, arises from this inability to be consistent. In their isolation, however, both moments become absurd. Just as the utter expediency of the beautiful thrusts it into irreconcilable contradiction with its purposelessness, Veblen's conception of the economic comes into contradiction with his idea of a good society.

not to man 'as such' but rather to man as he is determined by society and in his social manifestations. Walter Benjamin once wrote that it is as erotically important to the man for his beloved to appear in his company as for her to give herself to him. Veblen would have joined in the bourgeois jeering at this remark and would have talked about conspicuous consumption. But the happiness that man actually finds cannot be separated from conspicuous consumption. There is no happiness which does not promise to fulfil a socially constituted desire, but there is also none which does not promise something qualitatively different in this fulfilment. Abstract utopian thinking which deludes itself about this, sabotages happiness and plays into the hands of that which it seeks to negate. For, although it strives to purge happiness of the social stigma, it is forced to renounce every concrete claim to happiness and to reduce human beings to a mere function of their own work. Even the commodity fetishist who has succumbed to conspicuous consumption to the point of obsession participates in the truth-content of happiness. Although he denies his own living happiness and replaces it with the prestige of things--Veblen speaks of 'social confirmation'—he reveals against his will the secret that lies hidden in all pomp and ostentation, the fact that no individual happiness is possible which does not virtually imply that of society as a whole. Even malice, the flaunting of status, and the drive to impress, in which the social moment of happiness inexorably manifests itself under the principle of competition, contain the recognition of society, of the whole, as the true subject of happiness. Those features of luxury which Veblen designates as 'invidious', revealing a bad will, do not only reproduce injustice; they also contain, in distorted form, the appeal to justice. Human beings are no worse than the society in which they live--therein lies the corrective to Veblen's misanthropy. But his misanthropy is also a corrective. It defames the bad will even in its most sublime impulses because it remains stubbornly loyal to a good will.

It is deeply ironic, however, that Veblen's loyalty is compelled to take the form which he so vigorously condemns in bourgeois society, that of regression. In his mind, the only hope lies in the prehistory of man. All the happiness which for him is excluded by dreamless realism, by pliant adaptation to the conditions of the industrial world, is reflected in the image of a paradisical golden age. 'The conditions under which men lived in the most primitive stages of associated life that can properly be called human, seem to have been of a peaceful kind; and the character—the temperament and spiritual attitude—of men under these early conditions of environment

and institutions seems to have been of a peaceful and un-
aggressive, not to say an indolent cast. For the immediate purpose
this peaceable cultural stage may be taken to mark the initial phase
of social development. So far as concerns the present argument, the
dominant spiritual feature of this presumptive initial phase of culture seems to have been an unreflecting, unformulated sense of
group solidarity, largely expressing itself in a complacent, but by
no means strenuous, sympathy with all facility of human life, and
an uneasy revulsion against apprehended inhibition or futility of
life.' Veblen interprets the demythologizing and humanity which
characterize mankind in the bourgeois era not as indications of increasing self-consciousness but rather as a reversion to this primal
state. 'Under the circumstances of the sheltered situation in which
the leisure class is placed there seems, therefore, to be something of
a reversion to the range of non-invidious impulses that characterize
the ante-predatory savage culture. The reversion comprises both
the sense of workmanship and the proclivity to indolence and good-
fellowship.' Karl Kraus, the critic of linguistic ornament, once
wrote 'Origin is the goal'. Similarly, the nostalgia of Veblen, the
technocrat, aims at the resurrection of the most ancient; the feminist
movement is for him the blind and incoherent effort 'to rehabilitate
the women's pre-glacial standing'. Such provocative formulations
seem like insults to the positivist's sense of fact. But here one of
the most curious conjunctions in Veblen's theory manifests itself,
that which joins positivism and the Rousseauistic theory of a primitive ideal state. As a positivist who admits no norm but that of
adjustment, Veblen sees himself faced with the question why one
should not also adjust to the givens of 'the principles of waste,
futility and ferocity', which according to his conception comprise
the 'canon of pecuniary decency'. 'But why are apologies needed?
If there prevails a body of popular sentiment in favour of sports,
why is not the fact a sufficient legitimation? The protracted discipline of prowess to which the race had been subjected under the
predatory and quasipeaceable culture has transmitted to the man
of today a temperament that finds gratification in these expressions
of ferocity and cunning. So, why not accept these sports as legitimate expressions of a normal and wholesome human nature? What
other norm is there that is to be lived up to than that given in the
aggregate range of propensities that express themselves in the sentiments of this generation, including the hereditary strain of prowess?'
Here, with a grin not unlike Ibsen's, Veblen follows his reasoning
to the point where it is in danger of capitulating to the world as
it is, to normal barbarism. His solution is surprising: 'The ulterior

norm to which appeal is taken is the instinct of workmanship, which is an instinct more fundamental, of more ancient prescription, than the propensity to predatory emulation.' This is the key to his theory of the primitive age. The positivist permits himself to conceive of human potentiality only by transforming it into a given, something which actually existed in the past. There can be no justification of a reconciled life without that life being more 'given', more positive, more existent than the hell of existence. Paradise is the positivist's aporia. Veblen invents the instinct of workmanship only incidentally, in order to bring paradise and the industrial age together under a common anthropological denominator. As he would have it, men earned their bread by the sweat of their brow even before the Fall.

It was in theories of this kind, impotent and self-caricaturing props in which the idea of the different tries to make its peace with adjustment to the eternally same, that Veblen most exposed himself. It is easy to deride the positivist who strives to break out of facticity. Veblen's entire work is permeated by the motif of spleen. It is one big joke at the expense of that 'sense of proportion' that the positivistic rules of fair play demand. He is insatiable in seeking elaborate analogies between the customs and institutions of sports and religion, or between the aggressive codes of honour of the gentleman and the criminal. He cannot even refrain from complaining about the economic waste involved in the ceremonial paraphernalia of religious cults. He has an affinity with the reformers of life. Often enough his primitivistic utopia degenerates to the crude belief in the 'natural', and he preaches against so-called follies of fashion like long skirts and corsets, for the most part attributes of the nineteenth century which the progress of the twentieth has swept away without thereby bringing the barbarism of culture to an end. Conspicuous consumption becomes an *idée fixe*. To understand the contradiction between this and the sharp insights of Veblen's social analyses, one must consider the cognitive function of spleen itself. Like the image of a peaceful primeval age, spleen in Veblen—and not only in him— is a haven of potentiality. The observer who is guided by spleen attempts to make the overwhelming negativity of society commensurable with his own experience. He seeks to make tangible the impenetrable and alien character of the whole, but it is precisely this quality which lies beyond the grasp of direct, vital experience. The *idée fixe* replaces the abstract general concept in that it rigidifies and stubbornly preserves specific and limited experience. Spleen expresses the desire to compensate for the lack of authority and evidence inherent in a merely mediated and derived knowledge of what is most immediate—real suffering. But this suffering originates in the oppressive social system as a whole and can therefore be elevated to knowledge only in abstract and mediated form. Spleen rebels against this. It draws up schemes for dialogues with Mr. Knownothing. They fail because social estrangement consists precisely in excluding the objects of knowledge from the sphere of immediate experience. The subject's loss of experience in a world dominated by 'more of the same', the premise of Veblen's entire theory, designates the anthropological side of the process of estrangement which since Hegel has been grasped in objective categories. Spleen is a defence mechanism. Always and everywhere, even as early as Baudelaire, its gesture is accusing. But it denounces society in its immediate manifestations and attributes society's guilt to its phenomena. The commensurability of knowledge and experience is purchased at the cost of the insufficiency of that knowledge. In this respect spleen resembles the petty bourgeois sect which attributes the world's downfall to a conspiracy and at the same time frankly admits the absurdity of that with which it is obsessed. When Veblen saddles a surface phenomenon like barbaric lavishness with total responsibility, the very disproportionality of his thesis becomes an element of its truth. It aims to shock. This expresses the incommensurability of this world and the potential experience of it. Knowledge accompanies itself with sardonic laughter over the fact that its actual object evades it as long as it remains human knowledge; only as inhuman knowledge would it be equal to the inhuman world. The sole avenue of intellectual communication between the objective system and subjective experience is the explosion which tears both apart and momentarily illuminates in its glare the figure they form together. Inasmuch as this kind of criticism pounces on barbarism at the nearest street corner instead of consoling itself in the realm of general concepts, it retains, in contrast to less naïve theory, before which it makes itself ridiculous, a memento of what began to be neglected with the conception of 'scientific socialism' and finally disappeared in what Karl Kraus called 'Moskauderwelsch', Bolshevik jargon. Narrowness is not only the complement to broadness; sometimes it is a wholesome antidote to the all too broad overview. As such, it justifies itself in Veblen. His spleen stems from his disgust with the official optimism of the spirit of progress, whose part he himself takes in so far as he swims with the stream of common sense.

Spleen dictates the particular character of Veblen's critique. It is one of disenchantment, of 'debunking'. Veblen eagerly follows a traditional procedure of the Enlightenment, that of exposing religion as a 'hoax of the clergy'. 'It is felt that the divinity must be of a peculiarly serene and leisurely habit of life. And whenever his local habitation is pictured in poetic imagery, for edification or in appeal to the devout fancy, the devout word-painter, as a matter of course, brings out before his auditors' imagination a throne with a profusion of the insignia of opulence and power, and surrounded by a great number of servitors. In the common run of such presentations of the celestial abodes, the office of this corps of servants is a vicarious leisure, their time and efforts being in great measure taken up with an industrially unproductive rehearsal of the meritorious character-istics and exploits of the divinity.' The manner in which the angels are blamed here for the unproductivity of their labour has something of secularized swearing, but also something of the joke which fizzles. The hardened man does not let himself be bothered by the slips, dreams, and neuroses of society. His humour is like that of the husband who forces his hysterical wife to do housework in order to drive those crazy ideas out of her head. While spleen stubbornly clings to the estranged world of things, making the treachery of objects responsible for the subject's misdeeds, the attitude of de-bunking is that of the person who does not let himself be taken in by the treachery of objects. He strips them of their ideological masks in order to be able to manipulate them better. His rage is directed against the damned swindle rather than against the bad state of affairs. It is no accident that the debunker's hate turns so readily against all mediating functions; swindle and mediation be-long together. But thinking and mediation as well. The hatred of thought has its roots in debunking.[4] True criticism of barbarian culture, however, cannot be content with a barbaric denunciation of culture. It must recognize overt uncultured barbarism as the *telos* of that culture and reject it, but it cannot crudely proclaim the supremacy of barbarism over culture simply because barbarism has ceased to lie. Honesty as the triumph of horror echoes in formula-

[4] Consciously, Veblen is quite free of this hatred. But anti-intellectualism is objectively contained in his struggle against the intermediary functions of society as well as in his denunciation of 'higher learning'. In a debunker like Aldous Huxley it gains the upper hand. His work is largely the self-denunciation of the intellectual as a swindler in the name of an integrity which amounts to the glorification of nature. It is very possible that the narrowness of Veblen's theory can ultimately be explained through his in-ability to think through the problem of mediation. In his physiognomy the zealotry of the Scandinavian Lutheran, which admits no intermediary be-tween God and inwardness, blindly prepared itself to enter the service of a social order which liquidates the mediations between the commanded production and the coerced consumers. The two attitudes, that of radical Protestantism and that of state capitalism, have anti-intellectualism in common.

tions like that about the industrial unproductivity of the heavenly hosts. Such jokes appeal to conformism. The person who laughs at the image of beatitude is closer to the powers that be than is the image, however distorted by power and glory it may be.

Nevertheless, there is a good and wholesome element in Veblen's insistence on the facts, in his tabooing of all images. In him the resistance to a barbaric life has migrated into the strength to adjust to the merciless necessity of that life. For the pragmatist of his type there is no whole, no identity of thinking and being, not even the notion of such an identity. He repeatedly comes back to the position that 'habits of thought' and the demands of the concrete situation are irreconcilable. 'Institutions are products of the past process, are adapted to past circumstances, and are therefore never in full accord with the requirements of the present. In the nature of the case, this process of selective adaptation can never catch up with the progressively changing situation in which the community finds itself at any given time; for the environment, the situation, the exigencies of life which enforce the adaptation and exercise the selection, change from day to day; and each successive situation of the community in its turn tends to obsolescence as soon as it has been established. When a step in the development has been taken, this step itself constitutes a change of situation which requires a new adaptation; it becomes the point of departure for a new step in the adjustment, and so on interminably.' Irreconcilability prohibits the abstract ideal or makes it appear a childish phrase. Truth can be reduced to the smallest step; what is true is what is nearest, not what is farthest. Against the demand to adopt the interest of the 'whole' as opposed to the particular interest, however it is understood, and thereby to transcend the utilitarian narrowness of truth, the pragmatist can rightly contend that the whole is not definitively given, that only the nearest can be experienced and that therefore the ideal is condemned to be fragmentary and uncertain. Against this argument it is not sufficient to invoke the distinction between the total interest of a good society and the limitations of practical utility. The existing society and the other society do not have two different kinds of truth; rather, truth in the latter is inseparable from the real movement within the existing order and each of its moments. Hence the contrast between dialectics and pragmatism, like every distinction in philosophy, is reduced to a nuance, namely, to the conception of that 'next step'. The pragmatist, however, defines it as adjustment, and this perpetuates the domination of what is always the same. Were dialectics to sanction this, it would renounce itself in renouncing the idea of potentiality. But how is potentiality to be conceived if it is not to be abstract and arbitrary, like the utopias dialectical philosophers proscribed? Conversely, how can the next step assume direction and aim without the subject knowing more than what is already given? If one chose to reformulate Kant's question, one could ask today: *how is anything new possible at all?* In the sharpening of this question resides the seriousness of the pragmatist, comparable to that of the physician whose readiness to help is conceived in terms of the similarity of man and animal. It is the seriousness of death. The dialectician, however, should be the one who is not resigned to this fate. For his position the either-or of discursive logic dissolves. Whereas for the pragmatist the bare facts remain 'opaque items', as which they cannot be comprehended but only classified, the dialectician sees himself confronted with the cognitive task of dissolving those phenomenal residues, the 'atoms', by means of the concept. Nothing, however, is more opaque than adjustment itself, which the imitation of mere existence installs as the criterion of truth. The pragmatist insists on the historical index of all truth, and his own idea of adjustment has such an index. It is what Freud called 'ananke'—scarcity. The next step is one of adjustment only as long as scarcity and poverty prevail in the world. Adjustment is the mode of behaviour which corresponds to the situation of 'too little'. Pragmatism is narrow and limited because it hypostasizes this situation as eternal. This is the significance of its concepts of nature and life. What it wants for man is 'identification with the life-process', a mode of behaviour that perpetuates the process by which living beings exist in nature as long as nature does not provide them with sufficient means of subsistence. Veblen's outbursts against the 'sheltered', whose privileged position allows them to a certain extent to avoid adjusting to a changed situation, amounts to a glorification of the Darwinian struggle for existence. It is nothing less than the hypostasis of scarcity, which in its social form has now been made obviously obsolete by the very technological development to which, according to Veblen's doctrine, human beings are supposed to adjust. Thus the pragmatist falls prey to dialectics. The only adequate response to the present technical situation, which holds out the promise of wealth and abundance to men, is to organize it according to the needs of a humanity which no longer needs violence because it is its own master. In one of the finest passages of his work, Veblen recognizes the connection between poverty and the persistence of the bad situation: 'The abjectly poor, and all those persons whose energies are entirely absorbed by the struggle for daily sustenance, are conservative because they cannot afford the effort of taking thought for the day after tomorrow; just as the highly prosperous are conservative because they have small occasion to be discontented with the situation as it stands today.' But the pragmatist, himself regressive, clings to the standpoint of those who cannot think beyond tomorrow, beyond the next step, because they do not know what they will live from tomorrow. He represents poverty. This is his truth, because men are still constrained to be poor, and his untruth, because the absurdity of poverty has become manifest. Today, adjustment to what is possible no longer means adjustment; it means making the possible real.

Literature and General Culture
Seymour Betsky

from

Universities Quarterly, vol. 14, 1960.

LITERATURE AND GENERAL CULTURE

S E Y M O U R   B E T S K Y

Professor of English, Montana State University, U.S.A.

THE first meeting of the Conference on 'Literature and General Culture' was held at the regular session of the Modern Language Association of America (M.L.A.) in December 1958. The purpose of a Conference is to explore the advisability of originating a fresh field of inquiry not already incorporated in the Association.[1]

A certain urgency prompted the inquiry. In part that urgency was personal, so that I must take sole responsibility for the idea of the inquiry, for the formulations and for the conduct of the meeting to this point. At the same time I hoped that my interest in the problem was only representative: that others shared with me a concern about literature in relation to culture; and that others thought that the pooling of talents and specializations in a field so large might win a sense of control, where now most of us feel only submergence.

That intensity of interest proved justified. In order to ensure an attendance of thirty-five, I circulated about seventy invitations. With the invitations I circulated in mimeographed form the first formulations: an attempt to chart the field of inquiry. Virtually every one of the invitations was accepted, and where the individual indicated that he would be unable to attend, he wished to be kept in touch with its progress. Many of those who accepted invitations requested additional ones for colleagues. At the meeting, a few minutes after the doors were opened, the room was filled to overflowing and the doors had to be closed. Some of the most distinguished scholars, critics, historians, sociologists and publishers in America attended that meeting.

The abundance of materials I provided proved, in the event, unwieldy for a mixed group—I took the liberty of inviting many non-M.L.A. members—to organize in the space of about one hour. The results of the first meeting were therefore inconclusive. However, the group expressed a strong desire that the idea be continued for 1959. This time the group was kept to some fifteen, meeting in Chicago. The results were better, as I shall indicate. Clearly there is a feeling that the inquiry ought to be launched forthwith. There remains only some uncertainty about the best way to launch it.

We appear to have reached this point in our deliberations. In America, there is considerable interest, the extent of which we have so far not estimated, in 'culture'. We have amassed a large bibliography.[2] Articles on aspects of 'culture' seem to be increasing in national magazines, in those little magazines carefully examined and 'digested' by the national magazines (itself a significant aspect of the cultural process) and in specialist journals. There seem also to be an increasing number of programmes devoted to the subject on T.V.

What is most astonishing is that America is still without basic formulations. Each separate article or book or discussion seems to drop into the maw of the huge machine for discussion, is given its moment—some more extended—of notoriety, and disappears. America has not even begun to find agreement about basic formulations: *it does not know what it is looking for*. It has difficulty 'placing' the problem historically. To date no individual or group of individuals has, with an eye on the present situation, begun the inquiry into the American historical past, charted the important phases historically, gauged the nature and particularly the tempo of change. American specialists in *British* literature beginning with Elizabethan times (little work has been done with pre-Elizabethan Britain) are just now beginning to collect some of the documents covering the profession of letters, patronage, audiences and publishing conditions. But each specialist remains within his specialization and fails to establish continuity with what precedes or with what follows. Nor have Americans come to the resolution—indispensable, as I think—that the best guides for their present purposes are in Britain. They are happy each to make his 'contribution to knowledge' in the standard way. Moreover, American specialists in twentieth-century American literature, where the problem of culture is felt to be acute, have failed adequately to trace the problem in historical terms. Indeed, the problem seems to have been relinquished to the sociologists with (in more cases than I should like to admit) something of a sneer at what academics call 'sub-literature'. The field of serious literature has become the world of 'aesthetic experiences', divorced from any first-hand connection with

American civilization as 'culture' appraises that civilization. This in a nation where cultural debasement extends further, perhaps, than in any country we know. American sociologists cannot be trusted, for all the good work they have done, for two essential qualifications: critical ability that answers to the demands of the better critics; and a developed sense of history, where they can see themselves in a tradition of inquiry.

Nevertheless, a very rich literature on the general subject by scholars and critics of letters exists. The inquiry into 'literature and general culture' came into existence for this very reason; and for the added reason that the time seemed to have arrived for a collaborative effort. We need to agree upon major formulations. We need to suggest where scholarly and critical effort must go now and in the future.

There is need, there is urgency, about the problem, at least for those of us who feel that serious writing itself—the better poetry, drama, fiction and prose—is threatened with extinction by certain developments. We sense, without quite being able yet to demonstrate, that the discipline of letters, which means intellectual and emotional life and death to those of us who support them in profession or as vocation, is becoming so marginalized in our national life, or is now so tainted, that our very sense of having a function in communal or national life may be seriously questioned. We have the feeling that nobody cares whether the world of letters, as it answers to our demand for standards, lives or dies. We appear to have reached a point where there is only vestigial respect—a kind of cultural itch surviving from certain habits now in process of dying. In direct and in subtle ways this sense affects our personal lives and our commitments to scholarship, criticism and teaching.

Admittedly, those of us who are more sanguine adopt different formulations and attitudes. So far these differences, when they have been expressed in the two meetings to date, happily look more to exchange than to the assertion only of basic disagreement.

I have alluded to my own conviction that our best guides are to be found in Britain. I say this for the reason that the inquiry into 'Culture and Environment', begun almost thirty years ago in Britain, contains some of the best formulations available. That material needs to be reviewed, consolidated and brought up to date. (The recent books by Richard Hoggart, Raymond Williams and Margaret Dalziel, excellent in their ways, fail to establish effective continuity with that work.) Almost nothing is known of it in America.

Again, one agreement seems common: that 'letters' constitute one of the best indexes we possess to the culture of a civilization. And British literature at all levels represents one of the most remarkable achievements of which we know—an achievement readily available to Americans through a common language.

What follows, then, is a summary of the materials that appeared recently as a 'Report of Progress' and was distributed to individuals who have shown an interest. Those who attended the Chicago meeting had a year to consider the early formulations, and a short time to consider the 'Report of Progress'.

Nobody in the group has to this point questioned the need to give priority to *good critical practice* wherever, relevantly, it might be found: responsible and adequate judgments of literature at all levels. It was clear that, while an abundance of practice might be found for the better literature, there was little to be found for the contemporary best-sellers and for sub-literature. We possess in abundance excellent descriptive accounts covering subject matter and form, methods of production and audience. But we have not pooled our energies to discover a critical method adjusted to it, and particularly demonstrations of that method.

One highly significant agreement seemed to be common in both meetings: that there has been an astonishing paucity of good critical practice for major writers beginning roughly with the last part of the nineteenth century. We have not bothered to see where that practice might be found and what it looks like. I am here referring to the criticism which has offered the indispensable terms for considering which writers are significant and or less significant: criticism that has stood the test of time. We appear to have fixed on certain writers—T. S. Eliot, Yeats, Conrad, Lawrence, Joyce, James, Hemingway and Faulkner are representative—as 'major'. But we have paid little attention to the total process by which the stature of a writer arrived. The Chicago group felt that we would be without our bearings in the judgment of the lesser literature unless we spelled out in some detail the nature of such judgments, the individuals responsible, the implications as they related to inferior literature and the total machinery of dissemination, particularly in publishing and in universities. Moreover, we ought to do this work historically. So far we possess a very adequate history of theoretical criticism. But we do not possess the beginning of a history of practical criticism of the best kind—practical criticism devoted to the judgment of the worth of poetry, drama, fiction and prose as separate works appeared, as well as to the revaluation of that work with the passage of time.[3]

In addition to good critical practice, there is a need to find some working description of the relationship of literature to culture. Is it enough to say, as a kind of working description before we call attention to the most useful books and articles, that literature at all levels expresses the shared assumptions, spoken and unspoken, of a writer and audience; and that in the better literature we possess not only a critical appraisal of these shared assumptions effectively dramatized in the work out there, but also a critical appraisal with considerable range? The better literature, written and oral, of a particular nation at a particular time is one of the best indexes we possess of the total way of life of that civilization because it constitutes an appraisal, Arnold's 'criticism of life'. Can we say, next, that a civilization committed to 'religion' makes no distinction between religion and culture, since religion is culture in the sense of a way of thinking that both describes and evaluates; but that when a civilization ceases to use religion as a guide to national life, a number of disciplines, each increasingly specialist, fills the vacuum, each appraising the life of that civilization according to the procedure of the discipline? Where religion 'prevails', literature is often a powerful adjunct. Where religion no longer prevails, literature tends to become a substitute.

Can we say that the better literature offers effectively realized and significant appraisals of the total material, spiritual and intellectual life? Can we say that the inferior literature offers in its way 'inferior' assumptions, 'inferior' realizations and 'inferior' appraisals? Thus, if we come to know the total literature of a civilization at all levels, we have made the indispensable beginning and may then move outward to other disciplines for support, qualification and correction. Moreover, if we can determine what literature the *national audience* supported—provided, of course, that we can describe that national audience adequately—we may distinguish between the 'best-seller' who was Shakespeare or Jonson or Dryden or Bunyan or Congreve or Swift or Pope or Fielding or Dickens (representatively) and the 'best-sellers' of the nineteenth and twentieth centuries.

However, if we read literature *primarily* for discovering cultural patterns, we will be mis-reading—mis-reading just as seriously as though we were reading literature for Freudian, Marxist or doctrinal-religious patterns. Our procedure must, above all, answer to the demands of good critical practice. The writer, inheriting certain modes, conventions and models, uses the language available to him in order to create the imaginatively ordered work of literature, successful and/or significant in varying degrees. He reaches out to an audience. That audience contains individuals qualified to read the work of literature as literature, able to focus on the nature and degree of realization and, finally, to judge its significance. In practice, judgments about significance will inevitably take the critic to the writer's civilization, aspects of which he is appraising. If the world of 'culture' is the subject of appraisal, then the better literature is one of the most effective instruments available.

The nature of the responsiveness to, and the judgment of, *all* the levels of literature must be examined in some detail as part of any programme involving 'literature and general culture'.

If we can find some agreement about the better and inferior writers at a given historical moment, we can focus on the writer and ask some of the following questions: What was his formal education like? To what degree did his formal education encourage an interest in letters? What about the more significant influence of the informal education in the smaller and wider community as it bore on letters? How and why did a writer fix on the resolution to become a man of letters in the serious sense? In the less serious sense? Can we compare the different occupations and professions open to him at the time; compare the status and compensations offered to men of letters compared with men in other occupations and professions? In our day, for example, the 'intellectual' who wishes to go into sciences, pure and applied, has an enormous range. Moreover, he may apply all his training (or most of it) in a practical way in business and government where the rewards are considerable. Again, the sheer number of ways of making a substantial living in our standard-of-living civilization—in production, consumption, distribution—are incalculable. What might be the terms of comparison here with the past?

Then, too, a serious writer is aware that the number of ways of using language, in the world of imagination, in the world of practical journalism, in the world of advertising, and in the worlds of government and business, are likewise incalculable. How does this enormous group of writers who write purely and simply to make money compare with a similar group in Elizabethan times? To narrow down the inquiry: Can we discover how many writers now write for all the different genres outside of serious literature (comic books; inferior films; inferior stage dramas; inferior T.V. and radio; marketable fiction of all kinds; popular songs)? How many of these people have been trained in colleges and universities? What models did they use in order to train themselves? What would a comparison with the past look like?

Can we make a special study of the language available to the writer in these terms of comparison-contrast? Let us put it this way: Shakespeare's language made available to him the experience of sharing the total life of his England, at all occupational and social levels and taking in all the orders of experience. Throughout the history of literature we are aware of the degrees to which certain writers entered immediately into many 'worlds'—Bunyan, for example; or the degree to which certain writers cut themselves off from particular 'words'—Restoration playwrights, for example. In our day, however, the machinery of 'communication' appears so to have debased the quality of the experience of so much of a writer's world that a serious writer feels a revulsion, an indignity—unless, of course, he use satire—about treating that experience in his work.

What can we say about the writer in relation to his profession? In the particular historical era, to what degree was a writer forced by economic necessity to find a substitute 'vocation' in order to exist? When did the gravitation of a considerable number of writers into universities begin? Is it only an American phenomenon? What has been the history of the profession of letters as it relates to this problem?

Can we say something in detail about the audience for the different levels of literature in terms of class, profession or occupation, habits of attention, degree of formal and informal education? Shall we make a special point about the world which the writer and his audience shared—or failed to share—in common? Can we say that in a world where religion prevailed, whatever the differences in sects, the writer and his audience shared a considerable range of reference in common, of conviction in common, and even of difference in common? Can we say that the very absence of specializations in almost incalculable number (in our day the proliferation of specialization in the total world of letters constitutes one of the most serious obstacles to common action) made the task of the writer in the past an easier one in relation to audience? Can we say that the audience shared a similar 'knowledge' about political institutions, and differences of political beliefs? About social institutions and social beliefs? Of ideas in philosophy, science? About its economic modes? About topical allusions of all kinds? Can we next make the comparison between a pre-industrial civilization at a particular time where the degree of sharing, at least as it concerned the better literature with some range, must seem impressive to us, as against our industrial civilization?

Can we say at each level what standards a given writer kept in mind as he wrote or recited? What models? Can we discover what were the attitudes of writers towards the so-called 'guardians of letters', provided we can speak with some confidence about that portion of qualified individuals in whose keeping were these standards? When do we first meet the phenomenon of considerable distrust on the part of writers towards these guardians? Shall we begin with Goldsmith? The Romantics? Earlier? And what shall we say about the standards in the writing of inferior literature?

Can we identify these guardians for the different kinds of literature, even for sub-literature? What was the nature of 'standards' for the guardians? Did certain standards prevail at any time, and did the inferior literature tend to apologize for itself in the light of standards? Shall we speak about a gradual decay of standards with increased commercialization, or shall we say that standards have on the whole remained stable?

Can we say that the commercialization of literature produced a new phenomenon: the 'middleman of culture'? He is the individual who came to rely on a small body of qualified critics, and when the time was right tried to sell certain writers to a wider audience, as *Time* magazine does in our day. Is this an accurate description for certain writers since, say, the end of the nineteenth century: Conrad? Forster? Eliot? Woolf? Faulkner? Lawrence? Yeats? Joyce? Others? If this description is accurate, what are the implications?

We need, relatedly, a history of the progress of literature as it moved from a certain balance between patronage and the market in the Elizabethan age to a very different balance through the centuries up to our day. What are the most important books and articles?

Ought we to address ourselves candidly to this question: Is the situation for letters in relation to general culture one that is so different for an industrial civilization, certainly in its later phases, that we are dealing with something unprecedented, historically? Or can we find more similarities than differences in any comparison of past and present? Our present task, it would seem, is to find agreement among scholars about the major phases of the industrial revolution. If we perceive that literature registers a response to urgent pressures in a particular civilization, each writer following his unique urgency and each writer uniquely talented, then we may come to see that what we call 'Romanticism' in Britain was a response to phases of emergent industrialism, complicated, even in the early stages, by the influence of the French Revolution and the advance of science and scientific method. (In France and in America, the beginning phase is quite different; yet in time industrialism, democracy and science prevail in each nation.) If we discard the term 'Romanticism' and substitute instead some word or phrase to capture the earlier and later phases, we can see in 'letters' a changing responsiveness of a radical kind to these phases, particularly since the situation for letters itself undergoes radical transformation. Here, then, might be the terms of our discussion: Can we say that the goal of industrialism has come to be the goal of raising, extending, and defending the standard of living (needs, including health, comforts, luxuries, securities, diversions) of a nation? Can we say that such a goal has now become virtually exclusive, so that serious literature has no significant role to play? To spell this out further, can we say that each individual is expected—through direct or indirect pressure— to make a contribution, large or small, to the production, the consumption, or distribution of a standard of living item? Can we say that a considerable number of individuals are thus able to made an *intellectual* contribution towards this goal: e.g., describe how it might be done more effectively, understand its nature more adequately, suggest how one might 'adjust' oneself to its peculiar ecology? Further, that the work of such intellectuals has a considerably greater function in our civilization, particularly as that work borrows from science and the scientific method, than letters? Can we say, too, that 'literature as commodity' figures in statistical preponderance as a 'diversion' (i.e., the Hollywood entertainment industry); and that the diversion industry has become so huge, so proliferating, so manipulatory that it heavily overshadows—perhaps reduces to insignificance—what we call the better literature, i.e., the literature of integrity that tries to capture one world honestly, in detail, in subtlety, in richness, in relation to history, and uses as indispensable instrument the living language? If this is so, can we say that the American national mind is destroying effectively what we consider to be one of the most significant commentaries on its way of life?

Can we say that each nation is convinced for the first time in recorded history that it can achieve a decent living standard, and so control its destiny, by the use of secular intelligence applying the method of rational, scientific inquiry? If this is so, what is the effect of such a view, interpenetrating national life, on the role of serious letters?

Relatedly, the goal of the French Revolution was the goal of the freedom of the individual to raise his living standards without regard to class or religion or race. The French Revolution has produced its great army of liberals. In fact, much of the serious literature of our time is devoted, directly or indirectly, to these liberal goals. Do not most liberals feel that the pursuit of letters which does not bear on liberal goals is a distraction? (I speak here as a 'liberal' myself committed to the goals of the French Revolution, who yet feels two things: that the goals of liberalism themselves might be destroyed by a decay of standard in the implementation of these goals, where inferior ideas prevail in the total market; and that the danger of uncorrected liberalism might be nothing more nor less than the destruction of those standards of the past out of which considerable achievements came, including the achievements of liberalism itself.)

Can we say that, in the implementation of our living standards, science, pure and applied, has had a decisive role? That science is looked to as a guide to living: in psychology and psychiatry as the science of man; in sociology as the science of group living in its many forms; in political science as the science of political group-living; in economics as the science of economics; in philosophy as validating the scientific method as the only reliable method for 'knowledge'; in education as a training more in the use of scientific method, with an eye to vocational practice, than in literature and the humanities; in law as legal science; in medicine; in government and industry as an indispensable ally for rational inquiry into problems? Can we say that literature is seriously on the defensive, since very few self-respecting intellectuals see in literature a form of 'knowledge', but only a form of misleading 'fiction' or, at best, an 'aesthetic experience' of the palate variety?

Can we say that industrialism has in so many ways that need to be described intensified our sense of overwhelming complexity? Can this very sense of complexity—so much to be known; such an endless proliferation of specialization; such a sense of problems on a national and international level; such an awareness of the complexities of urban living; such a sense of the sheer dynamism of mobility and change in institutions and forms of knowledge (to name only a few)—be said to make the pursuit of letters more difficult for the writer, the critic and audience? Aren't we faced with a built-in irony of history where a literature 'adequate' to a difficult civilization will have an increasingly smaller audience? Isn't this situation unprecedented?

It is clear, too, that changing relationships developed between literature and the press; literature and the development of specialist, informative non-fiction in periodicals and books; literature and advertising. What I have in mind is the way in which, step by step, the world of reliable and/or unreliable forms of 'information' and 'knowledge' competed against literature in the open market. Whereas men of letters could turn to forms of journalism, higher and lesser, before the 1870's and 1880's, after these decades they appear to have lost the world to others, specialists and journalists both. Is it true that only the 'familiar essays' (perhaps a dying form) and literary criticism survive tenuously out of a richer past? Is it not also true that there has been as much an increase of 'sub-expression' of ideas of all kinds as of sub-literature?

I have been arguing, implicitly, that the situation for letters in a pre-industrial civilization is in every respect different. In discussion groups, however, those who would argue more for similarity than for difference constitute perhaps as large a number. At any rate, we may agree about the general lines of inquiry.

Such an inquiry into literature and general culture is enormously complex. My own feeling is that American minds have had difficulty with the problem because they have not perceived the degree of complexity: the inquiry will be short-sighted if historical awareness is short-sighted.

At the Chicago meeting, there was a strong feeling that we ought to make a beginning and that we ought to allow our inquiries to impel us along. We would try to consolidate our findings periodically.[4] We decided that we would move in two directions.

In the first place there was a strong feeling that we ought to be considering papers, not discussion alone, as a means of furthering our inquiry.

And secondly, we should begin to compile a critical bibliography of the better books and articles covering the following phases of our inquiry:

(a) Good critical practice, particularly of best-sellers and sub-literature, but also practice covering the better writers.

(b) General and specific studies where the relationship of literature to general culture takes the emphasis, as distinct from other possible approaches, e.g., 'history of ideas'. Specific pieces on precisely the relationship between literature and general culture.

(c) General and specific studies of audience.

(d) General and specific studies of the total careers of particular writers, with a view towards answering the questions proposed.

(e) General and specific studies of the 'guardians of letters'.

(f) General and specific studies of the market for letters in relation to and/or distinct from patronage.

(g) General and specific studies where 'letters' are studied in relation to other disciplines in the context of 'culture', and not so much in terms of intellectual distinction.

NOTES

[1] Part of the discussion, therefore, was devoted to whether 'literature and general culture' might not be merged into the section on 'Literature and Society', for some years now a division of M.L.A. with a rotating Advisory and Nominating Committee, Bibliography Committee and Officers: and at whose regular yearly meetings papers were read. A Conference is limited to thirty-five invited members. It meets yearly until the Executive Committee of M.L.A. decides whether it ought to be formally incorporated.

2 For instance, two chapters in the recent book on *Contemporary American Scholarship*, edited by Lewis Leary (New York 1958): 'The Public Arts and Private Sensibility', by Patrick D. Hazard, the 'Literary Audiences', by Lennox Grey; separate pages devoted to aspects of culture in *Mass Culture*, edited by Bernard Rosenberg and David Manning White (Glencoe, Illinois 1957); a bibliography in Hugh D. Duncan's *Language and Literature in Society* (Chicago 1953) —these are only representative. Representative also are the books by David Riesman, William H. Whyte, Jnr., Jacques Barzun, Richard Altick, James D. Hart, Arnold Hauser, Joseph Wood Krutch, Gilbert Seldes, Max Lerner and C. Wright Mills.

3 Mr. Michael Wolff of Indiana University, an editor of *Victorian Studies*, thought that such work might go forward with promising results for the Victorian period. Mr. Joseph Frank of the University of Rochester reminded us of the considerable difficulties for literature before the eighteenth century.

Mr. James B. Hall of the University of Oregon, the secretary for the meeting and himself a writer of fiction of some distinction, told the group that he had recently completed a study of some hundreds of short stories from American slick magazines. This was the kind of paper, the group felt, that might relevantly make a contribution: it was done by a serious writer with a sense of standards; it followed the procedure of qualified criticism; and it made judgments of 'realization' and 'significance'.

4 I am happy to say that at the meeting in Chicago, Mr. W. J. Harvey, an editor of *Essays in Criticism*, currently teaching for the year at Reed College, Oregon, indicated that, should a nucleus for the inquiry begin in America, he would do whatever he could to duplicate the effort in Britain. Mr. R. J. Kaufmann, American representative for the *Critical Quarterly* offered similar encouragement, as did Mr. Hennig Cohen, editor of the *American Quarterly* and Mr. Michael Wolff, editor of *Victorian Studies*.

Two Working Papers in Cultural Studies
Paper 1: A Humane Centre
Paper 2: Max Weber and the 'Cultural Sciences'
Alan Shuttleworth

from

Occasional Papers No. 2, 1966, Centre for Contemporary
Cultural Studies, Birmingham University.

INTRODUCTION

These papers were presented by Alan Shuttleworth to two Centre Seminars in the Winter Term, 1965 and the Spring Term, 1966. They have since been substantially revised.

At the beginning of the 1965/66 academic year, we introduced for all members of the Centre a weekly seminar on 'Selected Texts'. The purpose of this seminar was to build up a common body of background reading in the different disciplines adjacent to 'cultural studies'. We felt the need for at least one weekly occasion when we could focus sharply on the problems of method and purpose in our work, with discussion centering on one relevant text. In this way we hoped to give depth and breadth to our research projects and to build up a common vocabulary of concepts.

The first task was to give some historical depth to the field of enquiry, and we made a start from the literary/social end of the spectrum, taking certain representative texts from English writers and social critics in what - following Raymond Williams's book - we called the 'Culture and Society' tradition. These included Blake, Cobbett, Paine, Burke, Coleridge and the Romantics, Carlyle, Mill, Arnold, Ruskin, Morris, Tawney, Lawrence, Eliot and Leavis. This tradition represented a critical response to the industrial revolution and the growth of a mature capitalist civilization in England - a transformation which, as Williams pointed out, is indicated among these writers by a preoccupation with certain key terms (industry, democracy, class, art and culture). The body of writing shows the way in which men with, broadly speaking, 'literary minds', reached out to make sense of and to criticise the new society. Many of the terms and key definitions which we use to describe the relation of culture to society were first offered by writers working in this tradition. They represented our first point of departure.

Then we turned to another, equally relevant, 'moment' in the response to industrial society - the origins of classical European sociological thought: what Alan Shuttleworth, in his second paper, calls "the late flowering of the German Culture and Society tradition." Here was another response - another 'kind of mind' - coming to grips with modern society and culture, and finding new terms and concepts with which to describe that society. In the time available, we tried to get as close as we could to this tradition, through the writings of Saint-Simon, Comte, Marx, Durkheim, Weber, Toennies, Mannheim. This work is continuing, with a somewhat different emphasis, in the third year.

The two papers printed here were offered to the Text Seminar as
(a) a critical account of the work of F. R. Leavis in the cultural
field, and (b) a summing-up paper on Max Weber, his exemplary qualities
for us, especially as shown in his essays on the methodology of the
'cultural sciences'. Alan Shuttleworth has used these two major
writers, each representative of two distinct traditions of thought, to
highlight some of the problems of method and purpose in cultural
analysis. He has tried to single out the unique contribution which
each writer has made to the field. He also suggests common points and
perspectives, and relates these to the Centre's needs as a 'humane
centre' of study and research. In looking at the work of Leavis and
of Weber in this field, he continually returns to the questions "Is
this the Centre's notion of a finished piece of work?" Implicit here
is the challenge to clarify and define the field better, and to pinpoint the points of transition as the frontiers between disciplines
are crossed. The two Papers do, therefore, extend and amplify the
argument, while at the same time helping to draw together themes
touched on in seminar discussion. A brief reference to the manner in
which this discussion has reshaped our own approach, is made, under
the section on "Definitions", in the Centre's Third Report (December,
1966).

Alan Shuttleworth read P.P.E. at Oxford, worked for a year on a
project in urban sociology, and then undertook research on the work of
Weber and Talcott Parsons as a post-graduate student in the Department
of Sociology, Birmingham. He took an active part in the work of the
Centre, and made a valuable contribution to its development, helping
to set up the Text Seminar and advising on research projects. He has
now taken up a teaching appointment at Manchester University, but we
hope that he will maintain a close and continuing association with
the Centre's work in the future.

Centre for Contemporary Cultural Studies,   Richard Hoggart
School of English,   Stuart Hall
University of Birmingham.

December, 1966

A HUMANE CENTRE

by Alan Shuttleworth

> The problem is to produce specialists who are in
> touch with a humane centre, and to produce a centre
> for them to be in touch with; but this centre is
> not best conceived as a standard 'educated man'.
> There will be 'educated men' with various stresses,
> various tendencies towards specialisation. (1)

In bracing itself for an encounter with sociology, and in attempting
a general survey and evaluation of the culture and society debate
from Coleridge to Leavis, this Centre should not adopt a merely
historical approach, placing each of the major figures in the tradition in relation to one another, pointing out their particular merits,
arguing how good they were in their time. Nor should we be concerned
just with a rescue operation, thanking God for their rhetoric, taking
out what is valuable, focusing on the idea of culture in its various
meanings which they did maintain against much opposition: we are
fortunate - this has been done for us. (2) The question we should ask
is this: here is a purpose, a style, a way of writing about culture
and society as a whole; we recognise its merits; how far is it the
highest aspiration of the Centre to produce similar work - similar in
purpose, style and method? Or do we have a different aim? I do not
suggest we should work in this mode all the time: but to what extent
are Coleridge's 2nd Lay Sermon, Carlyle's Past and Present, Eliot's
Notes, in accord with our idea of a finished piece of work; the kind
of work we think the Centre should be directed and organised towards
publishing? My answer is: similar in purpose, dissimilar in style
and method.

I begin with a discussion of Leavis's sketch for an English School
because in itself it could serve as a model for the Centre and because
through it I hope to focus certain problems of method and purpose
relevant to the tradition as a whole. The sketch for an English School
is noted, and relevant for us, for two features: its defence of "the
literary mind" as "the central kind of mind" and its assertion of the
need for combined literary and social studies, mutually guided by the
literary mind. Of the literary mind, Leavis says,

> It is of the essence of the scheme that the work
> of all kinds would be done by the 'literary mind'
> (to redeem that label from its injurious use); by,
> that is, an intelligence with the sensitiveness,

> the flexibility and the disciplined and mature pre-
> occupation with value that should be the product of
> a literary training. It is an intelligence so
> trained that is best fitted to develop into the
> central kind of mind, the co-ordinating conscious-
> ness, capable of performing the function assigned
> to the class of the educated. (3)

Note there that these claims are made for the literary mind on the
basis of two virtues: its sensitiveness and flexibility and its disciplined and mature preoccupation with value. It is these claims that
I want to spend most of this paper looking at.

As regards the combination of literary and social studies, Leavis
suggests that the School should concentrate on the study of a particular time and place - seventeenth century England - and that within
that period the student would be concerned with "something like the
whole history of the century, political, economic, social and intellectual." Though, of course, this work would proceed by means of
particular pieces of work, which would themselves be guided by the
various specialists, it would all be done "in the light of a dominant
preoccupation, a major guiding and sensitizing interest,"

> This is a summing-up, an evaluating survey, of the
> changes taking place in the period - the changes
> as they affect one's sense of England as a civili-
> sation, a civilised community, a better or worse
> place to have been born in, to have belonged to, to
> have lived in. (4)

This evaluating survey of the seventeenth century is in turn relevant
in so far as it helps produce a mature contemporary sense of value.

This is a very brief statement of Leavis's project, but the brevity
should not conceal the boldness of the series of positions which are
being maintained. Lying behind what is said here, he is, first of
all, arguing a case within literary criticism: that the literary
critic cannot be satisfied with the linguistic or historical clarification and interpretation of the text which is occupying him, but
must all the time be concerned to, driven to, judge it. Within his
own proper field, narrowly defined then, Leavis is insisting on this
evaluative strictness. That demand, in itself, has proved contentious
enough. But he is also arguing that the literary critic must extend
his interests beyond 'his own proper field.' On home ground, as it
were, the critic is concerned with works of literature: the case is
that he should become involved with the workings of society. Let us
be clear about what this means: it is not just that society's litera-

ture, seen as a whole rather than as separate pieces, nor even that
society's popular culture, which is to become the object of scrutiny.
It is the whole society. The project thus goes beyond literary
criticism, and yet, in a different sense, it remains too closely tied
to literary criticism to be identified easily as sociology. For the
dominant preoccupation of all the studies would be that same "disciplined and mature preoccupation with value" that Leavis regards as one
of the defining characteristics of the literary mind. That is why this
project is designed for an English School at all, rather than for any
other university department: it is to ensure that the academic work of
all kinds will not evade having to arrive at a judgement of value.

We ought to be quite clear about the position being defended here, and
to be able to distinguish it from positions which approximate to it
but do not make the final 'grand' claims. In his paper on <u>Sociology
and Literature</u>, Leavis does put forward some of these different positions,
without, however, drawing much distinction between them. First of all,
he makes a modest proposal to sociology. If you are going to enquire
into the sociology of literature, that is into the social conditions of
literary production, then

> you must have a more inward acquaintance with the
> works of literature from which you argue than can
> be got from a literary history or a text-book ...
> Investigations of the kind suggested could be pro-
> secuted - they are, indeed, likely to be conceived -
> only by a more sensitively critical reader of English
> poetry than most scholars show themselves to be, even
> when they are born to the language ... That is, no
> use of literature is of any use unless it is a real
> use; literature isn't so much material lying there
> to be turned over from the outside, and drawn on,
> for reference and exemplification, by the critically
> inert. (5)

Similarly,

> You cannot make changes in taste the centre of your
> enquiry without implicitly undertaking, as an essen-
> tial part of your work, a great deal of perception,
> discrimination and analysis such as demand a sensitive,
> trained and active critic. (6)

This much is, I think, agreed within the Centre: that in order to undertake a sociology of literature, or a sociology of popular culture or
the mass media, or a sociology of the history of taste, then only 'content analysis' of the same subtlety and discrimination is adequate as
would warrant a literary critical judgement. Here, clearly is a task

for the Centre: to train sociologists in literary criticism.

The literary critic can provide evidence for the historian and sociologist in a second sense: through the 'representative' quality of
great literature:

> The possible uses of literature to the historian
> and the sociologist are many in kind, and all the
> important ones demand that the user shall be able,
> in the fullest sense, to read. If, for instance,
> we want to go further than the mere constatation
> that a century and a half ago the family counted
> for much more than it does now, if we want some
> notion of the difference involved in day-to-day
> living - in the sense of life and its dimensions
> and its emotional and moral accenting - for the
> ordinary cultivated person, we may profitably start
> trying to form it from the novels of Jane Austen.
> But only if we are capable of appreciating shade,
> tone, implication and essential structure - as (it
> is necessary to add) none of the academically, or
> fashionably, accredited authorities seems to be. (7)

Here, again, I think there can be no doubt that the Centre can and
should do work of this kind and should attempt to improve the quality
of work done by others.

These are both more modest claims than those made in such passages as
the following (these amount to the same 'final grand claim' outlined
above). In developing the point about the sociology of literature, by
reference to the work of L. C. Knights, he continues to this more
advanced position:

> If it is asked of such an inquiry whether it is pri-
> marily sociological or literary it will be enough to
> answer that it represents the kind of sociological
> interest into which a real literary, or critical,
> interest in literature develops, and that, correla-
> tively, the sociologist here will be a literary
> critic or nothing. For to insist that literary
> criticism is, or should be, a specific discipline
> of intelligence is not to suggest that a serious
> interest in literature can confine itself to the
> kind of intensive local analysis associated with
> 'practical criticism' - to the scrutiny of the 'words
> on the page' in their minute relations, their effects
> of imagery, and so on: a real literary interest is an
> interest in man, society and civilisation, and its

>   boundaries cannot be drawn; the adjective is not a
>   circumscribing one. (8)

That is, what distinguishes the 'literary mind', as Leavis defines it
here, is not its subject matter but its method: the literary mind is
not confined to literary criticism. That, clearly, is a further
development of the argument than need be made. We could argue that
the literary mind has important insights to offer to the historian or
sociologist of literary taste, or even to the general historian or
sociologist, without going on to argue that the literary critic should
himself engage in work in those fields and that, when he does so, he
should bring to bear his full range of concerns, including his preoccupation with value.

Similarly, Leavis goes on to develop the argument that great literature
has a 'representative' quality; that it reveals aspects and complexities
of the society from which it emerged - aspects and complexities which
it is difficult or, perhaps, impossible to get at in other ways. He
enlarges that point in a way which is characteristic of the whole of
the culture-and-society tradition:

>   A social historian who appreciated the nature of
>   the vitality of the English language and of English
>   literature in the seventeenth century - and such
>   appreciation itself leads to sociological inquiries -
>   would, in defining and developing his interests, be
>   sensitised by more positively and potently realised
>   questions than any that have given life, form and
>   significance to English Social History: questions as
>   to the conditions of a vigorous and spiritually vital
>   culture, the relations between the sophisticated and
>   the popular, and the criteria by which one might
>   attempt to judge the different phases of a national
>   civilisation. To say this is not to envisage with
>   complaisance a habit of naive comparative valuation.
>   But social history will have shape and significance -
>   will have significant lines and contours - only so far
>   as informed by the life and pressure of such questions;
>   and as intent preoccupations it is towards comparative
>   valuation that they press, even if they actually issue
>   in none that is explicit, definitive and comprehensive.
>   What, as a civilisation to live in and be of, did
>   England offer at such and such a time? As we pass
>   from now to then, what light is thrown on human possi-
>   bilities - on the potentialities and desirabilities of
>   civilised life? In what respects might it have been
>   better to live then than now? What tentative concep-
>   tion of an ideal civilisation are we prompted towards

> by the hints we gather from history? It is with
> such questions in mind - which is not to say that
> he will come out with answers to them - that a
> social historian, in so far as his history is any-
> thing more than an assemblage of mechanically
> arranged external information, must define the
> changes and developments that he discerns. (9)

It is this 'grand claim' which the English culture-and-society tradition forces on our attention, for clearly this kind of evaluation of
a whole society, of a whole century was what they attempted; this was
their purpose. It was also, on the whole, the literary mind which
they brought to bear on this task, for, with one or two exceptions -
J. S. Mill, Tawney - the literary mind has been the central kind of
mind within the tradition. Or, rather, let me qualify that, and state
the main line of my argument: that ought to have been the characteristic
merit of this body of social writing, but it has not been. I would
argue that the literary mind, at its best, has important limits when
it comes to writing about society; but that in this tradition we have
very rarely seen the literary mind at its best. The tradition is,
accordingly, doubly limited.

So far, in relation to the sketch for an English School, and in relation to the culture and society tradition, I have been looking at
purpose. If we accept for our own work the definition of purpose which
Leavis has offered here, then we need to be very clear about the best
method and strategy for achieving it.

> The point is that everyone would have been required
> to come to fairly close terms - the work must be
> thorough enough to justify that claim - with other
> fields of special study, other trained approaches
> and other disciplines, than the literary. (10)

Fairly close terms? This is clearly an important practical problem.
How much sociology should students at the Centre be required to read?
The student would be put into contact with,

> such works of sociology, anthropology, history,
> political thought, and so on, as might, after due
> consultation and consideration ... be picked on as
> appropriate. (11)

That last phrase, coming from Leavis, is not as revealing as it would
be coming from anyone else. But how much sociology, anthropology,
history and political theory counts as "fairly close terms"? It has
to be close enough, remember, to justify judgement and evaluation.
Clearly, it involves something more than just reading Middletown and
The Wheelwright's Shop. Let me put the question another way: consider
someone already fairly eclectic in sociology, anthropology, history
and political thought; what would count for him as coming to "fairly
close terms" with literature and literary criticism? What would be
close enough reading to justify judgement and evaluation?

The literary student's acquaintance with these various disciplines
would have to be sufficient to enable him to judge and evaluate; it
would have to be sufficient, to serve any purpose, to enable him to
write a compulsory paper on "the process of change by which the England
of the Seventeenth Century turned into the England of today". As
should be clear, this is not just one paper among others which the
student would write; in a way, the whole purpose of the course is to
enable him to do so. Of this essay, Leavis writes,

> In such a piece of work, clearly, it would be pre-
> eminently the unacademic virtues that would be
> demanded and tested: a pioneering spirit; the
> courage of enormous incompleteness; the determina-
> tion to complete the best possible chart with the
> inevitably patchy and sketchy knowledge that is all
> one's opportunities permit one to acquire; the
> judgement and intuition to select drastically yet
> delicately, and make a little go a long way; the
> ability to skip and to scamp with wisdom and con-
> science. (12)

That is as clear a statement of what "fairly close" means as we get.
Is that as much, and as little, as all Centre students require? In
its way it is fair enough. It is hard to see how the logic of an
English School, with a general concern for values, could avoid requiring
such a piece of work at that level. But we are not merely considering
the undergraduates in an English School, and therefore the first stages
of their training in the uses of the literary mind. We are considering
a whole 150 years of tradition of the uses of the literary mind by
mature writers, aiming not at undergraduate essays but at a disciplined
valuation and judgement of a whole society, an entire century. Is
such a sketch sufficient to that task? Is such a skipped and scamped
'reading' sufficiently attentive to the 'text'? (And I am concerned -
with all possible allowance to our collective "wisdom and conscience" -
with how we as a Centre ought to write.) What sort of essay would the
equivalent reading in literature produce on "The process of change by
which the literature of the Seventeenth Century turned into the literature of today"?

Let me illustrate the pertinence of the questions raised so far. Is the Centre concerned with the evaluation of literary artefacts, whether high, middlebrow or popular, in and for themselves, and then offering these to the historian and sociologist as evidence; or is it itself concerned with these "as they affect one's sense of England as a civilisation, a civilised community, a better or worse place to have been born in, to have belonged to, to have lived in?" That is, how close are our aims to the aims of the tradition? The answer to this question affects the more immediate questions. Is the sociology of teenagers of any real, vital relevance to the Centre's work, or is it merely of incidental _interest_? How important is an understanding of the class and power structure of contemporary Britain and its shifts in this century for the press project? How can you meaningfully interpret James Bond without an understanding of the social process of affluence and the social structure of deference? If these issues are of vital importance to us, should members of the Centre attempt to acquire an 'undergraduate' competence in them, or should the Centre itself include sociologists doing their own work, on their own terms, on the sociology of teenagers, the class and power structure of Britain, the sociology of affluence? These are questions raised at all levels of the Centre's work - in individual projects, in the design of collective projects such as the press study, in the arrangement of seminars, in the range of items included in a possible journal and above all in the design and balance of the Centre's work as a whole. And they are not questions which can be answered by the Centre's having sociologists, if it is unclear about the work they should do.

We are clearly moving into a critical attitude towards the tradition here. Coleridge did occasionally write what one can only call undergraduate history essays — and they were appallingly bad. John Stuart Mill was a keen amateur historian of the French Revolution, though he wrote only minor book reviews on the subject. This amateur competence was not the basis of their acquaintance with their societies. Again, though J. S. Mill defended at length the view that all social thought and social writing should be based on scientific sociology, it cannot be said that any of his writing was. So neither amateur nor professional sociology or history seems to have been at work in the tradition. What then did discipline the social thought and writing?

First of all, it must be said that sometimes, and more frequently as the tradition progressed, and almost entirely in Eliot and Leavis, no discipline at all was at work in the social writing. Consider a passage from Culture and Environment, which I think Leavis would claim to be the centre of such a 'sketch', and note that this is not an isolated passage, unfairly taken out of a more complex, more qualified analysis, or one out of a number of stated lines of development, or at a different level of generality from the way he normally writes about society, or even written with the realisation that it is such a 'skipped and scamped sketch'; this, filled out a little and exemplified, is about all we get:

> Sturt speaks of 'the death of Old England and of the replacement of the more primitive nation by an "organised" modern state.' The Old England was the England of the organic community, and in what sense it was more primitive than the England that has replaced it needs pondering. But at the moment what we have to consider is the fact that the organic community has gone; it has so nearly disappeared from memory that to make anyone, however educated, realise what it was is commonly a difficult undertaking. Its destruction (in the West) is the most important fact of recent history - it is very recent indeed. How did this momentous change - this vast and terrifying disintegration - take place in so short a time? The process of the change is that which is commonly described as Progress. This is how George Sturt describes it ... (13)

Even treated as a sketch, that is very inadequate indeed. It should be no surrender of the important literary critical claims to recognise that it is precisely such passages which rightly inflame sociologists and allow them too easily to refuse all co-operation with literary critics. To avoid being stampeded into that position, we should try to be precise in noting the passage's weaknesses. One would expect Leavis to approach The Wheelwright's Shop precisely as "a sensitive, trained and active critic" prepared to undertake "a great deal of perception, discrimination and analysis." As such he might well have wanted to say something about Sturt's very distinct tone of voice throughout that book; about the way in which we never get the story of life in that village and workshop 'straight', but are always aware of Sturt's own insistent presence, standing between his material, sometimes revealing it for us very clearly, at other times - we can feel this in the reading - obscuring it, bending it, throwing a certain romantic haze over the whole proceedings. This task of analysis was one that Leavis was supremely qualified to undertake and ought to have undertaken. It would have caused him to make a much more sensitive use, and a much more controlled use, of the book. As it is, he simply takes the book as revealing the truth. He does not explore its repre-

sentative qualities; he _assumes_ them. And thus, time and again in
Culture and Environment, we lose that sense - elsewhere so characteristic of Leavis - of a man with a disciplined and strenuous concern
for values coming to the material, probing it, exploring it, trying,
working to make connections and to come to a difficult judgement.
Rather, we feel we are in the presence of a man with a fixed moral prejudice, lighting on passages that fuel those preconceived prejudices
and then being inflamed by them.

It is not so much the sentiments themselves that I am objecting to here -
just think how much more impressively (more subtly, complexly, particularly, modestly) Leavis makes that same sense of transition and
loss work for him (because he works for it) in some of his literary
criticism, in the essay on Bunyan for instance. Here the use of the
sentiment is merely self-indulgent: he allows himself to be carried
away by it, rather than himself bearing it to, and working with it in,
some particular time and place. And when he does confront something
local with it - advertising for instance - the sweep of history is so
massive, so general, covers so much, so clearly has only one moral
implication, that the effect is slightly ridiculous rather than
incisive. It is no real analysis of advertising to say that it is
representative, like everything else, of an epochal historical change,
moving irresistably in one direction, underway for at least two hundred
years.

The passage is so bad because it is the produce of no discipline. It
is not the result of any literary critical discipline, for literary
critical methods have been ignored. Nor has it been subjected to any
directly empirical discipline - it has not been required to face and
argue out of any particular facts. It uses facts in a merely illus-
trative way; and it has not been subjected to any theoretical discipline -
the use and meaningfulness and relationships of such terms as "organic",
"organised", "primitive", "community", "disintegration" has nowhere been
stated or defended, nor have these terms been challenged to assert their
meaning and utility in contrast to "individuality", "liberty",
"socialism", "capitalism", "welfare", "rationality" etc. _All_ we have
is evaluation.

Let us be quite clear that the application of the literary mind to
society does not mean this. Indeed quite emphatically it does not.
Consider this in the light of Leavis's own definition in the passage
quoted above; we have the preoccupation with value allright, but certainly not the flexibility and sensitiveness. Bearing in mind the
three different ways of writing about society established so far - the
'undergraduate essay', the educated sociologist working on his own
terms, and the passage from _Culture and Environment_ - listen to the
following passage from _Education and the University_ and consider what
other virtues, apart from a generalising rhetorical concern for values,

the literary mind ought to be able to bring to the study of society.

> The essential discipline of an English School is
> the literary-critical; it is a true discipline, only
> in an English School if anywhere will it be fostered,
> and it is irreplaceable. It trains, in a way no
> other discipline can, intelligence and sensibility
> together, cultivating a sensitiveness and precision
> of response and a delicate integrity of intelligence -
> intelligence that integrates as well analyses and
> must have pertinacity and staying power as well as
> delicacy. (14)

Before looking closer at the notions contained in that passage, I want
to pull back and look at the intellectual context out of which this
tradition of social writing and thought arose at the beginning of the
nineteenth century. Especially in the Romantics, we can see this
tradition developing in sharp opposition to the dominant, rationalist,
mode of thought. We can see in Coleridge, for instance, the move from
radicalism to conservatism, from enthusiastic support for the French
Revolution into bitter opposition, from Godwin to Burke. Contained
within that political move, and contained by it, was a switch in method
and basic modes of thought, a switch, in Coleridge's terms, from the
pure, abstract reason of the Enlightenment (and the equally abstract
understanding of scientific empiricism) to a new fusion or interplay
of reason, understanding and imagination. All thought, political,
social, psychological and educational, had been dominated by the model
of natural science, by the model of generalising thought; by the
desire to strip whatever was being studied of its particular, individual features and to treat only its universal aspects; to develop,
not concrete descriptions, but classifications and out of them general
laws. Thus instead of writing about the actual political systems
dominant in Britain, its history and its tensions, men wrote about the
universally valid natural rights of man and deduced from them a plan
for the perfect political system, perfect for all societies at all
times and in any situation. Instead of looking at what actual men did
desire, want, feel, value, esteem, they drew up a utilitarian list of
what all men would naturally desire. Instead of noting the visible
course of economic development, they posited 'economic man' and
deduced reality from their theorems. Reality was, at the most, classi-
fiable under three or four dichotomous sets: rational/traditional;
tyrannical/democratic; religious/scientific. Coleridge did not respond
only by offering a different model at the same level of generality, but
also by arguing that a true analysis must also grow out of the study
of the particular and must be informed as well by the imagination. All
three - reason, understanding and imagination - properly used, are ways
of disciplining thought and forcing it back to, not letting it evade,
the full confrontation with reality. Of course, much of Coleridge's

own writing on society is informed by none of these qualities: it is peculiarly unreasonable, lacking in understanding, unimaginative, a mere outrush of invective. But occasionally the analysis swells out, it becomes filled with the presence of the real Coleridge and we begin to see what might be possible.

I am thinking in particular of the Second Lay Sermon, where he is discussing the "causes of the present discontents" and the rise of capitalism. He has a first run through at an 'analysis' but the thought is so warped and twisted by a bitter and intense hatred of radicalism that he attributes all the changes and the ills of the society to the personal wickedness, intemperance and weak morals of the lower orders. There is no attempt to understand social process and structure in anything other than individual terms, and yet it is never to any particular person that he refers, but always to a general sort of person. There is really no attempt to analyse at all, but merely to judge and condemn.

But then he comes back to the subject again, and this time proceeds rather differently. He starts at a high level of generality by bringing forward some of the dominant contemporary interpretations, or rather metaphors, for the rise of capitalism: that it is "a self-regulating machine" with escape pipes and safety valves, or that "all things find their level." He acknowledges the general merit of the system - "that the power and circumstantial prosperity of the nation has been increasing." The implicit argument that he is presenting to us here is that of the most important rationalist thinkers of the time - the economists. They were not concerned with particular people and occasions, but with general processes, the general rise in production, the increase of manufactures. And Coleridge responds and states his method,

> Dare we unpack the bales and cases so marked,
> and look at the articles, one by one?

And to look behind the crude statistics of material prosperity is what he proceeds to do.

> But persons are not things - but man does not find
> his level. Neither in body nor in soul does the
> man find his level. After a hard and calamitous
> season, during which the thousand wheels of some
> vast manufactory had remained silent as a frozen
> waterfall, be it that plenty has returned and that
> trade has once more become brisk and stirring: go,
> ask the overseer, and question the parish doctor,
> whether the workman's health and temperance with
> the staid and respectful manners best taught by the

> inward dignity of conscious self-support, have
> found their level again.

He wants to move behind the generalisations and to look and to respond
to the particular human meanings involved. But it is not _that_ easy:
"staid and respectful manners" is just another cliché. We can tell _in
the writing_ that this is not a genuine experience which is being made
to work here. He immediately proceeds to tell us that he has seen

> a group of children in Dorsetshire, during the heat
> of the dog days, each with its little shoulders upto
> its ears, and its chest pinched inward, the very
> habit and fixtures, as it were, that had been
> impressed on their frames by the former ill-fed, ill-
> clothed, and unfuelled winters.

This is more deeply felt. He goes on immediately to cite "the old
labourer's savings", "the orphan's funds", "the fond confiding sister's
humble fortune." In all of this - again, we can tell it from the
writing - the tone is not right. Workmen with temperance and manners,
a group of children each with _its_ shoulder and chest, the _old_ labourer,
the orphan, the fond confiding sister, they are still not quite people.
We can see that it is not enough to offer a rhetorical concern for the
particular: it requires work and discipline to really use the particular
as evidence.

Now listen to this about the enclosures:

> The speaker was an elderly and respectable widow,
> who expressed herself with that simple eloquence
> which strong feeling seldom fails to call forth in
> humble life, but especially in women. She spoke
> English, as indeed most Highlanders do who speak
> it at all, with a propriety of phrase and a dis-
> crimination of tone and emphasis that more than
> compensated for the scantiness of her vocabulary.
> After an affecting account of her own wrongs and
> ejectment (which however, she said, bore with com-
> parative lightness on her, who had saved up her
> wherewithall to live, and was blessed with a son
> well to do in the world), she made a movement with
> her hand in a circle, directing my eye meanwhile to
> various objects as marking its outline; and then
> observed, with a deep sigh and a suppressed and
> slow voice which she suddenly raised and quickened
> after the first drop or cadence - "Within this space -
> how short a time back! - there lived a hundred and
> seventy-three persons: and now there is only a

> shepherd, and an underling or two. Yes, sir! ...
> I sometimes fancy that the very birds are gone -
> all but the crows and gleads! Well, and what then?
> Instead of us all, there is one shepherd man, and
> it may be a pair of small lads - and a many, many
> sheep! And do you think, sir, that God allows of
> such proceedings.

That woman is fully realized. Coleridge has succeeded in responding
and so the old widow begins to count for something against the conventional generalities. After one or two other such examples, Coleridge
moves, not as might be expected to a rhetorical indictment, but to a
more precise characterisation of capitalism than he had achieved before:

> We are - and, till its good purposes, which are
> many, have all been achieved, and we can become
> something better, long may we continue such! - a
> busy, enterprising and commercial nation. The
> habits attached to this character must, if there
> exist no adequate counterpoise, inevitably lead us
> under the specious names of utility, practical
> knowledge, and so forth, to look at all things
> through the medium of the market, and to estimate
> the worth of all pursuits and attainments by their
> marketable value. In this does the spirit of trade
> consist.

That is not a bad analysis for 1817! And finally,

> I was sometimes afterwards told by a very sensible
> person who had studied the mysteries of political
> economy, and was therefore entitled to be listened
> to, that more food was produced in consequence of
> this revolution, that the mutton must be eat some-
> where, and what difference where? If three were
> fed at Manchester instead of two at Glencoe or the
> Trosachs, the balance of human enjoyment was in
> favour of the former. I have passed through many
> a manufacturing town since then, and have watched
> many a group of old and young, male and female,
> going to, or returning from, many a factory, but I
> could never yet persuade myself to be of his opinion.
> Men, I still think, ought to be weighed, not counted.
> Their worth ought to be the final estimate of their
> value.

The response to particular human situations and experiences has here
become a form of argument. It is not 'poetic' feeling as opposed to

strict analysis: it is feeling <u>and</u> analysis, feeling aiding analysis.
It is not imagination as opposed to the truth: it is imaginative insight
helping us towards the truth. Nor is it a concern for the particular
as opposed to a concern for generalisation and theory: the whole movement of thought is from general to particular and back, hesitantly, to
the general again.

It is with this example in mind and aware of its historical importance
that I now want to take up again the question of the literary mind and
try to pinpoint its precise merit as <u>method</u>. I will look first at an
exchange between Wellek and Leavis over the importance of theory for
the literary mind. Wellek wrote to Leavis about <u>Revaluation</u>, making
the double criticism that Leavis had failed to theorise about his own
position, assumptions, values, etc., and that Leavis had failed to
recognise the importance of such theory in those he was evaluating,
especially the Romantics. Thus, in making the first point, Wellek wrote,

> I could wish that you had stated your assumptions
> more explicitly and defended them more systematically.
> I do not doubt the value of these assumptions and, as
> a matter of fact, I share them with you for the most
> part, but I would have misgivings in pronouncing them
> without elaborating a specific defence or a theory in
> their defence. Allow me to sketch your ideal of
> poetry, your "norm" with which you measure every poet:
> ... the only question I would ask you is to defend
> this position more abstractly and to become conscious
> that large ethical, philosophical, and, of course,
> ultimately, also aesthetic <u>choices</u> are involved. (15)

As regards the second point,

> This makes you underrate the coherence and even the
> comprehensibility of the romantic view of the world. (16)

And he makes the following particular points: first, in relation to
Blake's <u>Introduction</u> to the <u>Songs of Experience</u>,

> I think the poem has only one possible meaning, which
> can be ascertained by a study of the whole of Blake's
> symbolical philosophy. Here is my paraphrase ...

> The chapter on Wordsworth, excellent as it is in fine
> critical discrimination, shows the same lack of

interest in romantic philosophy. I cannot see why
the argument of Canto II of The Prelude could not be
paraphrased ...

I cannot see the slightest confusion in the opening
paragraph of Mont Blanc. It states an epistemological view of the world ... Shelley's philosophy, I
think, is astonishingly coherent. After an early
stage of 18th Century materialism he turned to
idealism in a subjective version ... Berkeley or
Berkeley through Drummond, Plato, the neo-Platonists,
the Gnostics, Spinoza, Shaftesbury, or the animistic
philosophy of nature developed by E. Darwin and
H. Davy from Newton are the names which can be found
among his wide reading and they are obviously his
spiritual ancestry. (17)

I have quoted Wellek's letter here at some length in a critical spirit
because, I think, it makes decisively, if unintentionally, a basic point.
In so far as I am a creature of a training, that is how I would attempt
to write. My training was precisely aimed at enabling me to 'paraphrase',
'state epistemological views of the world', show when influences from
Berkeley and Plato were at work, state 'norms', sketch 'ideals' and show
when they are operative in a situation. If I approached literature and
literary criticism armed with my disciplines, that is the very best that
I could reasonably hope to write. That is the very most that I would
expect from any student I sent to look at Leavis, Blake, Wordsworth or
Shelley. For my (and their) reading of the texts could only be 'fairly
close'.

I now want to quote at very great length from Leavis's reply, because
it is there that we can really see what the literary mind ought to be
able to bring to the study of society, and what it all too rarely has:
not just the concern for value alone, but something much more than
that. In his reply, Leavis recognises both kinds of absence from his
work, and defends this,

If I omitted to undertake the defence he desiderates
it was not from any lack of consciousness: I knew I
was making assumptions ... and I was not less aware
than I am now of what they involve. (18)

But he did not elaborate "a specific defence or a theory in their
defence," because he is not a philosopher but a literary critic,:

Philosophy, we say, is 'abstract' (thus Dr. Wellek
asks me to defend my position 'more abstractly'), and
poetry 'concrete'. Words in poetry invite us, not to

> 'think about' and judge but to 'feel into' or
> 'become' - to realise a complex experience that
> is given in the words. They demand, not merely
> a fuller-bodied response, but a completer respon-
> siveness that is incompatible with the judicial
> one-eye-on-the-standard approach suggested by
> Dr. Wellek's phrase: 'your "norm" with which you
> measure every poet.' (19)

This is the first thing: this responsiveness and this concern with the
particular and the concrete. Again,

> The business of the literary critic is to attain a
> peculiar completeness of response and to observe a
> peculiarly strict relevance in developing his res-
> ponse into commentary; he must be on his guard
> against abstracting improperly from what is in
> front of him and against any premature or irrele-
> vant generalising - of it or from it. His first
> concern is to enter into possession of the given
> poem (let us say) in its concrete fulness, and
> his constant concern is never to lose his complete-
> ness of possession, but rather to increase it. (20)

But, it should be clear, this is not only a way of insisting on the
engagement with particular things, it is also a way of organising one's
responses:

> The critic's aim is, first, to realise as sensitively
> and completely as possible this or that which claims
> his attention; and a certain valuing is implicit in
> the realising. As he matures in experience of the
> new thing he asks, explicitly and implicitly: 'where
> does this come? How does it stand in relation to ...?
> How relatively important does it seem?' And the
> organisation into which it settles as a constituent
> in becoming 'placed' is an organisation of similarly
> 'placed' things, things that have found their bearings
> with regard to one another, and not a theoretical
> system or a system determined by abstract considera-
> tions. (21)

It is this kind of responsiveness, and this way of organising responses
that the literary critic looks for in the work he is studying (this is
the way language works in literature), and it is the way in which he
seeks to proceed in his own work. Why? What basically is to be gained
by working in this way? And why, once the literary critic has worked
in this way, why should he not then come out into the open?

> If Dr. Wellek should still insist that I ought, even
> if I declined to elaborate the philosophy implicit in
> my assumptions, at any rate to have been more explicit
> about them, I can only reply that I think I have gone
> as far in explicitness as I could profitably attempt
> to go, and that I do not see what would be gained by
> the kind of explicitness he demands (though I see what
> is lost by it). Has any reader of my book been less
> aware of the essential criteria that emerge than he
> would have been if I had laid down such general pro-
> positions as: 'poetry must be in serious relation to
> actuality, it must have firm grasp of the actual, of
> the object, it must be in relation to life, it must
> not be cut off from direct vulgar living, it should
> be normally human ...'? If, as I did, I avoided such
> generalities, it was not out of timidity; it was
> because they seemed to be too clumsy to be of any use.
> I thought I had provided something better. My whole
> effort was to work in terms of concrete judgements
> and particular analyses: 'This - doesn't it? - bears
> such a relation to that; this kind of thing - don't
> you find it so? - wears better than that,' etc., (22)

And a little later on in the same passage,

> I feel that by my own methods I have attained a
> relative precision that makes this summarising seem
> intolerably clumsy and inadequate. I do not ...
> argue in general terms that there should be 'no
> emotion for its own sake, no afflatus, no mere
> generous emotionality, no luxury in pain or joy';
> but by choice, arrangement and analysis of concrete
> examples I give those phrases (in so far, that is,
> as I have achieved my purpose) a precision of
> meaning they couldn't have got in any other way. (23)

It is all of this, I take it, the fuller-bodied and complete responsiveness to the particular and actual, and the resultant discipline and
precision, which is contained in the word "sensitivity", which the
literary mind can, and the best literary minds have, brought to the
study of society. It follows that we no longer have that division of
labour whereby the sociologist and historian provide the facts, and the
critic lies back, ponders and issues an evaluation. What the literary
mind can offer, <u>whatever it studies</u>, is a disciplined mode of valuing:
each side of that equation implies the other, for the valuing is worth-
less without the discipline, the inquiry; and that kind of inquiry,
involving that sort of responsiveness, cannot proceed without commitments and judgements all the time. As Leavis himself points out else-

where, this does not mean that the critic accordingly sallies forth
brandishing his licence to judge,

> This means not self-confidence, but cultivated self-
> mistrust; not assertiveness, but disciplined and
> strenuous humility and docility - means curiosity,
> patience and accuracy. (24)

If we take with full seriousness what Leavis says in these passages, it
becomes clear, I think, how inadequate Leavis's own writing about society
is, how inadequate Eliot's is, how inadequate so much of the writing in
the tradition is. Not often since Coleridge do I remember encountering
an actual person, living and breathing, in this body of writing; nor
can I remember it mattering very often whether it was this year or that,
this city or town or that, that was being discussed; all too rarely
have we ever focused clearly enough on any problem, policy, or sphere
of society particularly enough. This of course, I should say, has by
no means been a problem of method alone: it has been closely related to
the conservatism and the academicity of the tradition. There is a way
of writing here, biographical, particular, actual, vivid, responsive,
on a human scale, which is aware of its own limitations, which, if we
are meant to take the claims for the literary mind seriously, ought
to be undertaken by the Centre. One can see its relevance, for instance,
to the study of teenage life, or to the effects of women's magazines
and other media. There is, also, precisely a need for such writing
within sociology, which is not to say that all sociologists would
approve of it.

Let me now begin to move towards a conclusion and see where all this
has got us. First, the starting point: it is clearly not disputed that
the central task of the Centre is to bring the literary mind to bear
on cultural artefacts of all kinds - high, middle and mass - to
identify the valuable and to mark movements and changes. That is a
limited task and here the literary mind is on, or near, home ground.
Secondly, the Centre is interested in simply asserting that literature, when read properly, and only when read properly, has important
status as evidence, and in inviting, and training, sociologists and
historians to use them. The problem arises when we consider how far
the Centre itself ought to work outside the cultural field narrowly
defined. If it ought, does it then go on to make the grand claim and
become involved in responding to and judging a way, or ways of life?
How close are we in purpose to the tradition and to Leavis's projected
English School?

There then arises the problem of method. If we have that concern for
values, how do we then proceed with the inquiry? I have argued that
the literary mind, if it is used to the full, is not just a magisterial
voice issuing evaluations: it is also a <u>method</u>, a peculiar way of working

in close, dense contact with particular material. This is a virtue
which arises out of the training in 'close reading' and in responsiveness to what is there on the page, but it ought to hold also when the
critic is going beyond that to inquire into ways of life and social
processes. The literary critic may not, perhaps, be so sure as the
sociologist in handling the generalising mode of thought, but he ought
to be much better than the sociologist in his sympathetic openness
and attentiveness to the particular, to what is there, to the stuff
out of which generalisations are made and by which they can be destroyed. This __ought__ to be the special merit of the literary critic.
It is a way of working which the Centre would do well not to sacrifice
in the forthcoming engagement with sociology.

The question I want to come back to now is where does sociology fit in?
What kind of amateur competence in sociology should people with these
concerns have and what use should they make of people working primarily
in sociology? How far out of their way do critics want to go: how far
should they? The sociology which is most important (and I should make
it clear in what follows that I am talking about the best sociology
and about the most distinctly sociological features of sociology: I am
trying, very barely, to state the features of the sociological mind
which pull it most sharply away from the literary mind) arose in response to precisely the same situation as did the culture and society
tradition - only it arose, to a degree in France, but mainly in Germany.
What we will be looking at, in the main, will be late flowerings of
the German culture and society tradition, both on its home ground, and
then after it was transported to America. It too developed as a response to industrialism and democracy, as an attempt to understand them,
and in opposition to natural-scientific, utilitarian, economic univer-
salism. Thus the German tradition insisted on the differences in
subject-matter and method between the human studies and the natural
sciences. The human studies were called in Germany, "the sciences of
the spirit" or the "cultural sciences". The subject matter of these
studies was not man as a biological organism or as a complex of chemi-
cals and atoms, but man as a spiritual, cultural being, feeling, thinking, knowing, willing, expressing himself. As Dilthey, the greatest
methodologist of this phase, wrote:

> Insofar as man experiences human states, gives
> expression to his experience and understands the
> expressions, mankind becomes the subject of the
> human studies. The interrelation of life, expres-
> sion and understanding, embraces, gestures, facial
> expressions and words by which men communicate with
> each other, permanent mental creations revealing
> the profundity of the creator to the man who can
> grasp it, and permanent objectifications of the
> mind in social structures in which human nature is
> surely and for ever manifest. (25)

This is the subject-matter: the appropriate method is the 'understanding' of 'meaning'. This, it was felt, in the Nineteenth Century, could only be done by the same concern as the literary critic with the particular, the actual, the full responsiveness to the individual, and by capturing, in all its uniqueness, the real-life process. The only difference here is that the Germans called this activity history. (26)

If the Germans had stayed content with that, we would have had no problem today about the relations between sociology and literary criticism. But sociology proper grew out of a modification of that position. While recognising that sociology, being the study of things human, was concerned with the understanding of meaning, Max Weber began the insistence, which has continued, that it still ought to be a generalising, classifying, and therefore theorising, discipline. Because, first of all sociology was not concerned primarily with the behaviour of individuals, but with the behaviour of groups, organisations, collectivities. Not all of a person's full individuality is ever contained in the organisation he is, for the moment, acting in; belonging to a group only involves certain commitments, certain ways of acting and we can understand these, and their meaning, and state them without understanding fully each individual in the group. This is what sociologists mean by a 'norm'. It is because of this that we are able to describe what capitalism is, what bureaucracy is, what the University of Birmingham is, in meaningful, human terms, without saying anything about anybody in particular. What we are stating is what sort of commitment to what kind of action members of this or that group typically make. Understanding what these institutions and organisations mean in the life of any individual is an important task, but it is not the sociologist's main task. This is the first sense in which sociology is a generalising discipline and has moved away from the method of 'the literary mind.' And the making of this kind of generalisation clearly involves a discipline and rigour which is different from that of the literary critic. It involves precisely expliciteness and summarising - though not perhaps necessarily in the form which Leavis objected to so strongly in Wellek. There is an important difference between Wellek's kind of 'history of ideas' and sociology.

But sociology generalises in another sense; it is concerned with classifications and typologies. Having found ways of describing groups and institutions, and therefore having abstracted from the real life process, it is concerned to compare and contrast, explicitly, these groups and institutions, both within any one society, historically, and cross-culturally, cross-nationally. To do this it is necessary to develop classifications and typologies, to be quite precise and explicit about the relationships between the various classifications and about precisely what counts as being a member of this or that type. The activity thus involves theory and theoretical defences. Once you do decide to resort to explicit classes and types in an attempt to keep the boundaries fixed, then you must start theorising in their defence. The results are well known: the abstractness, the inflexibility, the stilted, pseudo-scientific language, etc. At least one problem of this method is that much of the best sociology is unavailable to any but the specialist: the work of Durkheim, Parsons and much of Weber cannot be read without an enormous amount of time and effort.

Some of the sociology we will look at is as bad as I have argued some of the culture and society tradition is. Often it, too, is not disciplined by any genuine empirical enquiry and when the theory is not first-rate it degenerates into a disguised rhetoric. What the best sociology offers, however, is not so much 'the facts' - because the literary mind has its own ways of acquiring knowledge - but a classificatory, typological way of organising knowledge, and a way of making ideas explicit and theorising about them. Properly, it is because of this, not vice versa, that it uses sampling and questionnaire techniques, which are thus purposely abstract, incomplete, in a sense 'unreal'; they are precisely intended for generalising out from the flux and wholeness of a way of life. If sociology does not offer <u>the</u> facts however, it makes available a great wealth of special kinds of facts. But you cannot handle these facts 'neutrally': if you want the facts you have to take the method as well. This is not the time to defend that method. Here, I just wanted to clarify the nature of the confrontation.

NOTES

1. F. R. Leavis, Education and The University, p.28

2. See R. Williams, Culture and Society.

3. F. R. Leavis, Education and The University, p.55

4. F. R. Leavis, Education and The University, p.54

5. F. R. Leavis, The Common Pursuit, pp.195-198

6. loc.cit, p.198

7. F. R. Leavis, The Common Pursuit, p.203

8. F. R. Leavis, The Common Pursuit, p.200

9. F. R. Leavis, The Common Pursuit, p.202

10. F. R. Leavis, Education and The University, p.57

11. loc. cit. p.61

12. F. R. Leavis, Education and The University, p.60

13. F. R. Leavis, Culture and Environment, p.87

14. F. R. Leavis, Education and The University, p.34

15. René Wellek, letter to Dr. Leavis, in The Importance of Scrutiny, ed. by Eric Bentley, p.23

16. René Wellek, letter to Dr. Leavis, p.24

17. René Wellek, letter to Dr. Leavis, pp.24-28

18. F. R. Leavis, Reply to Dr. Wellek, in The Importance of Scrutiny, ed. by Eric Bentley, p.30

19. F. R. Leavis, Reply to Dr. Wellek, p.31

20. F. R. Leavis, Reply to Dr. Wellek, p.32

21. F. R. Leavis, Reply to Dr. Wellek, p.32

22.   F. R. Leavis, Reply to Dr. Wellek, p.33

23.   F. R. Leavis, Reply to Dr. Wellek, p.34

24.   F. R. Leavis, Education and The University

25.   W. Dilthey, Meaning In History

26.   And the school of thought most associated with this
       approach, 'historicism'.

MAX WEBER AND THE 'CULTURAL SCIENCES'

by Alan Shuttleworth

Max Weber is the dominant figure in what I have called "the late
flowering of the German culture and society tradition." Throughout
his voluminous works a constant major concern is the relationship
between ideals and values, especially in the form of religious systems,
and social and economic structure. Impelled to revise, perhaps refute,
Marx, he always tried to understand the wide range of societies which
he looked at in terms of their most basic beliefs, expressed in their
most sacred writings. This is clearly a body of work which the Centre
must attempt to understand and to which it should clarify its approach.
Thus, in looking at Max Weber's work, as in looking at the Culture and
Society tradition, I am concerned with its exemplary qualities for the
Centre. What can we learn from, say, The Protestant Ethic And The
Spirit of Capitalism about how we should ourselves proceed?

Consider, for instance, chapter two of that work, itself called
The Spirit of Capitalism. It is as short as it is ambitious. In it
he states the theme of his inquiry as being to discover "the spirit of
capitalism"; he identifies a central ('representative'?) expression of
that spirit in the writings of Ben Franklin and proceeds to attempt
his own characterisation of it. (1) It is worthwhile attending very
carefully to this. "The concept spirit of capitalism" is introduced
(almost, thrust at us) quite baldly, with no preliminaries, and we are
told that this is what we are concerned to discover and define. Simply
by imposing this one phrase on us he has, of course, determined the
essential form of the chapter: it is concerned both with a massive,
complex social transformation and with "spirit" - a term that has clear
connections with "ethos," "values," "ideals," and, perhaps, "culture."

Having barely presented this term he turns swiftly to Franklin's writing
and offers a number of passages for inspection. Immediately he concludes,

> That it is the spirit of capitalism which here
> speaks in characteristic fashion, no one will
> doubt, however little we may wish to claim that
> everything which could be understood as pertain-
> ing to that spirit is contained in it. (2)

Weber is not a diffident thinker. He then "pauses a moment to consider" the passages from Franklin and draw out "the peculiarity of this philosophy of avarice." The special meaning he has identified there is given a preliminary statement:

> The peculiarity of this philosophy of avarice appears
> to be the ideal of the honest man of recognised credit,
> and above all the idea of a duty of the individual
> towards the increase of his capital, which is assumed
> as an end in itself. Truly what is here preached is
> not simply a means of making one's way in the world,
> but a peculiar ethic. The infraction of its rules
> is treated not as foolishness but as forgetfulness
> of duty. That is the essence of the matter. It is
> not mere business astuteness, that sort of thing is
> common enough, it is an ethos. This is the quality
> which interests us. (3)

The peculiarity he has identified with such decisiveness and precision is that given in the words "ideal," "idea," "preached," "ethic," "rules," "duty," "ethos." He completes this phase of the movement of the thought by giving his own summary characterisation of this spirit as he has identified it. He moves first to the formulation, "Man is dominated by the making of money, by acquisition as the ultimate purpose of his life," and then produces his own distinct statement of "a calling,"

> And in truth this peculiar idea, so familiar to us
> today, but in reality so little a matter of course,
> of one's duty in a calling, is what is most charac-
> teristic of capitalist culture, and is in a sense
> the fundamental basis of it. (4)

The first thing likely to strike us about this half-chapter is the massiveness of the task attempted. It is not lacking in sheer bravado. At the same time we realise its centrality; Weber rightly refers to capitalism as "the most fateful force in the modern world." Of course, it is no accident that these two qualities go together, for the central tasks have a way of also being massive. I should make it clear that when I recommend Weber's work as "exemplary" it is not primarily these qualities that I intend. Before embarking on similar projects, we should at the very least remember the immense erudition that lies concealed behind this work - I am thinking both of Weber's own studies and of the German nineteenth-century intellectual tradition upon which he relied so heavily - and then consider our own. But, on the other hand, I would not wish to discourage anyone from trying to think about central matters.

More immediately, I am concerned with the way in which he seeks to understand this socio-historical development in terms of the ethics, ideals, values embodied in it. We might say that he interprets society as culture (in the widest sense of that word). Thus, and this is the point to which we should pay most attention, he moves in these few pages from the vast, generalising notion of 'the concept spirit of capitalism' to the very local literary product and then back to a conclusion at the general level. The basic work done to sustain this argument is of a literary critical kind: it is nothing more than the close reading of a text. But we should also note what distinguishes his reading from that which a literary critic might undertake. He is extremely selective. He nips in very smartly, picks up only what he wants and is then quickly out again - "This is the quality which interests us." In no sense is he concerned to give a full rendering of the text. It is also significant that he does not rest content with pointing to those features of the text which concern him. He does not allow the text to speak for itself (as Leavis, at a certain point, would): he insists on speaking for the text. He produces his own explicit, summary characterisation of the qualities in Franklin's writing which interest him, and from that point on the text is of no further interest.

It is this sort of attempt to move to an explicit characterisation of the change of values involved within certain major social transforma- tions that drives all Weber's work along. This will emerge even more clearly as we go on to discuss his method and his methodological writings. But before proceeding with that discussion, it will be use- ful to bring into focus a proposition of Leavis's and see how it stands in relation to what we know of Weber so far. I am thinking again of Leavis's notion in Education And The University that the work of all kinds in his proposed English School would be done "in the light of a dominant preoccupation, a major guiding and sensitising interest":

> This is a summing-up, an evaluating survey of the
> changes taking place in the period - the changes
> as they affect one's sense of England as a civili-
> sation, a civilised community, a better or worse
> place to have been born in, to have belonged to,
> to have lived in. (5)

As a statement of purpose this is much closer to what Weber is doing than most discussions of the problem of method in this area would allow. It is the concern to evaluate which is normally taken to distinguish the 'literary mind' from the social scientific. Most discussions of the relations between the two take that as their starting point. The popular stereotype of the literary man is that, trained in criticism and a minority high culture, he is concerned only to issue judgements and evaluations and that typically he looks down paternalistically on the masses and condemns their culture - "that which is commonly des-

cribed as Progress." The sociologist and social-psychologist, in contrast, repudiate all judgement as subjective and rely instead wholly on
the rules of empirical science to reproduce the truth. The concern
with evaluation is seen as the direct opposite of the empirical pursuit
of truth. The two bodies of work are thus held to be irrelevant, if
not intolerable, to each other.

The reality is more complex. What I tried to argue in the paper on
Leavis was that a proper evaluative approach has to be at the same time,
in an important sense, empirical and that literary criticism has its
own distinct ways of being both evaluative and empirical. We do not
merely judge: the evaluative summary, whether of a poem or a whole
social development, is intended as the purpose of the work. As such
it states the direction in which we move - and we do have to work to
get there. Literary criticism has its own way of working, of being
empirical, and sociology has nothing to teach literary criticism about
being attentive to the facts: quite the contrary. What I think emerges
from Weber's work is the other side of this case; the way in which any
truly significant sociological work must be based on a very deep concern with evaluation.

So far I have been attempting to establish connections - at the levels
of purpose and method - between the work of Leavis and Weber. But my
concern in discussing Weber is not simply to act as peace-maker. My
intention in urging his work upon you as exemplary in certain respects
is to point to qualities in it which are not to be found elsewhere, or,
rather, are not to be found so clearly and so well understood elsewhere,
and, particularly, are not to be found in Leavis or in the English tradition generally. In order to establish this point, I should like to
recap briefly the argument about Leavis, so as to make the contrast
more precise.

Leavis's writings on the literary mind emphasise on the one hand its
sensitiveness, its attentiveness, its responsiveness to the particular
work in question. It has in this way a special kind of precision. It
is all this, of course, that is referred to as 'close reading'. It is
movement of thought into the words on the page. This clearly is a
peculiar merit of this kind of mind. But there is a second mode of
thought which concerns Leavis:

> a serious interest in literature cannot confine
> itself to the kind of intensive local analysis
> associated with 'practical criticism' - to the
> scrutiny of the 'words on the page' in their
> minute relations, their effects of imagery and
> so on: a real literary interest is an interest
> in man, society and civilisation, and its boun-
> daries cannot be drawn: the adjective is not a

circumscribing one. (6)

It is this movement of thought which takes him out to the need for an evaluating survey of, say, the Seventeenth Century and which forces him to remark,

> In such a piece of work, clearly, it would be pre-
> eminently the unacademic virtues that would be
> demanded and tested: a pioneering spirit; the
> courage of enormous incompleteness; the determina-
> tion to complete the best possible chart with the
> inevitably patchy and sketchy knowledge that is
> all one's opportunities permit one to acquire; the
> judgement and intuition to select drastically yet
> delicately, and make a little go a long way; the
> ability to skip and to scamp with wisdom and con-
> science. (7)

This is obviously a very different kind of thought from that involved in close reading. The organisation and ordering required here go beyond that form of organisation which is built up by weighing this particular against that - this, doesn't it, stands in such relation to that. It is of course Leavis's very great merit as a literary critic that his thought does move in both directions, both inwards and outwards, from the particular to the general, and that he recognises in some of his more 'theoretical' writing that it ought to do so. But it must also be said that he does not give the generalising phase, or kind, of thought quite the attention and explication that he gives to "reading" and that his own generalising writing on society is weak. While it is true that in making judgements about broad social phenomena and long historical developments, the "pre-eminently unacademic virtues" must at some point be tested, we nevertheless need to be rather more precise than Leavis ever is about what is involved in this kind of thought and about how to discipline it. It is here that Max Weber has most to contribute and it is for this reason that I recommend his work.

There are three propositions which Weber, in his writings on method, is especially concerned to defend and which I will be looking at. First, he insists that sociology is not concerned with the properties of matter, animal, vegetable or mineral but with "meaningful actions". Its subject matter is quite distinct from that of the natural sciences. Its basic concern is with the way in which meanings, values, ideas shape human actions, personality and social relations. Sociology is the study of subjective meaning and must use an appropriate method - the understanding of meaning. Secondly, sociology is a science; that is, it is interested in classifying and conceptualising reality. Its focus of interest is not in the individual but in the typical. Third, as a science, sociology attempts objectivity. It strains towards making its conclusions "value free". If it is to be worthwhile, however, it must be "relevant for value."

Sociology, like all the 'cultural sciences', is defined by Weber as the study of meaningful action. That is, we explain human actions in terms of the purposes, ends, ideals, goals, intentions, desires which the individual is trying to realise in his action. We explain a present action in terms of the future state that it is intended to be a step towards. To explain an action, we have to see, in some sense, what is in his mind. This Weber calls subjective meaning.

Only secondarily are we then interested in the 'external conditions', the 'objective' facts of the individual's context. And there again, the aspect of that context which interests us most is what other people are doing, what they are thinking, what pressures they are putting on him, how they are trying to influence him. To know this we have to go, in the same sense, into their minds. Again, this 'human context', and the physical environment, are only fully relevant because the indivi- dual we are looking at is aware of them, by experience can understand them, and responds to them. The basic method of explanation in socio- logy, then, as in all the cultural sciences is the understanding or interpretation of subjective meaning. Thus, for example, if we want to explain the 1867 Reform Act we certainly need to know about the situa- tion within the Tory and Liberal parties, the state of the nation etc., but at some point the decisive step will be to go back to Disraeli and the other crucial actors, to grasp their various intentions, to see ideals and immediate goals developing out of their different experiences, try to show what their different actions in relation to that reform meant for them. So we go back to their speeches, correspondence, diaries and, in Disraeli's case, novels, where we see this meaning directly expressed. There is nothing very striking about this. The depth to which we penetrate the various consciousnesses may vary, but the manoeuvre itself is a normal procedure of political history.

The 'interpretation of meaning' is common ground for all the 'cultural sciences', or, as we might more readily say, 'cultural disciplines.' This is the point at which literary criticism and sociology most clearly meet. Nevertheless, there are also difficulties here. There is, from a literary critical point-of-view, something odd about the whole pro- cedure as it has just been outlined. It rests upon systematically arguing from the meaning that is expressed in the speech, letter, diary or novel to the meaning that is intended and to the ideas and purposes that are actually in the author's mind and to those which inform his action. We cannot assume that these are all identical. The 'literary' expression, the mind, and the attitudes guiding action stand in complex relationships to each other - it would be a very different world if we always did what we intended to do, or were always like our letters and speeches - and it is a step in reasoning to move from one to the other. This, of course, is well known in literary criticism

itself. Apart from anything else, this is why writing is such a
struggle: it is nearly impossible for most of us even to approximate
to the truth about ourself. That is one of the things great literature is about; that is why Leavis argues that such literature has a
'representative' significance that more mundane writing does not have;
that is why the opinions of each interviewee in a sample survey ought
not, on all questions, to be counted as having no more, and no less
weight than every other interviewee. Some people, and some writings,
are more truly revealing than others.

To refer to our previous example, the meaning expressed in those parts
of Franklin's writing which Weber considers might not have been at all
the same as the attitudes which actually moved him in the conduct of
his workshop and the control of his employees. It is an extremely
important methodological jump later on in the book when Weber moves
from the values expressed in the autobiography to the way of life -
capitalist society - embodying those values. It is not an impossible
jump - if that were so the whole argument would clearly fall apart -
but it is a jump, and we should note it. (8) To refer this point to
the Centre's own work: precisely one of the crucial points to be
explored in the study of teenage culture is the relationship between
the meanings and values expressed in dance, song, dress, speech and the
attitudes and experience of teenagers themselves. We need to find a
way of detecting how far teenage culture (in the narrow sense) is truly
expressive of teenage experience and how far it bends and twists it.

An extension of the problem occurs when our interest lies not in, say,
Disraeli's actions and aims but in the popular agitation prior to 1867.
For here we have to understand the collective consciousness of large
numbers of people in so far as it is directed towards the attainment of
reform. There is again here another crucial jump in reasoning from the
literary expressions of this man and that to the common experience and
shared aspirations of a group or movement. Precisely the problem here,
we might say, is to establish which literary products have 'representative significance.' The general point is that Weber's statement of
the subject-matter of the cultural sciences gives 'literary' expressions
a crucial status as evidence: but their status is never that of <u>evidence</u>.
His formulation does not simply turn sociology into the reading of
literature. (9)

The argument so far had been established in Germany before Weber, notably
by W. Dilthey. (10) But Weber's predecessors had pushed the argument
in a particular direction which he thought was mistaken. They had
argued that no one's mind or personality or experience was quite like
anyone else's. Each person was unique, and so too was each event, each
process, each historical movement, each literary expression. The only
way to be fully truthful then is to break down the conventional categories and classifications by which we type and obscure people and

actions and to recover and represent the full individuality of the person and events studied, to convey the true complexity and <u>difference</u> of the experience lying behind each action. This is a programme for history which still has appeal. It is an aim for history which finds a strong echo within literary criticism in such passages as this:

> Words in poetry invite us ... to 'feel into' or 'become' - to realise a complex experience that is given in the words ... The business of the literary critic is to attain a peculiar completeness of res- ponse. His first concern is to enter into posses- sion of the given poem ... in its concrete fulness and his constant concern is never to lose his com- pleteness of possession, but rather to improve it. (11)

Weber's point in response is simple. In literature, perhaps, where there is only a very limited number of novels, poems, etc., which invite that sort of response, then to speak of "completeness of response" and "completeness of possession" may be justified. But when our concern is to arrive at judgements about society, that is about the countless acts of millions of men, or about the multiple products of mass culture, or even about one's man life, then the programme is impossible and can only lead to incoherence. It is this dilemma of the German Historical School that leads Weber to insist upon his second major methodological argument: that sociology is a science. It is because he enters the problem in this way that he defines science in the way he does: science is distinguished from other forms of study for Weber because it proceeds by means of the explicit classification and conceptualisation of reality. It is not concerned with uniqueness, only with typicality.

I will present the argument here in some detail for this is the crux of the matter. Its relevance for one of the Centre's main projects - a study of changes in the popular Press over the last thirty years - will, I think, be evident. He begins:

> The type of social science in which we are interested is an <u>empirical science</u> of concrete <u>reality</u>. Our aim is the understanding of the characteristic uniqueness of the reality in which we move. We wish to under- stand on the one hand the relationships and the cul- tural significance of individual events in their con- temporary manifestations and on the other the causes of their being historically <u>so</u> and not <u>otherwise.</u> Now, as soon as we attempt to reflect about the way in which life confronts us in immediate concrete situations, it presents an infinite multiplicity of successively and coexistently emerging and disappear- ing events, both "within" and "outside" ourselves.

> The absolute infinitude of this multiplicity is
> seen to remain undiminished even when our atten-
> tion is focused on a single "object", for instance,
> a concrete act of exchange, as soon as we seriously
> attempt an exhaustive description of all the indi-
> vidual components of this "individual phenomenon",
> to say nothing of explaining it causally. (12)

Or again, a little later,

> How is the causal explanation of an individual fact
> possible - since a description of even the smallest
> slice of reality can never be exhaustive? The num-
> ber and type of causes which have influenced any
> given event are always infinite and there is nothing
> in the things themselves to set some of them apart
> as alone meriting attention. A chaos of "existential
> judgements" about countless individual events would
> be the only result of a serious attempt to analyse
> reality "without presuppositions." And even this
> result is only seemingly possible, since every single
> perception discloses on closer examination an infi-
> nite number of constituent perceptions which can
> never be exhaustively expressed in a judgement. (13)

Sociology, or any other empirical discipline, cannot be a sample rendering of the facts. It must select and order the facts. This is the
basis of the logic that leads Weber in the Protestant Ethic to rip
through his material, tearing out the stuff he needs. He goes to the
material with the organising notion, "The Spirit of Capitalism" already
formed, it is this which drives and rigorously directs the course of
the inquiry. He emerges, of course, quite explicitly, with a one-sided
view of the history. Other things were happening in those years -
even within Franklin's autobiography - apart from the growth of the
spirit of capitalism as he has defined it. But that that is one of
the things that was happening has, has it not, been decisively demon-
strated. This kind of judgement, the preparedness to pick out one side
of the flux of events, to show part of the order existing within complexity, to cease at some point to be fully responsive, and to recognise
that this is what you are doing, is a necessary part of being empirical.
You cannot simply be responsive to the reality: it is also necessary to
bring to it an already fairly rigorous, precise set of ideas, interests,
concerns, and with these question it. This is only one phase of the
movement or process of empirical thought: but it is an essential phase.
To put this another way: the imagination can be the proper complement
of empirical thought, not its contrary.

So far, Weber has been describing what must happen, explicitly or implicitly, if an inquiry is to make any sense at all. He has not been trying to outline any startlingly new procedure, but merely to clarify methods actually in use. If you have avoided incoherence, then this is how you must have done it. As he continues, however, he does begin to make recommendations, and to evolve a novel - because explicit - procedure. It is this type of procedure that Weber calls ideal type analysis. The 'concept spirit of capitalism' is the classic example of an ideal type. The clearest definition of an ideal type that he offers is the following:

> An ideal type is formed by the one-sided accentuation of one or more points of view and by the synthesis of a great many diffuse, discrete, more or less present and occasionally absent concrete individual phenomena, which are arranged according to those one-sidedly emphasised viewpoints, into a unified analytical construct. (14)

Again, he gives a definition in the form of an example,

> one can delineate the (ideal type) of a "capitalistic" culture, i.e. one in which the governing principle is the investment of private capital. This procedure would accentuate certain individual concretely diverse traits of modern material and intellectual culture in its unique aspects into an ideal construct which from our point of view would be completely self-consistent. This would then be the delineation of an "idea" of capitalistic culture. (15)

Again, he says of this process of thought,

> It involves first the production of - let us say it calmly - "imaginative constructs" by the disregarding of one or more of those elements of "reality" which are actually present, and by the mental construction of a course of events which is altered through modification in one or more "conditions". Even the first step towards an historical judgement is thus - this is to be emphasised - a process of abstraction. This process proceeds through the analysis and mental isolation of the components of the directly given data. (16)

And he says a little later in that same passage that the basis of this process is "a matter of isolation and generalisation" which "transforms the given 'reality' into a 'mental construct'".

This is, in an important sense, a movement away from reality - transforming reality into a mental construct. Or, rather, it is a movement away from any particular bit of reality.

> In its conceptual purity, this mental construct can-
> not be found empirically anywhere in reality. It is
> a <u>utopia</u>. (17)

The 'concept spirit of capitalism' is a one-sided accentuation and simplification of attitudes that did have historical force. But no one
firm or individual was ever motivated by pure, unalloyed capitalist
spirit. That attitude always exists in fact as part of a more complex
reality and is thereby modified. In the same way, for instance, no-one
was ever pure 'scholarship boy'. Again, one of Weber's most well-known
and penetrative ideal types is that of bureaucratic organisation: no
area of social life has ever been completely and totally bureaucratised,
nevertheless bureaucratisation represents a powerful force and tendency
within modern life.

How this might work - to bring a number of these points together - is
suggested if we look at the example Weber goes into in most depth in
these essays - Goethe's letters to Frau von Stein, where he shows some
of the different directions in which it would be possible to trace out
their significance. The first phase is the preliminary 'reading' of
the letters:

> In order to see the various logical standpoints from
> which the "facts" of cultural life may be scienti-
> fically considered, let us take an example: Goethe's
> letters to Frau von Stein. It is not - let us clear
> this up in advance - the perceivable "fact" before
> us, i.e. the written paper, which is treated as
> "historical." This paper is rather only the means
> of knowing the other fact, namely, that Goethe had
> the sentiments expressed there, wrote them down and
> sent them to Frau von Stein ... This "fact" which is
> disclosed by an "interpretation" of the "meaning" of
> the letters - undertaken ultimately by "scientific"
> procedures - is in truth what we have in mind when we
> refer to these "letters". (18)

Having completed this preliminary reading - which seems to be something
in between linguistic clarification and 'close reading', though Weber
clearly regards it as quite unproblematical - he proceeds to show how
we might look for their significance. First our interest might be
straightforwardly historical, that is, we might be concerned to fit the
correspondence into an historical account of Goethe's life and give it
some weight as an important event in his life. We might, by looking in

this direction, find that the correspondence had influenced him in a
number of significant respects. This would be the normal historical
biographical procedure. But the letters might not have had this direct
effect on his life - or hers. In that case, secondly, we might be
interested in them because they are characteristic of Goethe, because
we can

> derive from them insights into a type of conduct
> and outlook on life which were peculiar to him
> throughout his life or for a substantial period
> and which influenced markedly his literary expres-
> sions and personal traits which interest us his-
> torically. The "historical" fact which would then
> be integrated as a real link in the causal nexus
> of his "life" would be that "outlook on life" - a
> conceptual complex of grouped qualities. (19)

We thus move away from the particular letters and the particular responses that they contain or elicited to this and that on various occasions, his various attitudes to her, the cat, Monday morning, Saturday
afternoon, etc. We are now concerned, not with the particular, but
with the "outlook on life" typical of Goethe and which we have formulated for Goethe. (The self-confidence of sociologists is clear.)
This is now a "collective concept" and an abstraction. It is this outlook on life which we regard as being expressed in the letters, or, put
another way, we regard the letters as "'symptoms' of that outlook on
life." Third, we might be interested in the letters as typical, not of
Goethe only, but "of the pattern of life of certain German circles of
that period." We might then use the letters "as a conveniently usable
paradigm of that type, as, in other words, a means of knowing the
'characteristic' features of the mental and spiritual attitudes of those
circles." (In Leavis's terms, we might say that here we would be
treating the letters as a representative cultural document in much the
same way as Leavis himself recommends that we use Jane Austen's novels
if we want to understand a certain kind of late-eighteenth century
family life.) Or, fourth, at an extremely high level of generality,
"a psychiatrist interested in the psychology of love-relationships
might view them from a variety of 'useful' viewpoints, as an 'ideal-
typical' illustration of certain ascetic 'disturbances'." And so on.
Here, in the second and third procedures that he outlines, are in summary form, the basic procedures of Weber's thought: the movement from
a literary expression to a judgement about, or formulation of, the outlook on life or values that it is "symptomatic" of, or the way of life
of a group that it expresses. This movement of thought - the explicit
statement of the values embodied in a literary product, a form of
activity, a way of life - Weber calls, in this context, "value-interpretation" and "value analysis". He means to distinguish it sharply
from 'philological' and 'textual-linguistic' interpretation. Value-

interpretation "analyses and 'psychologically' interprets the letters."

> It teaches us to "understand" the intellectual,
> psychological and spiritual context of that corres-
> pondence; it develops and raises to the level of
> explicit "evaluation" that which we "feel" dimly
> and vaguely. For this purpose, interpretation is
> not all required to enunciate or to "suggest" a
> value judgement. What it actually "suggests" in
> the course of analysis are rather various possible
> relationships of the object to values. (20)

Such interpretation does not result in the enunciation of a simple
value-judgement for or against: rather,

> The meaning of interpretation consists in disclosing
> to us the possible "evaluative standpoints" and
> "evaluative approaches." (21)

Value-interpretation or, what amounts to the same thing, the ideal-type
analysis of subjective meaning, reveals the general evaluative stand-
points at work in particular activities or particular patterns of life.
As such it refuses to see the world, it is unable to see the world, as
an existential chaos. Rather it shows the ways in which values are at
work in the world. It shows the moral and artistic commitments which
lie behind an exchange of letters. It shows that the writings of Ben
Franklin have involved the making of choices; Franklin has had to
choose and has decided to go this way rather than that; he has turned
against many of the possibilities of human development and, in his
writing, expresses himself as decisively committed to one peculiar
value-standpoint. It is Weber's argument that commitment, as it is
expressed there, has, so far, also seen the dominant commitment of the
whole of Western society. Value-interpretation does not go on to make
our choices for us. But it shows us that choice is possible and what
choices are, potentially, open.

It will be clearly remembered that Weber's 'ideal-type' analysis of
Franklin's work can make no claims to being exhaustive. He is only
concerned with one aspect of the work and analyses that alone. Certainly, another student looking at the Autobiography could find different
qualities there and could 'value-interpret' them in a manner which might
well take him very far away from capitalism and towards establishing
quite new connections. After Lawrence's essay, for instance, one could
well value-analyse its naivety and move towards an ideal-type of that.
Indeed, it is impossible for value-analysis ever to be exhaustive.
There is no finite list of values in existence which we can use once
and for all to conduct an inventory on the world's literature and give
each a 'value-coding'. (That, roughly, is the sort of thing some socio-

logists frequently attempt.) It is impossible for ideal-type analysis
ever to be exhaustive because it is quite explicitly one-sided, accen-
tuating and exaggerating one of the qualities present. Life in capitalist society is clearly not all the time, unalloyed, nothing but
doing one's duty in a calling. The ethic does not have such a total
grip as that: the system is not so complete. All Weber claims to have
established is that the idea of duty in a calling is one of the dominant values which has affected and still does profoundly affect us.

The ideal-type of capitalism which Weber puts forward might, then, be
said to be a utopian exaggeration of this one aspect of our world.

> It is possible, or rather, it must be accepted as
> certain that numerous, indeed a very great many
> utopias of this sort can be worked out, of which
> none is like the other, and none of which can be
> observed in empirical reality as an actually exis-
> ting economic system, but each of which however
> claims that it is a representation of the "idea" of
> capitalist culture. Each of these can claim to be
> a representation of the "idea" of capitalistic cul-
> ture to the extent that it has really taken certain
> traits, meaningful in their essential features, from
> the empirical reality of our culture and brought
> them together into a unified ideal-construct. (22)

There are, of course, difficulties here that cannot be resolved by clarifying the notion of the ideal type itself, but only by showing that the
movement of thought to the construction of an ideal type is only one
phase in the whole process of thought. But we might acknowledge here
that the characteristic weakness of sociology is an over-willingness
to conceptualise, to spawn abstract classifications, in short, to produce ideal types.

It is precisely at this point, of course, that serious historical objec-
tions are raised. The historian might wish to answer Weber that he is
fully aware, thank you, that he is to be thoughtful, use his imagination,
that he cannot merely photograph reality, but that he manages to do this
without the explicit conceptualisation and abstract reasoning which seems
to be so characteristic of much sociological thought. Weber acknowledges
this argument,

> If the historian (in the widest sense of the word)
> rejects an attempt to construct such types as a
> "theoretical construction", i.e., as useless or dis-

pensable for his concrete heuristic purposes, the
inevitable consequence is either that he consciously
or unconsciously uses other similar concepts without
formulating them verbally and elaborating them logically or that he remains stuck in the realm of the
vaguely 'felt'. (23)

He argues that the historian, whether he likes it or not, when he uses
terms such as 'individualism', 'imperialism,' 'feudalism', 'mercantal-
ism', etc., is using ideal types. Of course they do not have to be
explicitly defined. "In a particular instance the course of a concrete
historical event can be made vividly clear without its being analysed
in terms of explicitly defined concepts. And it will accordingly be
claimed for the historians in our field, that they ... speak the
"language of life" itself." But Weber is suspicious of these merits:

> Every type of purely direct concrete description
> bears the mark of <u>artistic</u> portrayal ... Valid
> <u>judgements</u> always presuppose the <u>logical</u> analysis
> of what is concretely and immediately perceived,
> i.e., the use of <u>concepts</u>. It is indeed possible
> and often aesthetically satisfying to keep these
> <u>in petto</u> but it always endangers the security of
> the reader's orientation, and often that of the
> author himself concerning the content and scope of
> his judgements. (24)

The charge of abstraction, failure to use 'the language of life',
stilted scientific jargon, etc., do not weigh very heavily on Weber's
mind. I am not at all sure that he shouldn't take this argument a lot
more seriously than he does. Another way of describing the ideal-type
procedure is to say that - instead of using the "language of life
itself" to characterise and describe what you are studying, and being
aware while you are doing so that each word has a rich and complex
past, is fattened with associations and nuances, and that certain of
the crucial words, "democracy", "reason", "freedom", are by this
extremely open-ended and ambiguous - you choose to redefine as you
please and limit the meaning of the words that are crucial to your
analysis. Instead of taking the word "democracy" as it comes, staying
with it and fighting it, you choose for yourself a precise list of the
conditions of being democratic. Such a list is an ideal type. One of
Weber's most characteristic phrases is "I intend to mean by ..." and
then a definition. Some later sociologists have been extremely cavalier
in the way they have chosen to redefine rather important words. But it
should be noted that this whole procedure is essential to most of the
well known sociological empirical methods, which are often based on
using a handful of questions as a means of classifying people into such
types as democratic/authoritarian; tough-minded/tender-minded; scien-

tific/unscientific, etc.

A point which concerns Weber much more is that we should forget that we are being abstract, that is, forget that an ideal type is always a one-sided accentuation and simplification of reality and can never exhaust its infinite richness. An ideal type is an interpretation of reality, and therefore not the same as reality itself. The confusion of theory and reality, the concepts with the actual history, is an ever-present danger for sociology:

> This confusion expresses itself firstly in the belief
> that the "true" content and the essence of historical
> reality is portrayed in such theoretical constructs
> or secondly, in the use of these constructs as a pro-
> crustean bed into which history is to be forced or
> thirdly, in the hypostatization of such 'ideas' as
> real 'forces' and as a 'true' reality which operates
> behind the passage of events and which works itself
> out in history. (25)

There is a final danger in this form of analysis, a danger which Weber only mentions briefly but which has been much discussed in recent years. In undertaking ideal type analysis we are always abstracting from the flux of events, gathering together many varied particular things occur-ring over a time span and considering them only in so far as they are the same, share one common characteristic, can be regarded as being of the same type or class. We are thus, as Weber puts it,

> dealing with ideal-types as abstract concepts of
> relationships which are conceived by us as <u>stable</u>
> in the flux of events.

One important further danger, then, of confusing our classifications with reality is that we will make the world appear to be a more stable place than it really is. Thus, for instance, in the <u>Protestant Ethic</u> <u>and the Spirit of Capitalism</u>, Weber operates with one fixed concept of the protestant ethic, ignoring the complex and subtle changes within protestantism during its history. This is an inevitable consequence of ideal type analysis: it only becomes a danger when we cease to be aware that it is happening.

All of these - the over-generous spawning of concepts, the reification of concepts, abstractness, the static bias - are the characteristic faults of sociological analysis. They are the usual ways in which ideal type analysis is misused and the Centre should certainly look out for them in its sociological reading. But that this form of analysis can be misused is no form of argument against the analysis itself. What tends to cause all these errors is a failure to remember the proper place of the theoretical movement of thought within the whole process of thought. The generation of ideal type concepts is not the end point of thought, but one phase within it. Ideal types are nothing more, in this sense, than heuristic devices. In the establishment of an ideal-type, one simply uses empirical material for illustration in order to make the type clear, and to show that the type has some preliminary viability.

> The danger of this procedure which in itself is entirely legitimate lies in the fact that historical knowledge here appears as a _servant_ of theory instead of the opposite role. (26)

This procedure must then give way to another,

> Using this construct as a heuristic device for the comparison of the ideal type and the "facts".

The ideal type thus becomes,

> a mental construct for the scrutiny and systematic characterisation of individual concrete patterns. (28)

So we must proceed from the establishment of "theoretical constructs using empirical data illustratively" to "historical investigations which utilise theoretical concepts as ideal limiting cases." It is this whole _process_ of thought which Weber is concerned to define, the battle between theory and reality, between our thought and the real stuff:

> For none of those systems of ideas, which are absolutely indispensable in the understanding of those segments of reality which are meaningful at a particular moment, can exhaust its infinite richness. They are all attempts, on the basis of the present state of our knowledge and the available conceptual patterns, to bring order into the chaos of those facts which we have drawn into the field circumscribed by our _interest_. The intellectual apparatus which the past has developed through the analysis, or more truthfully, the analytical rearrangement of the immediately given reality, and through the latter's integration by concepts which correspond to the state of its knowledge and the focus of its interest, is in constant tension with the new knowledge which we can and _desire_ to wrest from reality. The progress of cultural science occurs through this conflict. Its result is the perpetual reconstruction of those concepts through which we seek to comprehend reality. The history

> of the social sciences is and remains a continuous
> process passing from the attempt to order reality
> analytically through the construction of concepts -
> the dissolution of the analytical constructs so con-
> structed through the expansion and shift of the
> scientific horizon - and the reformulation anew of
> concepts on the foundations thus transformed. (29)

I must come, finally, back again to the problem of purpose. How does
this way of understanding subjective meaning, and producing types of
meaning - of outlooks on life, of ethics, of spirits of social forces -
help us, how, crucially, does it inform the purpose stated by Leavis
which I quoted at the beginning? It is one of Weber's great merits as
a writer on method that he does ask this question, and that the question
is central to the way he proceeds. Fundamentally, the scientific task
of the clarification of the world is its own purpose. Its aim is to
move beyond that fixed perception of the world which convention and
common-sense and ordinary language makes self-evident and yet to show
the world, not as a chaos, but as an order, and the particular social
world which we inhabit as a unique and distinct order having such and
such characteristics. We show by ideal type analysis, or value-interpretation, that within the apparent chaos of particular actions, immediate purposes and local situations, there are principles, values,
attitudes to life at work; and we characterise them. By doing this we
are not merely clarifying the world: that is not a sufficient end in
itself. We are preparing the way for action:

> (We proceed) by making clear the competition of numerous
> possible evaluations in their practical consequences -
> that these and these ultimate positions are conceivable
> with reference to this practical problem. The real sig-
> nificance of a discussion of evaluation lies in its con-
> tribution to the understanding of what one's opponent or
> one's self really means - i.e., in understanding the
> evaluations which really and not merely allegedly separate
> the discussants and consequently in enabling one to take
> up a position with reference to this value.

> Science can make the (acting person) realise that all
> action and naturally, according to the circumstances,
> inaction imply in their consequences the espousal of
> certain values - and herewith - what is today so often
> overlooked - the rejection of certain others. The act
> of choice itself is his own responsibility. (30)

NOTES

1.   It is worth noting that in the rest of the chapter he then proceeds to take the spirit of capitalism, so defined, and to compare and contrast it with certain of the other attitudes, dominant in history, to economic activity. He finishes by connecting the spirit of capitalism as it existed in that eighteenth century teaching with the modern capitalistic order.

2.   Max Weber, The Protestant Ethic and The Spirit of Capitalism, p.51

3.   loc. cit.

4.   Max Weber, Prot. Eth., p.54

5.   F. R. Leavis, Education And The University, p.54

6.   F. R. Leavis, The Common Pursuit, p.200

7.   F. R. Leavis, Education And The University, p.60

8.   In a more extended discussion of Weber's work, I should want to begin a much fuller criticism of certain crucial aspects of his work from this point. Such a criticism would not, I think, seriously modify the basic points I am trying to establish here.

9.   A point worth noting here, though it is slightly off the main line of the argument, is that Weber does little to clarify what is perhaps the point of most interest to the literary critic. He seems to take it that 'reading' itself is unproblematic: that the understanding of meaning in the first place raises no problems. Sometimes he refers to "insight" and "empathy" as required; elsewhere he speaks of "the 'interpretation' of meaning - undertaken ultimately by 'scientific' procedures," without saying what those procedures are.

10.   See especially, W. Dilthey, Meaning in History, ed. by P. Rickman.

11.   F. R. Leavis, Reply To Dr. Wellek, in The Importance Of Scrutiny, p.31-2, Ed. by Eric Bentley.

12.   Max Weber, The Methodology of the Social Sciences, p.72

13.   Max Weber, The Methodology of the Social Sciences, p.78

14.   Max Weber, The Methodology of the Social Sciences, p.90

15.   Max Weber, The Methodology of the Social Sciences, p.91

16.   Max Weber, The Methodology of the Social Sciences, p.173

17.   Max Weber, The Methodology of the Social Sciences, p.90

18.   Max Weber, The Methodology of the Social Sciences, p.138

19.   Max Weber, Methodology, p.139

20.   Max Weber, Methodology, p.143

21.   Max Weber, Methodology, p.144

22.   Max Weber, Methodology, p.91

23.   Max Weber, Methodology, p.94

24.   Max Weber, Methodology, p.107

25.   Max Weber, Methodology, p.94

26.   Max Weber, Methodology, p.102

28.   Max Weber, Methodology, p.100

29.   Max Weber, Methodology, p.105

30.   Max Weber, Methodology, pp. 14, 53

The Cultural Debate
Anthony Hartley

from

A State of England by Anthony Hartley, Hutchinson,
London, 1963.

6

THE CULTURAL DEBATE

In my profession as a writer I have never asked myself how I may be of service to the whole. But always I have only sought to make *myself* better and more full of insight, to increase the content of my own personality, and then only to express what I had recognized as good and true.

GOETHE

Sie haben volle Gesichter,
auch Lippen mit Rouge baiser,
wer wollte als Rächer und Richter
hier sagen: Entschminke dich, geh?

They have plump faces and lips with Rouge baiser lipstick too; who would wish to say here as avenger and judge: Go on, take off your make-up?

GOTTFRIED BENN

Before entering into the present debate concerning the quality of English culture it is as well to be reminded by the quotation from Goethe which I have set at the head of this chapter that those who create culture—art, music, literature, philosophy and science—must necessarily be more indifferent to society than society is to them. This does not mean that they do not care what happens in the world around them, but it does mean that for them the supreme value must be their own power of self-expression in words, paint or notes of music, their own struggle with the enigmas of Nature or the paradoxes of the human situation. It is this creative egotism which has always made it so difficult to press writers and artists into the services of causes foreign to their inner imperative. For them the supreme importance of what they have to say provides the only hypothesis which can enable them to continue their exacting task of creation. They can no more cast doubt on it than a doctor can doubt the utility of saving people from death. In both cases a value has to be assumed in order to enable work to be done, and thereby justifies itself whatever philosophical points can be made against it. To believe that poets are the unacknowledged law-givers of mankind is the only alternative to believing them to be ineffectual angels.

It seems useful to state this clearly at the outset, since so much recent discussion of English culture has centred on the way in which culture is received and diffused by society rather than on the way in which it is created by the artist. In the dialectic between society and the artist it is always the first term that is analysed, and this, of course, is not altogether surprising.[1] Most of those who consider the subject have a well-founded suspicion that nothing very much can be done about the processes which take place inside the artist's skull. Many of those concerned for the stability of society would like to brainwash him; some of them have actually succeeded in silencing him; but nobody has yet been able to force him to sing their own song and to sing in tune. The lamentable fiasco of orthodox Soviet literature shows the limits of what can be done in this field, however totalitarian the intention of the controllers.

It follows from this that *from the point of view of those producing culture* all such expressions as 'bourgeois culture', 'working-class culture', etc., are misplaced metaphors drawn from sociology or politics. Artists, writers, musicians primarily express themselves and not their class or the historical situation, and, though Marxists may contest the 'objective' truth of this statement, a belief in their task of self-expression is certainly the most important motivating factor impelling onward those concerned with artistic creation. This confidence that *I* (and not history) am writing a novel, that *I* (and not the imperialist-capitalist-bourgeoisie-in-their-decline) am painting an abstract picture is another part of the creative hypothesis, and an important one, since it throws into relief certain

---

[1] This also applies to the relationship between society and the consumer of culture—of mass-culture above all. Most recent utterances on the subject neglect the very real forgetfulness of self and stirring of the imagination entailed in the enjoyment of the most hackneyed film or television play. There is a thrill in these things which is not necessarily that of the drug addict and in which, because human psychology is neither particularly logical nor its transitions particularly apparent, it is easy for society to miss an emotion of a higher nature than the shoddy work that stimulated it.

ambiguities in the use of the word 'culture' which have bedevilled recent argument on the subject.

DEFINITIONS OF CULTURE

The placing of an adjective before 'culture' assists a confusion of meanings which is sufficiently important to require elucidation here, tedious though this may be. In fact, there is a vital distinction to be made between *culture* and *a culture*, which the use of terms such as 'bourgeois culture' tends to obscure. In the latter ethnological use of the word, when, for instance, we speak of 'Aztec culture' or 'Dyak culture', there is implied a total unified way of life informed by common beliefs and made possible by the strongly integrated tribal societies to be found among primitive peoples. To talk of 'modern English culture' or 'cultural activities' is to mean something quite different: those creative and largely intellectual activities which are recognized as dictating the aesthetic and, to a considerable degree, the moral tone of a civilized society. When Raymond Williams defines 'working-class culture' as 'the basic collective idea, and the institutions, manners, habits of thought and intentions which proceed from this', he is using culture in its ethnological (or sociological) sense.[1] It can, of course, so be used, but then the user must be careful not to carry over into it any presuppositions from its original application to primitive societies, and nobody who has read Mr. Williams's arguments in favour of a 'unified culture' can say that he has entirely escaped that danger. Indeed, his thesis appears to run so contrary to the known facts of cultural history that it can most easily be explained by a prior assumption that a culture held in common is the norm from which present and past variety represents a deplorable deviation.

Nor should it be thought that, say, the Transport and General Workers' Union is the product of working-class culture in the same way as Cézanne is the product of bourgeois culture or that the two are comparable in any respect. In fact, in an advanced community the expression of attitudes such as Mr. Williams's 'basic collective idea' or 'basic individualist idea' will itself have been formed by culture in the more restricted sense. If a vague belief in equality is part of the English working-class ethos it is because of Rousseau, because of Bentham, because of Marx—in other words, behind it stands a tradition of radical thought

[1] *Culture and Society 1780–1950* (Chatto and Windus, 1958), p. 327.

which has filtered down through society until it is reproduced in a more or less unrecognizable form in pub talk of 'we' and 'they'. The culture of a modern society is the result of purposeful and voluntary thought and creative activity in a way in which, let us say, the traditional sexual taboos accepted by a savage are not. Today's *culture* can produce *a culture* tomorrow, and, if the position of English culture is to be discussed, the emphasis must be on the more restricted meaning of the word, as it is only through a rise in the quality and an enlargement in the dissemination of culture considered as thought, literature, science and the arts that any improvement of culture considered as a total way of life can be expected.

The confusion caused by this terminological difficulty is tiresome, and, as I have already said, it becomes particularly obtrusive when some such phrase as 'the product of bourgeois (aristocratic, working-class) culture' is used to describe an individual artist or work of art. It is philosophers, scientists, writers, artists and musicians who produce *a culture*, whether aristocratic or bourgeois, and not the other way round. When Matthew Arnold emphasized the part of effort contained in the idea of culture it was this impulsion given to society by a minority which he had in mind.[1] Whether he likes it or not every writer and artist inculcates standards, if not for his own age, then for ages after him.

In so defining *culture* I do not mean to deny that it may be influenced by the total way of life of the society from which it springs. Obviously it is so influenced. All that I am trying to suggest is that it differs from *a culture*, and that the two expressions cannot be used as if they were identical, nor can characteristics of the one be applied to the other. Unfortunately, when the article is omitted the two usages can appear identical. A phrase such as 'medieval culture' contains two concepts, although in this case they are less far apart than they would be in the case of a more aggressively individualistic society. But, naturally, there is interaction. In *The Divine Comedy* Dante produced an expression of

---

[1] 'The moment this view of culture is seized, the moment it is regarded not solely as the endeavour to see things as they are, to draw towards a knowledge of the universal order which seems to be intended and aimed at in the world, and which it is a man's happiness to go along with or his misery to go counter to—to learn, in short, the will of God—the moment, I say, culture is considered not merely as the endeavour to *see* and *learn* this, but as the endeavour, also, to make it *prevail*, the moral, social, and beneficent character of culture becomes manifest.' *Culture and Anarchy*, ed. by J. Dover Wilson (Cambridge University Press, 1960), pp. 46–7.

what came near to being the total life of his age (while possibly understating the grosser side of the medieval character), but also (and perhaps more importantly) he formed the Italian language by his example in such a way that the purity of his style became part (and not the least active part) of the total life of ages after him. The makers of culture can be said to order and transmit to future time the total life of their age. This they could not do were they completely divorced from it, but neither could they do it if they did not stand a little way off from it. *Culture* can provide most of the spiritual data of *a culture* and simultaneously a principle of transmission, so that the particularities of an age can take their place in a general inheritance. Of *a culture*, *culture* is usually what is left to us. It is certainly what is relevant.[1]

CULTURE INTO POLITICS

With this definition of culture in mind it is easier to discuss its situation in England today as well as the various proposals that have been made for the improvement of that situation. In my last chapter I put forward the idea that the Welfare State has been widely considered to be a cultural failure in that the expectations which had been raised by it have not been fulfilled. I do not intend to repeat the instances of that failure which I gave, but I should like to point to one important development in the political sphere which seems to stem from it as well as from that lessening interest in pure politics which is a result of Great Britain's post-war diminution of power.

Writing in the *Manchester Guardian* in August 1958, David Marquand pointed out that young Socialists at Oxford tended to see the reforms, which they would wish to carry out, more in cultural than in economic or political terms. A similar diagnosis is implied by Mr. Williams when he writes:

'We should be much clearer about these cultural questions if we saw them as a consequence of a basically capitalist organization, and I at least know no better reason for capitalism to be ended. It is significant that the liveliest revolt against the existing system, particularly among the new young generation, is in precisely these cultural terms.'[2]

[1] Cf. Dr. Leavis's definition quoted above, p. 52, n. 1.
[2] *The Long Revolution* (Chatto and Windus, 1961), p. 339.

From a different direction we have 'Taper' affirming in the *Spectator* that he would vote for any party which would introduce a series of reforms, most of which can be described as cultural in quality. And Mr. Crosland's book *The Future of Socialism*, while containing in its conclusion proposals for better welfare services, greater equality and more efficient management of the national economy, also has sections headed 'Liberty and Gaiety in Private Life' and 'Cultural and Amenity Planning'. No doubt this represents a return to Ruskin and Morris, but these are not considerations which have been much in the minds of reforming politicians since then. To do them justice, they have been too busy with other things.[1]

In an earlier chapter I drew attention to the comparatively tame character of those 'causes' which nowadays compete for the support of liberal intellectuals. These are frequently to be found existing in a domain where moral conviction blends into taste, the ethical into the cultural. For instance, the argument most frequently used against the continuance of capital punishment is that it is barbarous and produces a barbarizing effect on the society which makes use of it. The case for the abolition of hanging is argued from the admitted unpleasantness of the operation in preference to lines of attack which are perhaps logically more cogent— for instance, that the death penalty assumes a perfection in the English system of justice which has certainly never existed in any human insti- tution. Even without the Evans case it was always quite obvious that innocent men were liable to be condemned to death, for the same reasons that innocent men are known to have been imprisoned for burglary. Similarly such diverse subjects of public dispute as the implementation of the Wolfenden Report, the behaviour of the Royal Family, the censorship of books and plays, are discussed along lines which can broadly be called cultural. Reform in many fields is not so much claimed to be 'right' as the old system is felt to be 'ugly' or 'stuffy'. Even the increased emphasis in progressive political programmes on social, as against economic, equality raises an issue which has more cultural than political implications,[2] though, no doubt, political action would be required to produce it. In the first Aldermaston march (before the movement was

[1] I imagine that Mr. Crosland's conception of liberty and gaiety would differ greatly from the 'Merry England' which Ruskin and Morris had in mind. The contrast is not without its piquancy.

[2] 'It is by the humanity of their manners that men are made equal.' Matthew Arnold, 'Equality', *Mixed Essays*, p. 68.

changed into a weapon against the present leadership of the Labour Party) there was an atmosphere of aesthetic choice rather than of sturdy moral conviction, and it was this feature of the march which struck most independent observers.

What I am suggesting here is not that there is no moral fervour involved in these causes but that the way in which they are chosen and subsequently furthered by their devotees is quite unlike that in which, say, a Victorian teetotaller chose and furthered total abstension. The Puritan fire has gone out of us. In practice ethics have usually been a matter of taste—of good taste in the strict sense of the word; there is never time for anything other than an instinctive reaction. Nowadays, in the absence of transcendence what is left to us is manners, a mode which assumes relativity and a necessity for practical compromise in human relations. Manners are a way of respecting other people, and it is unlikely that causes selected by the criteria which they provide will be pursued with great fanaticism. The Victorians were humanitarians; we are humane—and in this distinction there is expressed a real, if still partial, passage from moral feeling to taste.

At a time when manners and taste decide choices, which might otherwise be made upon moral grounds, culture and the creators of culture (in its narrower sense) will take on an increased social importance. Since there is no assured and generally accepted system of values, art and science provide a source of directives on matters which their qualifications for considering are not obvious.[1] At the present time the views of artists, writers and scientists are widely thought to be of value on subjects —such as foreign affairs or the reform of the Civil Service—about which they frequently know nothing. And, by a complementary process, many of those whose job it is to write about politics do so from the standpoint of someone considering a cultural object, a play or a performance on television.

This blending of politics into culture is to culture's advantage—to the advantage of its influence, not necessarily of its quality. Politics itself, however, will tend to suffer from the association, the ultimate result of

[1] The process by which moral issues are decided and presented in cultural terms can give rise to ambiguities. Dr. F. R. Leavis has produced a system of Puritan morality in the form of a study of the English novel—The Great Tradition (Chatto and Windus, 1948)—but it is not quite certain who is using whom. In a general way it can be said that moralists now prefer to call themselves literary critics. As Daniel Halévy once wrote, 'Qui jugera les hommes de lettres?'

which is the state of mind that is to be found among many young supporters of C.N.D., where banning the Bomb, Socialism, good modern architecture and the accoutrements of Bohemianism all take on something of an equivalent importance as gestures against everyday conformity. In this mêlée the political loses its priority, and that in the very sphere of action where its claim to be considered first is irrefutable. What is done is dictated more and more by tone and less and less by belief organized towards an end, and tone is the direct product of culture in its widest sense and has its original source in culture in its narrower, but intenser, meaning. Combine this trend with the diminution in interest of purely political causes and it is clear that the Oxford students who see the reforms they wish to achieve in cultural rather than political terms are more representative of their time than those who hammer away at the political issues of thirty years ago. This does not mean that they are likely to be more successful in getting what they want, but that they provide a convenient example of the change which has come over the English left since the war.[1]

T. S. ELIOT

Criticism of the present state of English culture has usually come from those holding left-wing political views. On the right—quite apart from that element in Conservatism which simply desires to keep things as they are—there is a more empirical attitude towards reform. To this state of mind having dogmatic ideas about culture is dangerous and their realization not a legitimate domain for political action, while the fact that issues such as 'equality' or the advantages and disadvantages of an élite are raised by such questionings in itself makes them suspect. The word that most often occurs when a person of a genuinely conservative cast of mind discusses culture is 'tradition', and this is not necessarily the hallmark of literary or artistic reaction. A large number of those most closely associated with the study and judgement of art and literature are conservatives in this sense and none the worse for it. They are concerned to see continuity between past and present, and they are suspicious of general cultural theories, partly because so many of them are presented in terms of arid dogma and appear to be an infringement of their liberty.

[1] Much the most important and original aspect of New Left Review is its utterances on cultural questions. These are what give it its narodnik tone.

Similarly, many creators of culture, though themselves revolutionaries in their practice of their art or science, dislike being asked to think about culture in general terms. They think of themselves as writing a poem or painting a picture or discovering an unknown virus rather than as changing the course of culture, and they see all too clearly the impossibility of legislating for cultural improvement except in the most indirect way.

The only conservative theory of culture at present current in England is that to be found in the writings of T. S. Eliot. His view of culture envisages a unity in diversity, the unity coming from an informing religious belief and the diversity from a social hierarchy of functions which is not inflexible, but will continue to exist, whatever scope it may afford to the individual for change from one class to another. From the top of the cultural pyramid are transmitted refining and educative influences, from its base arise the harshness and the strength needed for creative work. All its constituents participate in a greater or less degree in a common cultural tradition which is common just because its mainstay is a system of religious belief to which all can adhere though with unequal understanding. Holding the view that Mr. Eliot does of the importance of tradition in cultural creation, it is hardly surprising that he should view with some scepticism the prospects for planned cultural improvement. The idea of one moment in time trying to divert the course of the continuum has in it something of the disproportion between Canute and the sea.

The merit of Mr. Eliot's theory of culture is that it places in the foreground the aristocratic element involved in its creation. And it is possible to assent to this without drawing any of the consequences which right-wing political philosophy has been accustomed to deduce from it (the great error of theorists on the right has usually been to judge political phenomena by the cultural criterion). On the other hand, it is hard to imagine how religious belief can be a unifying factor in modern culture. Historically, it is, no doubt, the case that culture has traditionally been based on religion, and in particular the common Christianity of Western Europe has certainly been a fortunate thing for Western culture. But we are now in a position where religious belief is breaking down, and, just as in the field of ethics we have to do without transcendence and rely on manners instead, so in the field of communication we must discard common belief and rely on a common language: that is, a common method of experiment in belief. So that our culture will depend not so much upon what people believe as upon how they believe it. Ever since the nineteenth century poets have used myths as a research student uses hypotheses—not because they were necessarily true, but because they have sufficient probability to help in the creation of poetry. Now for our culture in its widest sense the unifying factor may be one of tone. It is hard to see how it can be one of direction. The restoration of the conditions which Mr. Eliot would regard as ideal for a society's culture would imply a sort of lifting of ourselves up by the hair, an exercise in spiritual gymnastics which the educated Englishman of the twentieth century seems peculiarly unfitted to undertake.[1]

At the opposite pole from Mr. Eliot's serious and austere cultural ideal lies a decadent conservatism in which respect for tradition either hardens into a dry scholasticism or encourages a sentimental nostalgia. Both these attitudes, so inhibiting to creative originality, are to be found as ingredients in the literary instruction usually meted out at universities. I have already remarked upon the extent to which nostalgia was rife in England during and after the war, no doubt encouraged as much by a desire for luxurious living as by any very consistent view of a causal connection between country houses and mandarin prose. In fact, any such connection would be hard to establish and dangerous to proclaim. One need have no particular objection, apart from a fleeting twinge of envy, to someone speaking of the delightful time he has had and the delicious food and drink he has consumed, while carrying on a witty and cultivated conversation, but it should be recognized that all this has little to do with the making of art or literature—let alone science— and may even actively discourage it. Genius has the digestion of an ostrich, but if you forbid it to live on anything except peaches-and-cream in a society where there is little of either you will be condemning it to a starvation diet. In this case respect for tradition will be stifling and culture killed by hallowing rather than by a failure to appreciate it.

Of course, the direct Puritan aversion to considering cultural values as anything other than marginal in the scheme of things is also damaging,

[1] I am not sure that the idea of culture arising out of religion is true historically. A culture is necessarily informed by the religion which dominates it, but culture in the more limited sense seems to arise when religion has passed the zenith of its intensity. Tragedy, for instance, appears to be the result of a clash between declining religious belief and an independent ethical judgement. The relationship is dialectical rather than causal.

and, in local government at any rate, is particularly prevalent on the right, where it combines with a dislike of state or municipal action in this field to quash what schemes are put forward to buy 'modern' pictures for a city gallery or abstract pieces of sculpture to place in playgrounds or schools. Recently, Conservative members of the Nottingham City Council have done their best to ensure that their town shall not have a municipal theatre. The vulgar right-wing attitude towards culture is that we don't want anything of that sort here—an attitude which is vociferously supported by a section of the Press—understandably because any general rise in the level of English critical sense would put them out of business.[1]

CULTURE AND THE NEW LEFT

From Mr. Eliot to the 'popular' Press is a far cry, and his theory of what English culture should be remains isolated, having found few disciples and arousing little discussion. It is from the left that most of the criticism of present trends in English culture has come. The most coherent theory of our present cultural state is to be found developed—with varying degrees of intelligence—in *New Left Review* and (with far more power and subtlety) in the writings of Richard Hoggart and Raymond Williams. With differences of emphasis and greater or less confusion of terminology the main points of the theory which can be deduced from these sources (and which has become the doctrinal mainstay of Mr. Marquand's young Oxford Socialists) are as follows:

(1) There should be more culture. (More state support for the arts, science, etc.)
(2) English culture (and particularly the culture of the working

[1] It is difficult to generalize about the respective hostility to culture of right and left in England. Manchester, for example, with a Labour majority on the council is certainly less imaginative and progressive in its support of culture than the more Conservative Liverpool. What is true is that Conservatives are more likely to object in principal to expenditure on cultural amenities—especially at a local level. On a national level the Conservative Party has a better record than Labour, Mr. Macmillan's government being the only administration since the war to raise the grants for museums and galleries to a more adequate level. Nor is indifference always to be blamed on a handful of stupid councillors. The derisory sum of money raised by public subscription in the city of Manchester to acquire a Rubens shows that suspicion of art also operates among the general public and is not confined to the startlingly modern. The Rubens in question went to Liverpool.

classes) is being corrupted by an unscrupulous use of the mass-media of communication by commercial interests who are ready to use debasing material to attract large audiences. They have forced commercial television through Parliament and would legalize horror comics if they thought that this would sell an ounce more of detergent. (The corollaries of this include attacks on the popular Press, independent television, advertising agencies, Hollywood and, quite often, on America, regarded as the great prototype of this corrupting process and of the capitalism that is said to engender it.)

(3) English culture should be 'unified'. (This involves the abolition of 'élite' culture and 'élite' education as well as the approval of such activities as jazz or Association football, which are assumed to be in some sense 'popular', and the advocacy of a certain measure of *proletkult* in art and literature.)

These theories are very much the fashion nowadays and fragments of them are likely to crop up in any general discussion of English culture. They are, therefore, worth looking at with some care, both with the aim of elucidating the presuppositions which they conceal and of estimating to what extent they are a sound basis for that improvement we all desire to see. Usually another point is added to the three I have outlined. Writers and artists generally (not scientists!) are recommended to become 'committed'—a piece of advice which usually boils down to a commitment to advocate the beliefs of the critic from whom the recommendation comes. If, on the other hand, as in a recent book on the subject, so wide a definition of 'commitment' is adopted that it comes to imply merely the possession by the artist of some coherent world view, this is no more and no less than has been required of him for many centuries. As used in this country 'commitment' means either propaganda or platitude, and there is little point in putting it alongside the other, relatively serious issues raised by the debate on English culture.[1]

---

[1] In France, of course, *engagement* is a more serious matter. Sartre's theory of literature is supported by an elaborate philosophical and psychological apparatus, which few English adepts of 'commitment' show much sign of having mastered. Sartre would take the view that only the manifestation of attitudes which he himself approves or, at any rate, does not condemn can constitute a 'commitment'. A Fascist 'commitment', say, would be a contradiction in terms in so far as the word is used as an expression of approbation. The literary theory contained in *Qu'est-ce que la Littérature?* is one of Sartre's weakest productions. The holes in it are so numerous that it would be superfluous to point them out here.

The first of the statements about English culture which I have listed above takes us back to the cultural failure of the Welfare State. It is a plea for getting rid of those Puritan and Philistine inhibitions which make culture and those who produce it of marginal importance when it comes to distributing public money. This is a sentiment with which it is easy to agree, though it should be added that those who share it do not always seem to realize to what an extent the Puritan attitudes they are attacking form a whole. The same set of values which makes a Treasury official or a town-clerk consider culture as expendable also keeps them from seeking personal financial gain from their positions. There is a paradox involved in demanding more Puritan rigour in the behaviour of the police force and less in that of divorce-court judges. However, it is impossible not to agree that our national expenditure on culture is something of a scandal, even if we throw in education, and once embarked on a discussion of this kind one becomes aware that the preservation or destruction of Puritan values is not a matter of choice. They are already dissolving, and in future we may well find ourselves with better architecture and a less honest Civil Service.

On the other hand, there is a curious contradiction which stands in the way of effective public aid to the arts. As has been suggested in the last chapter, the committee system of patronage is unsuited to the discovery of great artistic originality. Nevertheless, it is fairly cheap and easy for the state or a city to keep a novelist or painter while he produces a novel or a painting. What they cannot be sure of is the quality of the end-product; most probably it will be fashionable and derivatory with just a sufficient touch of modernity to make the patron committee feel it is getting something *avant-garde*. In the field of town-planning or the financing of opera, however, the case is altered. The state can be reasonably sure that it can keep an opera-house going. The city can be certain of imposing a relatively decent standard of town-planning upon a district due for development. In these instances the authorities in question are the only forces which can carry out such projects at all, so that questions of comparative quality enter into the argument only secondarily. But, since this kind of activity costs very large sums of money, and (as regards town-planning) is subject to pressure from financial interests, it is far harder to initiate than the simple subsidy to the individual. So that any attempt to gain public support for culture is faced by the paradox that the easiest forms in which that support can be given are liable to render poor returns, while those which might guarantee a rise in standards are the most difficult to get started and carry through. Public help for the arts (and science does not concern me here, since there are many directly utilitarian arguments which will always ensure it help and support from the state) is best given for objects which fall into the public domain, but which, for that very reason, require the kind of money no private individual can afford and are liable to all the constrictions and economies normally affecting government or municipal expenditure.

Arnold Wesker has recently called on the trade unions to interest themselves in subsidizing English culture, and there is certainly a case to be made for appealing to all wealthy corporations, whether trade unions or companies. But these can hardly take on the sort of cultural improvement which is needed in the public sector, while, on the individual level, they are hardly more likely to choose the best young novelist for the receipt of their bounty than a governmental committee. This is not a reason for their doing nothing, but it is a reason for not expecting too much from the result. Probably the best course they could pursue would be to give their money—which, if the Exchequer had an atom of sense, would thereby become exempt from tax—to increase the funds of those institutions which suffer from governmental parsimony. Fifty thousand pounds given to the Tate Gallery would be better spent than the same amount of money frittered away on the local 'festivals' which have now become something of a disease, or on repertory companies which are never going to establish themselves.[1]

The view of present-day English culture which concentrates attention on its failures in what I have called the public domain as well as on the lack of guidance and encouragement on the part of the state is, indeed, a partial one. In fact, the producer of culture in this country cannot be said to be particularly badly off. If he is a writer he will have the vast English-speaking market overseas open to his works as well as a growing market at home. If he is an artist or a musician he will find that the appetite for art and for music is growing, that sections of the population

[1] What Mr. Wesker actually has in mind in the way of practical steps to improve English culture is gruesomely revealed in a recent article 'The Secret Reins' (*Encounter*, March 1962). Here he quotes with approval the idea of holding 'Trade Union Weeks' described as 'a mixed bag of events from lectures on the industrial health service to mannequin parades and folksinging evenings'. After this it is no surprise to find the authentic handwoven note creeping into his reference to 'a tiny, worried trades council'. *Lucky Jim* might have been written in vain!

which never did so before the war are now going to concerts and buying pictures or reproductions of pictures. The existence of an enlarged and expanding audience for serious reading is indicated by the success of Penguin and Pelican books—perhaps the most significant symptom that mass education is producing some result. This new audience also represents a change in taste, but, by comparison with the twenties and thirties, this change is towards being more, not less, serious. There is a preference for archaeology rather than connoisseurship, for history rather than autobiography. Perhaps we have gone some way towards recapturing a Victorian gravity and passion for self-improvement. If that is so, we shall gain other things as well.[1]

These hopeful aspects of contemporary English culture—and I could have mentioned many more of them—have largely been neglected by the left-wing cultural theorists. It is fairly easy to see why. If one believes with Mr. Williams that 'We should be much clearer about these cultural questions if we saw them as a consequence of a basically capitalist organization' then it is obvious that the quality of English culture is going to be condemned from the start, since we can all gather without too much trouble what Mr. Williams feels about 'a basically capitalist organization'. It is no surprise when he concludes 'and I at least know of no better reason for capitalism to be ended'.[2] Moreover, because these theorists are interested in getting something done about the condition of English culture and because the only machinery which they believe to be available for such action is that afforded by the state, they have naturally concentrated their attention on the cultural failure in the public sector and neglected the modest grounds for optimism with which the condition of the individual writer or even reader might have provided them. It is true that when their eye roved in the direction of the individual it was caught by a far more sinister and spectacular phenomenon: the effect on him of the material with which he has been so liberally bombarded through the media of mass communication.

---

[1] I am told that Mr. Connolly's *Enemies of Promise* (Routledge, 1938) is now a popular book among people in their early twenties. This, however, does not invalidate my point (and, besides, I am all for anyone liking *Enemies of Promise*): there is no reason why seriousness of mind should prevent anyone enjoying a very readable book which is also rather serious beneath the glitter of its prose.

[2] *The Long Revolution*, p. 339.

As was hinted in the last chapter, merchants of advertising space hold something of the same position in the mythology of the left today as was held by armaments manufacturers in the twenties and thirties. They (heads of television networks, directors of advertising agencies, newspaper proprietors, publishers of pulp literature, film producers) are said to be corrupting public taste and morals in a number of ways. First, directly by making an appeal to the baser instincts of their audience, by pumping it full of eroticism and violence in the most extreme case, more usually by feeding it enervating and sentimental nonsense or inculcating a false ideal of middle-class 'gracious living'. Secondly, indirectly, by distracting their audience from using its leisure in more creative types of activity than the absorption of mass-produced fantasies and by destroying valuable local or regional characteristics. Thirdly, by subjecting the British people to a stream of advertising material creating a demand for goods which they would otherwise not want (or not want to the same extent), thereby producing a frame of mind intent on 'keeping up with the Joneses' and diverting national resources from other and more useful tasks.[1] These criticisms are associated with attacks on a system which places the power to influence the public mind in the hands of a few rich men. The tone of English life, so it is said, is being lowered for purely commercial reasons without any consideration of the possible effects of the material put out through television, film, Press or paperbacks.

How much of this is true? Some of the more far-fetched accusations can be dismissed fairly rapidly. Despite the fact that magistrates have been blaming pernicious literature ever since the Victorian penny dreadful and the cinema ever since it came into being, there is little real evidence to suggest that the misdeeds of juvenile and not so juvenile delinquents are caused by what they see or read except in the most indirect way. Whatever the reaction to a gangster film or a horror comic may be,

[1] 'To permit the free operation of a whole industry devoted to increasing consumption among the satisfied while others are still starving is against all humanity and decency. . . . If the answer to the vicious nonsense of advertising seemed to be a thumping tax, then the higher it was the more would Britain be able to sink in the capital development of poor countries.' Wayland and Elizabeth Young, *The Socialist Imagination*, Fabian Tract 326 (London, 1960), p. 12. This suggestion seems more remarkable for sound moral sentiment than for acquaintance with economics. However, it lives up to the title of the pamphlet.

everything goes to support the view that it is not of the simple 'X = X' type. Indeed, an urge to violence seems as likely to be sublimated as encouraged by the sight of it on the screen or the printed page. This is not to say that watching sexy or sadistic spectacles is an occupation to be recommended to the young—perhaps the real case against pornography is that it is *ersatz*: like taking saccharine in coffee—or that it can never produce assault and battery. But I would suggest that the mass-media cannot fairly be blamed for delinquency until something more is known about the way people react to their reading and viewing.[1]

Far more serious than any incitement to violence is what Dr. Leavis (in 1930!) has called 'that deliberate exploitation of the cheap response which characterizes our civilization'.[2] The world which the controllers of the mass-media present to their audiences is not necessarily or even frequently evil, but it does usually consist of a Lowest Common Multiple rather than of a Highest Common Factor. Much of the output of cinema, Press and television is intellectually enervating and morally void. Those who plan the programmes are admittedly out to make money, and there is little reason to believe that they are restrained by anything other than the fear of possible complications if they go too far. Even the B.B.C. can stoop to putting on a thoroughly objectionable programme like *This is Your Life* which draws its audience by a nauseating display of its victim's inner emotions. The introduction of commercial television may be responsible for the corporation's abandonment of what it used to claim were its standards, but that does not make the thing any better.

As for the newspapers, they are now far away from their original objective of letting their readers know what was going on in the world around them or of expressing opinions sincerely held by their editorial staff. Here Mr. Hoggart has a very relevant comment:

> 'When I was a boy the older generation of working-class people used often to say, as evidence of the truth of some fact, "Oh, but it was in the papers." That phrase seems to me now almost entirely unused. One goes on reading the papers, even the political parts, so

[1] I believe that one view suggested by recent investigations is that they hardly react at all. Which is both reassuring and depressing.

[2] *Mass Civilization and Minority Culture*, p. 11. Let me say once again that practically all the valid points in the New Left's view of English culture represent a politicizing of things Dr. Leavis was saying thirty years ago. And they were said then with far more subtlety and intelligence. This debt has not been acknowledged, but it is worth pointing out its size.

long as they are made human and personal. At the back of the mind, in matters inviting any form of genuine belief, there sounds an echo from a bottomless unbelief.'[1]

And the reaction is what might be expected: 'It's all lies in the papers.' 'It's all propaganda in the papers.'

This situation is part of the moral consequences of Lord Northcliffe, but, speaking as a journalist myself, I find it impossible to contemplate without feeling both anger and shame. Anger because this destruction of a real Press, this insult to the intelligence of real readers, add up to a betrayal. And shame because what is said to be a profession is so lacking in professional standards, so bemused by its own complacent *mystique* that it fails to do anything about putting its house in order. At the moment the English national daily Press consists of *The Times*, which is a characteristic institution with very different merits and defects from other newspapers, the *Guardian*, which does us all credit morally, if not invariably technically, and the *Daily Telegraph*, which presents its news on a decent level with a recognizable bias to the right on political issues. On Sundays there are three 'quality' newspapers, only one of which makes much attempt to do the job of a daily, the other two trusting to their magazine features to win a circulation and advertising war that appears to be imminent. As for the rest of the national dailies and Sundays, for the moment (and despite a praiseworthy effort to raise the level of the *Daily Herald*) they are part of the entertainment industry. Instead of news there is 'human interest' (which would be better called 'inhuman interest'!). Instead of opinion based on conviction there is a spurious moral indignation, which often participates in precisely those things which it claims to condemn.[2] And, behind the newsprint, there is frequently the invasion of privacy, the hounding of individuals at tragic moments in their lives, the distortion of words uttered by the innocent and naive.[3] The 'popular'

---

[1] *The Uses of Literacy* (Pelican ed., Penguin Books, 1958), p. 229.

[2] Anyone who is interested in moral tone should note how 'popular' journalists often become unable to write without a hypocritical ambivalence even when there is no necessity to do so. Their prose loses the possibility of conveying sincere emotion.

[3] The death of the late Gilbert Harding illustrates conveniently what kind of fare is offered by the mass-media to their audiences. Just before he died he was seen by television viewers to break down during an interview and say that he wished he were dead. After his death certain newspapers took the occasion to discuss his private life under the usual cloak of quoted rumour and denial. I leave it to my readers to find their own words for what they think of these incidents.

Press, of course, constantly asserts that it fulfills a salutary function by the exposure of abuses which could not be revealed to a wide public were they not mingled with a certain amount of sensationalism and scandal to make the mixture palatable. But it is certain that there is more ambiguity in their attitude than they would admit. One has only to ask oneself whether the *Daily Mirror*'s support of the Labour Party is weakened or strengthened by its particular brand of journalism. And the answer is not in doubt: were the ideals of British Socialism ever to be put into complete effect, the 'popular' Press might reasonably be expected to fade away, and, though we may, therefore, admire the disinterestedness of the *Mirror*'s political line, there remains an obvious conflict between the advocacy of democratic values and their presentation in a way that betrays so low an opinion of what the average man can be expected to digest. And the *Daily Mirror* is in many ways the best of the 'popular' papers, occasionally producing an article or leader which is a real reflection of the inchoate opinions and desires of the English man-in-the-street. It is the formula which is false.

As to the exposure of abuses, it might be asked what great abuses have been exposed by the 'popular' Press over the last ten years, and I am afraid that the question would be a difficult one to answer. The law of libel puts a most effective stopper on that crusading for cleaner local government which forms so staple a food of American papers, but it does not do much to prevent the persecution of anyone whom an editor or a proprietor may care to persecute—always with the best legal advice.[1] The coverage of foreign news in the 'popular' Press is lamentable, the space given to topics such as education, trade union affairs or science not much greater, while any starlet can be sure that her doings will attract more attention than they warrant. In fact, when it comes to closing down newspapers I sometimes wonder what all the fuss is about. Most of them have long ceased to be anything but an industry (and are frequently described as such at board-meetings), and nobody would expect an unprofitable industry to be kept running. What wanted doing about Fleet Street should have been done years ago and by journalists

---

[1] The editor of a small local paper cannot afford to take the financial risk involved in comment on Councillor X's acquisition of land scheduled for development or Councillor Y's exertion of undue influence in the allocation of council houses. Even if he is sure of his facts, the present state of the law of libel makes the result of any suit too uncertain. A crusader would soon go out of business.

themselves: the taking of active steps to establish and enforce decent standards of professional behaviour. But the journalists have done nothing —the Press Council excites the derision it deserves—and when a chill wind blows from the managerial side it is difficult to feel that any bastions are being stormed which had not been surrendered long ago. The garrisons have marched out with their bonuses flying.[1]

It must be admitted, therefore, that there is a great deal of truth in the charges of degradation and demoralization which are sometimes brought against the 'popular' Press. If, in fact, nobody is demoralized or degraded it is because people are mentally a good deal tougher than is sometimes thought. One of the more cheering features of contemporary England is the way in which the advice of the Press is fairly generally ignored on political issues, the substratum of sturdy disbelief noted by Mr. Hoggart. But this hardly absolves those who lower standards for profit or, more frequently in the case of the individual journalist, because they have only a vague idea that standards exist. If a man is given to firing pistols in the street it is desirable that he should be dissuaded from doing so even though he may not have hit anyone. What is remarkable and pitiable in Fleet Street is its increasing abandonment of the very attempt to influence opinion, its descent into melodrama or clowning.

THE CONTROL OF MASS-MEDIA

The mass-media do, I think, stand condemned by much of the matter they purvey. Usually their controllers do not make even the minimum effort required to appeal to the strength of their audience rather than to its weakness. I have spoken of the Press, since it is the mass-medium I know best, but the condemnation which the 'popular' Press deserves could also be directed against many television programmes, as well as certain types of book and film. On the other hand, it would be unfair to adopt the theory which blames the mass-media for the decline in English

---

[1] When it was recommended by a committee that criminal cases going to a superior court should not be reported in the Press at the magistrates' court level to avoid possible prejudice to a future jury the main comment of the National Union of Journalists was that this might put some court reporters out of work. The union's concern for its members is understandable, but, to say the least, there were other points which might have been considered in relation to that particular issue. If the N.U.J. wishes to be taken seriously then it must behave with some regard for the wider consequences of the practice of journalism.

regional and working-class culture. As has already been argued, in so far as these are not simply the product of a romantic view of the past, they were bound to be destroyed by universal education and the development of communications as well as by the necessity in a modern industrial civilization for a high degree of mobility of labour. The mass-media are, in fact, a symptom of the process which has abolished an older England rather than a cause of it.

Similarly, the idea that television and the films are preventing people from spending their leisure in some more creative way is also based on too rosy a view of what went on before the advent of the latest phase of modern industrial development. The original industrial revolution which, amongst other achievements, made television possible, also uprooted the English masses from their old rural, communal life and destroyed their folk culture. Remnants of this latter lingered on throughout the nineteenth century and into the twentieth (especially in isolated communities such as mining villages), but in general the English working classes became increasingly *déracinés* and had little possibility of using their leisure in any creative way. It may be that a number of working men went to the Mechanics' Institute who are now lured away by the silver screen, but the majority did not. They went elsewhere—most frequently to the pub—and, as between what used to go on in London working-class districts on a Saturday night fifty years ago and what goes on now, it cannot be said that the advantage is necessarily with a time that knew no television. Indeed, it could be claimed that the mass-media have damaged upper middle-class culture more than they have harmed the working classes' use of leisure. It is, after all, in Surbiton and Purley that the television aerial is ubiquitous. However, even in this class of society and in the eighteenth century Shakespeare was accompanied by the musical glasses. So he is today, but the music is different.

The third main charge against the mass-media, the immorality and importunity of the advertisements which make them go round, depends for its justification on economic rather than on cultural considerations. If the existence of a large and expanding market is essential to the modern industry of mass production (as it certainly is), then obviously anything which keeps that market in existence by drawing the attention of the consumer to the product in question is a good thing. As a political scientist not especially given to sympathy with a society of mass consumption has written:

'Being thus connected with the standard of living, with which it has a relationship of interdependence, advertising must be considered as an instrument of economic and commercial progress. It is not necessarily a factor of artistic progress. . . . But, socially, its role is not harmful—quite the contrary.'[1]

The apparatus of modern publicity is one of the numerous consequences of the development of industrial mass production, and to attack it in isolation from the process of which it is a symptom is to take a superficial view of its significance. The importance which a number of intellectuals and journalists have attached to it is another example of a tendency to be diverted by irritating detail.

In Britain, moreover, the heads of industry, no less than the heads of trade unions, have been conditioned by the depression when customers were limited in number, and it is too much not to expect them to fight for their share of an expanded market with all the weapons at their disposal. There is nothing particularly immoral about this: they owe it to their workmen as much as to their shareholders. And the idea that it is wrong for manufacturers to compete in sales at home because there are people short of essentials in other parts of the world is admirable considered as a gesture, but only as that. It is not so much home consumption which holds up aid to underdeveloped countries as the balance of payments difficulty. To cope with that it is necessary to export (and, incidentally, to advertise one's exports), and to export competitively it is necessary to have a large home market (this is not to deny that it can be too large, but the difference is one of emphasis). Moreover, while advertising may put something on to the product's price, that is part of the presentation—like packaging or display—and, in any case, it would be quite impossible to envisage a kind of self-denying ordinance by which all manufacturers agreed not to advertise. Such an arrangement would never last for a moment.

A large home market and a large export market (both of them incited by advertising) are the conditions of keeping British industry going, both by widening its scope and by offering the bait of higher living standards to those working in it. This may be selfish, but then so are human beings. All that democratic states can do is to adapt themselves to the nature of their citizens—capable, no doubt, of sudden acts of generosity,

[1] André Siegfried, *Aspects du XXème Siècle* (Paris, 1955), p. 62.

but liable to flag in their exertions if they cannot improve their own immediate lot by their work. You may as an individual moralist preach the virtues of austerity and abstention (which are real), but you must not expect to be obeyed by the majority of men without coercion from the state. And states do not coerce their citizens unless they stand to gain by it as a power in the world's affairs. The dragon publicity is the reflection of a consumer society, which benefits the British state and the majority of Englishmen and with which the latter are perfectly contented, and it is not likely to be slain by any St. George in our time.

It might be better if reformers concentrated on improving advertising instead of agitating for its abolition or subjection to a tax which would simply be an added tax on industry. The two things that are glaringly wrong with it at the moment are that it is frequently very inaccurate or simply uninformative and that it is also often offensive aesthetically. A poster in an Underground station announcing a film at the local cinema is actively useful, since it would be impossible to discover what is on without it and its complements in the Press. But slogans about toothpaste winked at toothpaste users in lights of surprising ugliness, or howled at them over the television sound system at the wrong moment, often produce an effect of misinformation similar to that of being told of a film playing at a non-existent cinema. Nobody expects advertisers to point out the snags in their own product, but they can at least provide *some* real and relevant information about it. To deceive consumers is irritating for them and immoral and foolish on the part of the deceivers— foolish because such tactics certainly attract their own penalty.[1] Yet it ought not to be beyond the wit of man to effect an improvement in advertising standards. It should be possible to devise a code both as to veracity and sightliness, which could be enforced by law, and this is a task to which attention could reasonably be given, but which is only of marginal cultural interest.

There is also some misunderstanding behind the statement that the increasing concentration of the instruments of mass persuasion in the hands of a few men is a dangerous phenomenon. Dangerous it may be—past experience of press lords seems to indicate that megalomania is one of

[1] As regards the morality of advertising, it is difficult not to agree with André Siegfried that it is 'moral to the same degree to which public speech is moral'. Op. cit., p. 81. And, like the public speech of a politician or lawyer, its success will depend on its maintaining a relationship to truth which is not one of identity, but can hardly be one of dissociation either.

the occupational risks of the profession—but not in the way that is usually claimed. An owner of mass-media is not a Goebbels; a William Randolph Hearst is about as far as he goes—which, God knows, is far enough. In other words, it is his lack of belief and unoriginality of mind in the field of general ideas—that same unoriginality which puts him in touch with his audience—which prevent him from threatening society by unscrupulous propaganda. If Kings were philosophers, then the power they wield might be put to really harmful use. As it is, the *Daily Mirror* roars the language of the right wing of the Labour Party (which it calls 'the people'), a language far more respectable than that employed by its competitors, but quite as unexciting. The end result of a concentration of the means of mass communication in a small number of hands is more likely to be a decline in quality, a lessening of the consumer's choice and, ultimately, the closing of newspapers, cinemas and television studios the minute they become unprofitable than any deliberate sapping of the national mind with a view to replacing it by some more subservient organ. Those who provide the diet of newsprint and celluloid, of viewing and listening, for so many millions of people are less pernicious and, above all, less potent than is commonly thought by their critics.

These brief reflections on the part played by the mass-media in our cultural life seem to me to lead to the conclusion that what harm they do consists in the enervation, rather than the corruption, of the national mind. It is certain that, though one may agree with Hannah Arendt that entertainment pure and simple cannot be condemned for failing to establish 'values', yet the devotion of television, wireless and newspapers to it does make less demand on the audience than would be justified even from the point of view of maximum entertainment effect.[1] Much of the stuff purveyed by the mass-media is not good of its kind, having all the

---

[1] 'The truth is we all stand in need of entertainment and amusement in some form or other, because we are all subject to life's great cycle, and it is sheer hypocrisy or social snobbery to deny that we can be amused and entertained by exactly the same things which amuse and entertain the masses of our fellow men.' *Between Past and Future* (Faber, 1961, p. 206). One can agree with this, while still believing some forms of entertainment and amusement to be better than others and finding the separation here implied from other forms of mental activity a little artificial. On the other hand, I find the insistence in the same essay on the dangers of popularization through the mass-media of 'cultural objects' exaggerated. To say that the danger is that 'the life process of society . . . will literally consume the cultural objects, eat them up and destroy them' (loc. cit., p. 207) is to be carried away by an image. My feeling is that, if *Hamlet* can survive Lamb's *Tales from Shakespeare*, it can survive anything.

sogginess and sentimentality of the British 'B' film. In this connection it is significant that there is evidence of a steep drop in the use of television by school-children between the ages of fourteen and sixteen—a drop which may partly be caused by increased activities outside the home but which could also be motivated by boredom with the material presented.[1] To be subjected to a perpetual stream of light programme is not particularly good for anyone, but it is not particularly amusing either. The one field where television has genuinely raised standards is that of news and comment on news. Here the careful impartiality and the relatively adult presentation are streets ahead of what is printed in the 'popular' Press and, one might suppose, will one day force the latter to reform itself. And the reason for this exception is a simple one: programmes with political implications provide the one area where the commercial companies and also the B.B.C. feel themselves vulnerable to parliamentary pressure. Sensationalism or falsification would soon lead to political intervention. Hence the fact that, while television news programmes are nowhere near as good as a really serious newspaper, they are much better than what is produced by any other kind. Governmental and parliamentary control, however, does not and cannot extend to matters of taste, nor can it create vitality where none exists.

Supposing it to be admitted that the influence of the mass-media may be for the worse a difficult question is posed: what is to be done about it? Institute a censorship? But the very same intellectuals who denounce the effect of television and horror comics followed one another into the witness-box to testify to their detestation of any form of censorship in the case of Lady Chatterley. Give back to the B.B.C. its monopoly of television? But the B.B.C. is said to have sold itself to the principalities and powers of English life, and is denounced for being 'stuffy' and 'priggish'. The fact is that those whom we have seen attacking the remnants of Puritan feeling when it manifests itself in a restrictive attitude towards culture are involved in a paradox. The freedom which they claim

---

[1] Cf. *The Leisure Activities of School Children:* a Report of an Investigation by Mary Stewart and the students of a Holborn Advanced Tutorial Class (London, 1958). The figures given in this W.E.A. pamphlet show that, of children with television in their homes, the average number of viewing nights per week diminishes between the ages of fourteen and sixteen and over as follows: grammar-school boys: 5·0 to 3·8; grammar-school girls: 4·9 to 3·4; secondary-modern boys: 5·2 to 3·3; secondary-modern girls: 4·7 to 3·4.

for the work of art and the artist will also be used by the mass-media—principally the freedom to be devastatingly silly—and this they can prevent only by recourse to new restrictions. Attacking the Puritan Philistine, they find themselves face to face with the commercial Philistine from whom they can escape only by developing the principles of a new political Puritanism. And experience suggests that the remedy is unlikely to be much better than the disease. Commercial Philistines have their disadvantages, but at least they do not enact legislation.

Moreover, supposing that it were decided to institute some kind of machinery to control the output of the mass-media, in the name of what principles could it be operated? The creation of any such censorship takes for granted an ethical unanimity which simply does not exist in present-day English society. It is true that there might well be a ban on various techniques (such as subliminal advertising) which are intended to attack the subconscious mind—a measure recently advocated by Aldous Huxley—but any measure going beyond this would raise the question of what we actually want the mass-media to do, and on this there could be no agreement. Of course, many of those who propose such control either directly or by implication have a very definite idea of how they would wish it to be operated: in accordance with their own theories of social good. After the Puritan Philistine and the commercial Philistine we should then have the reign of the ideological Philistine, which is to be seen in a perfected form in the Soviet Union. And if anyone is prepared to contemplate this eventuality he might think for a moment of the kind of person who would be found on the committee of, say, an English Writers' Union. Control of 'popular' culture can be carried out only as a consequence of a strong set of beliefs, which will also affect literature, art and probably science as well, since the believer will not draw distinctions of artistic or intellectual quality but will heed only the content, while usually oversimplifying and misunderstanding it. What begins with the condemnation of seaside picture postcards is likely to end with the condemnation of *Ulysses*, since in practice it is hard to find a legal criterion by which to distinguish between them. Not only would those concerned with the operation of such a control not know when to stop, but it is very unlikely that they would even want to stop. Theirs would be the frame of mind that lumps Nietzsche with the Nazis and objects to *Dr. Zhivago* just because its 'message' is conveyed with subtlety, power and distinction. This is the intolerance that led Claudel to deny Gide's talent and keeps Joyce from being published in his native country. A national ideology can be said to have some advantages, but it is in the cultural field that they are least obvious, and to desire a consensus of belief that does not exist is, in any case, either quite useless or a potential threat to freedom of thought and speech.[1]

UNIFIED CULTURE

This argument as to the undesirability of the ideological control of the mass-media is also relevant to the third item in the cultural programme of the New Left: the necessity of what is called a 'unified culture' or a 'common culture'. For any culture (taken in the widest sense of the word) to be genuinely 'unified' it must be informed by a structure of beliefs rigorously held in common. Indeed, inasmuch as this aspiration towards a 'unified culture' is not simply an attack on educational inequality, it seems to be a hangover from the anthropological use of the word culture. Primitive tribes often do have a culture unified and integrated by a strongly held series of myths and taboos. However, at quite an early stage there is a differentiation of function and also of hierarchy. From a state in which everyone indifferently tells stories or hunts game or makes arrows we pass to a state where these employments are specialized and are considered as of different degrees of value. A society in which everyone shares the same cultural experience is the exception rather than the rule even among primitive peoples, and the range of that experience tends to become wider as the society develops. Even in a social system as unified as that of the Middle Ages by the thirteenth century Dante had considerably less in common with an Italian serf than, say, Montezuma would have had with the average Aztec, and ever since then Europe has been divided with increasing clarity into a cultural élite and

[1] Contrary to what is usually thought, such total systems of belief are at something of a disadvantage in many parts of the world we live in. Modern civilization is so imbued with Western rationalism and a tradition of discussion that unifying total belief can be felt only as a mutilation. In our awe before Communism we often forget that, as compared with Christianity or Islam, it has had little success in imposing its system of ideas. Now after a hundred years they have already lost their force, though they may well have their maximum theological effect in countries such as China which do not share the Cartesian tradition. If anyone wishes to produce the absolutely stable totalitarian society of Brave New World he will have to use the genetic and psychological methods of conditioning which Mr. Huxley has described.

the rest (the moment at which this became most strikingly apparent we call the Renaissance). Civilization has always been marked by cultural diversity and differentiation of function—what we call progress has been in that sense—and it is only the unspoken assumption that unity is the normal state of culture that could lead anyone to imagine that it would be a good thing were there to be less variety and more 'common culture' than there is today. No system that one can think of would make of an artificially 'unified culture' anything but the enslavement of a creative minority to forces which would inevitably express themselves in bureaucracy. Ikhnaton would be subject to the priests.

Advocacy of a 'unified culture' is usually associated with the claim that only thus can the horizontal cleavage which is supposed to exist between the tastes of the various classes of English society be reduced or eliminated. No doubt such a cleavage is an unfortunate phenomenon, but it cannot be said that England is unique in this respect or that our social differences are greater than those which separate a highly educated Frenchman from a Parisian worker (for instance, there is the vast difference between working-class French and that spoken by an extremely literate upper class). Moreover, the gap is being lessened by the mass-media themselves which are producing a 'unified culture' of a sort and, incidentally, proving that the thing cannot be regarded as an unmixed blessing even by its warmest partisans. Culturally England is being divided into intellectuals and the rest. What we are seeing is the equalization of everything below a rather high cultural level, and this process does not reflect class differences in the usual sense, since, though intellectuals generally live like the professional middle classes, they cannot be entirely identified with them. And once the term 'common culture' is seen to refer to the relationship between the intellectuals and the 'rest' (whether upper class, middle class or working class), then it becomes quite clear how dangerous and deceptive an ideal it is.

It is on this question of the relationship between intellectuals and the 'rest'—a problem which includes that of the intellectual's role in society— that a final criticism of the cultural theories which I have been discussing must rest. In his play *Roots* Mr. Wesker has given an account of that relationship, which has been widely praised and which is revealing as to the conceptions of the intellectual's status that are still current among the English left. The intellectual in *Roots* is Ronnie Kahn who, as the play opens, is engaged to Beatie Bryant, the daughter of a family of Norfolk farm-workers. To her he has endeavoured to communicate his passions and his ideas from a knowledge of poetry to the habit of making love in the afternoon. Throughout the play we see her alternately boring and shocking her bucolic family by trying to pass on some of Ronnie's *ipsissima verba*. At the end of the play, just when he is due to arrive, Ronnie sends a letter breaking off the engagement and in the shock of disappointment Beatie finds herself uttering her own feelings for once instead of words put into her mouth by Ronnie. The play closes with her cry: 'God in heaven, RONNIE! It does work, it's happening to me, I can feel it's happened, I'm beginning, on my own two feet—I'm beginning . . .'[1]

This plot seems to imply several statements about the activities of intellectuals. Ronnie, it must be said, is not a terribly good intellectual. Most of the things he represented as saying either here or in the two other plays of Mr. Wesker's trilogy are the commonplaces of a vague populism, which makes up in moral fervour what it lacks in precise objectives. However, the most significant thing about him is that he should feel himself entitled, even compelled, to 'go to the people' with a message. His attitude towards Beatie has certainly been all too 'dominative'—to use a word much in disfavour with Mr. Williams and his followers— and the final moral of the play revolves around Mr. Wesker's determination not to let him get away with it. Ronnie's letter to Beatie breaking it off emphasizes masochistically the weakness and neurosis of intellectuals ('most of us intellectuals are pretty sick and neurotic . . . and we couldn't build a world even if we were given the reins of government . . .'), although the final *dénouement* of the play might be thought to show that he had done her some good after all. In fact, Mr. Wesker's view of the relationship of Ronnie to Beatie lands him in a difficulty. While approving of Ronnie's concern for carrying culture to others, he nevertheless seems to have realized the priggish side of such didacticism. Ronnie must, therefore, let Beatie down so that the weakness of the intellectual can be shown up and she can come out from under his influence shocked into articulacy by her disappointment. The advantage of this pattern is that it allows its creator to eat his cake and have it. Ronnie is both ineffective and effective. Beatie is both uninfluenced and influenced. The intellectual's guilt complex, which played so large a part in the movement of the thirties, has been systematized here into a theory of cultural transmission,

[1] *Roots* (Penguin ed., 1959), p. 77.

a resemblance which is partly concealed by Mr. Wesker's more realistic picture of the working classes.[1]

The fallacy in the theory of the relationship of the intellectual to society which can be gathered from *Roots* seems to consist in simultaneously exaggerating and diminishing his role. It is not the primary duty of an intellectual to go round as a kind of cultural missionary bent on converting the heathen. His primary duty is to improve the quality of his thought, and, if he is a creative artist, of his works. And if he takes any other view of his task in life he will not have anything worth saying to communicate—this, incidentally, seems to be the case with Ronnie Kahn. It is, in fact, the business of an intellectual to be a 'good' intellectual and only then to worry about his relationship with a possible audience. The first objective of the utterance of thought must always be to make it clearer to the thinker himself, and any theory of cultural transmission which places the emphasis on intellectual hot-gospelling will diminish both the status of the creative intelligence and the content of what it has to convey. However, once a thinker has arrived at a conclusion he ought not to be deterred from expressing it by any fear of displaying 'dominative' cultural attitudes. It is his duty to dominate, to say what he has to say and get it heard, to find some to listen now and many in the time to come. Guilt is as bad a motive for abandoning the necessary arrogance of the intellect as it is for wishing to change other people's lives. It would be easier to respect Ronnie Kahn if he had the courage of his didactic convictions. As it is, *Roots* seems to me to shirk the real problems involved in the relationship between an intellectual and 'the rest'. If the former is to produce an effect on the society in which he lives he must worry more about what he has to say than about whether he has the right to speak.

Mr. Wesker's play, in fact, typifies the dilemma which faces all those who adopt the cultural theories of the New Left, which I have been

[1] Mr. Wesker's new play, *Chips with Everything*, deals with the same problem of cultural transmission—only in this case there is no Beatie to start talking for herself at the final curtain, and realism about the possibilities inherent in the British working classes has changed to pessimism. This was probably an inevitable evolution, since Mr. Wesker seems always to have thought too much of them in one way and too little in another. He has an urge to improve them, but is unable to respect their own values—which are inarticulate and can be affected by cheap sentiment and false glamour, but are values for all that. He can neither like the English worker nor let him alone. And this dilemma is far more banal than the admirers of his plays would have us think. It is, in fact, the typical intellectual's dilemma.

discussing. To lead or not to lead? To teach or not to teach? These questions are not usually put directly, but the attempts to avoid them are revealing, leading, amongst other things, to that confusion between *culture* and *a culture* which is so useful to anyone who wishes to disguise the fact that culture is made by small creative minorities. Yet, a consideration of culture which places the emphasis on anything other than creation is false and also dangerous. For the majority of men will shackle the forces of change if they can, and if the marching wing of humanity has privileges (among others the ability to exist without the approval of society) it is because they need them for the work they have to do: the austere and ungrateful task of producing ideas that are unwelcome to their contemporaries but find an echo in the future. Here we return to the quotation from Goethe with which this chapter opened, to the idea of gradual self-perfection, of the preservation within oneself of an inheritance which is implicit in the Latin root of the word 'culture'.

Holding this view of the nature of culture, I cannot accept the theories which have been expressed with such sincerity by Mr. Williams. Even in the form in which he has put them forward they imply a culture controlled by bureaucracy and unified by ideology. And these remedies seem to me worse than the evils they are intended to cure. In a civilization which has gone as far as ours towards differentiation and variety the constraint of an orthodoxy would be felt as tyrannical by the first-class mind or, worse still, welcomed as a drug by the second-rate, while the control of the mass-media carried out in its name would lead to the results we have seen elsewhere. I do not say that Mr. Williams or even the writers in *New Left Review* necessarily wish to bring about censorship or impose a uniform ideology on their fellow countrymen, but I would claim that their cultural theories can never be put into practice unless they are willing to adopt some such measures as these. That being so, either those theories are mere speculation or else they represent the possibility of something undesirable, which is clearly discernible though unperceived by the theorists. Putting the argument at its simplest, they can be rejected in the old-fashioned name of liberty or whatever that quality is which enables the mind to avoid the potentially stifling pressures of the world around it.[1]

[1] These criticisms of the New Left largely repeat those I made in an essay called 'Philistine to Philistine?' which appeared in *International Literary Annual, No. 2*, edited by John Wain (Calder, 1959). Since then I have been glad to see some support

However, disbelief in the possibility or desirability of a culture 'unified' by the pressure of a series of beliefs held in common and scepticism as to whether the evils engendered by the mass-media warrant draconian restrictions do not exempt anyone from the duty of suggesting remedies for the malaise which hangs over our cultural life at the present time. In fact, as has been suggested, things are not so bad as they are said to be, but that does not mean that no improvements can be made. But these reforms should be by their nature of such a kind as to ensure the offering of the widest possible cultural variety in the hope (or in the faith) that the choice would be a right one. It is not by closing the access to horror comics that we should arrive at a solution for whatever problem they represent. It is by making people no longer wish to read them. It is not by discouraging 'pop' music that we shall encourage the taste for classical, nor by censoring gangster films that we shall increase the audience for Shakespeare (if the Elizabethans had censored the tragedy of blood we should have had no *Hamlet*). The trouble with the theories about culture, which I have been discussing, is that their emphasis has been far too much upon complaint and their remedies restrictive. All too often there seems to be a desire to replace living things by dead, to silence a vital, if vulgar and commercialized, form of entertainment and replace it by the cloistered calm of the municipal museum in some small provincial town. Detailed suggestions for cultural improvement too often conjure up a picture of one of those terrible organizations by means of which national states purvey their wares in literature, art and science. There are pictures in some safe modern style on the wall, books well reviewed in the Sunday newspapers on the shelves and a 'great man of letters' speaking slowly on British institutions to an audience of earnest students and Anglophil old ladies. There is little that is living there. What live matter there is will come in a question at the end of the lecture or a conversation after it is over, though, since the lecturer will meet only local notables at the subsequent cocktail party, this latter spark is unlikely to be struck.[1]

for my arguments from a different angle in Richard Wollheim's Fabian Tract *Socialism and Culture* (London, 1961). It is refreshing to find a professed Socialist quoting John Stuart Mill in order to refute the case for a 'common culture'.

[1] How unrewarding gatherings of intellectuals can be will be known to anyone who has taken part in them. Perhaps we need to know someone well—either

It would be too easy to point out all the defects in the organizational approach to culture. At the dead point where the official and the fashionable meet and blend (as they are bound to do) there is, so it seems to me, a bitter lesson to be drawn by those interested in improving cultural standards. Patronage (and especially state patronage) has always run the risk of making five derivative works of art bloom where one bloomed before, and anyone who wishes to study what consumption of talent and deviation of critical opinion fashion can cause should look at the history of the English theatre since the war. At a time when, say, Brecht is fashionable and any budding playwright writing Brechtian pastiche knows exactly in what papers he can safely expect a favourable notice it is fairly easy for anyone with subsidies to give to multiply the theatres at which such efforts can be seen. Whether this is worth doing can be a matter of dispute, but it is certain that what is difficult, and what will not, in fact, be done by official patronage any more than by straight commercialism, is to anticipate the next fashionable genre or winnow the rare grains of originality from the present one.

To 'do something' about cultural conditions in England demands a more sustained effort than is involved in the subsidies of the Arts Council and the creation of municipal theatres. It requires an infinity of individual actions upon the minds and emotions both of those whom I have called 'the creative minority' and of those who are not among their number. It requires, in short, that general and individual action which is usually described as education. If a mediating factor, a means of transmission is necessary between the intellectuals and the rest of society, then that is just the role that we expect of education in its widest sense. In this connection it will not so much be education directed towards a creative contribution to culture—for no educational system can be sure of producing the exceptional man; it can only enable him to do his work—as towards a realization that such a contribution must be made by someone if society is to survive, that that someone cannot be enlisted on the side of any project external to his purpose—it is he who will make the projects of fifty years hence—and that to produce the conditions under

personally or through his work—before he can speak to us in a manner we can understand. Then, indeed, conversation becomes exciting and significant—like a dialogue of one half of the mind with the other. The difference between this sort of thing and the ordinary boredom of cultural assemblies is something like that which we feel as between hearing just one more university lecturer and listening to a genuine teacher.

which he can survive is the one imperative duty on us all. Whether in literature, art, science, philosophy, commerce or politics, the original man is the one factor in our state we cannot do without. For that reason he deserves respect, and not only for that reason. It remains true that while only a minority can participate in those daemonic processes by which the total way of life of their fellows will be shaped and informed, yet there is a sense in which their achievement—and, above all, the manner of their achievement—must serve as the only goal and yardstick of humanity. Man, it is said, is a creator before he is anything else, and the thought should never be far from us in our discussion of culture that the individual act of creation personifies in exemplary form the myriad of small gains and satisfactions which, while they do not change the world, nevertheless represent life's advantage for the mass of men. Without the small effort, hardly apparent outside the personal sphere, man must lose his self-respect and with it his humanity.

> 'Den schlechten Mann musz man verachten,
> Der nie bedacht, was er vollbringt.
> Das ist's ja, was den Menschen zieret,
> Und dazu ward ihm der Verstand,
> Dasz er im innern Herzen spüret,
> Was er erschafft mit seiner Hand.

'The incompetent man who never considers what he is doing deserves nothing but contempt. What makes a human being is just this, that he can feel in his inmost heart what he fashions with his hands, and that is what his wits were given him for.'[1]

---

[1] Schiller, *Das Lied von der Glocke*, ll. 15–20. The translation is quoted from *The Penguin Book of German Verse* (Penguin Books, 1957), p. 261.

People and Culture
Alan Shuttleworth
with
A Response to People and Culture
Stuart Hall

from

Working Papers in Cultural Studies, 1, 1971.

Reprinted by permission of the authors.

PEOPLE AND CULTURE
Alan Shuttleworth

**A.S. has been Senior Research Associate at the Centre since 1968, and is the
author of *Two Working Papers in Cultural Studies*. His present interest is in
the culture of violence in modern society. The paper is an important attempt
to define the field of Cultural Studies in a humanist context. Central to the
argument is the contention that the culture of a people should always be
studied from the point of view of its connection with their personal thoughts
and experiences. The essay is followed by a response from Stuart Hall.**

THE MEANING OF 'CULTURE'

It is well known that in the last hundred years the meaning of the word
culture has been greatly extended. Culture in Matthew Arnold's sense — the
best that has been thought and said' (and the best that has been painted,
sculpted and composed, we should add) —had a very restricted meaning: the
word referred to the distinctively intellectual and artistic part of civilisation — the fine arts especially, the humanities, and also, perhaps, the
broader, more philosophical aspects of science. Definitely not a part of
culture were all the practical, technical, vocational and professional skills,
crafts and knowledges. In complete contrast, in the modern anthropological
(or sociological) sense of the word, we would be more inclined to say that
learned gentlemen have their culture, certainly: but, equally, technicians
have theirs. Every group in society, in other words, has a culture. Thus,
we can speak of the culture of a whole society or else of the culture, or
sub-culture, of a particular section of the society — working class culture,
youth culture, and so on. In this modern sense (it is not to be found in the
OED), culture means something like the way of life of a group in all its
aspects; or else all the products of a group, all the thought, speech and
writing, actions and artefacts produced by a group of people. From meaning the
best that has been thought and said, the word has come to mean everything that
is thought and said.

The extension of the meaning of culture has a complicated history, but part
of the energy behind the widening has been democratic. The argument here is
not that in matters of culture the majority is always right; it is, rather
that everyone always has some right. The core of the argument is that an
intellectual and imaginative life is not confined to one group in society
alone — those who have been specially gifted or who have been specially
trained for it. On the contrary, all human beings have such a life and all

social living is informed by the intellect and imagination of its members. There is not a thinking, creating minority and then an inert, mechanical, working mass. Instead, there are many ways of life, each with its own centre of thought, its own characteristic ideas and images, each producing distinctive expressions, products, activities and artefacts.

At one time, only a limited range of expressions — the best of the poetry, novels, drama, 'serious' music, ballet, and works of philosophy of a period — were thought to contain significant intellectual and artistic content. A group of interpretative studies — broadly speaking, the humanities — took those expressions as their field of study. It was an essential part of these disciplines to make qualitative judgements, to sort out the best. The rest, all other human expressions, were not thought worthy of study, were not thought to 'have enough in them' to make the effort of close and extensive inquiry worthwhile. We now shift our ground. **We hold that all the thought, and all the speech and writing, actions and artefacts, of all people express interesting, worth knowing, inner life. The interpretative study (struggling into existence of all human expressions) is cultural studies. This inquiry does not only select 'good' expressions for close study: it aims to be able to study any expression. It is an interpretative study in that its main effort is to understand and then state what images and ideas, what values, what mental life those expressions embody.**

■ **Thoughts and expressions.** We can put our starting position in slightly different terms. Any human activity, individual or collective, is always the product of ideas — at least, in part. A society, for instance, from the Birmingham University Motorbike Club to the Co-op to the nation state, is the embodiment or acting out or crystallisation of a set of beliefs and ideals. Men have ideas and then they act on them: that, in the simplest possible terms, is the story of human activity — at least, as I say, in part. That basic premise — we could call it idealism — inaugurates a whole field of studies: those which try to uncover the ideas behind the actions, to recover the thinking that has gone into making the public scenes that we regularly move among.

Ideas are found in two places: they are thought but not expressed, or they are expressed. On the one hand, a person may reveal his own ideas as little as possible. As far as he can, he may keep his ideas and ideals private, secret inside his own head. He may, for instance, be ashamed of what he thinks, or alarmed by it, or confused by it. That, as I say, may be extreme; but, certainly, no one reveals all his thought to all and sundry: most people are a bit wary about what they say in public. Thus, there are thoughts in people's heads which are not made public: we could call them **personal thoughts.** On the other hand, some ideas do get made public; they are expressed openly in some form. Some of these expressions are very perishable — talking, gesturing, *ex tempore* little dances, for instance. Other expressions achieve a relatively permanent public form — books, posters, graffiti, statues, gravestones, churches. Thus, ideas may exist as personal thoughts or they may be expressed and made public. **The two sets of ideas do not generally coincide.** On the one hand, what is commonly said does not straight forwardly reveal what people are really thinking — a lot goes on under the counter. Conversely, much of what people are thinking is not made available for others to share. Many people lead icelandic lives, shut in, unable to speak freely, numbed.

We began by saying that culture was all the products of a group, all the thought, speech and writing, actions and artefacts produced by a people. We are now separating the personal, unexpressed thoughts of a people from the speech and writing, actions and artefacts, that they have produced. We are separating **personal thoughts** and **public expressions.** The whole field of inquiries that we are envisaging, that we have called **Cultural Studies,** could thus be split from the start into two separate inquiries. On the one hand would be the study of personal thoughts. The aim of this study would be to describe, as far as possible, what people were thinking but were not, left to themselves, saying. Its basic method would be the extended interview. Recording how particular individuals see the world, getting down and making public the thoughts that would not otherwise be made known, that would be the sole end-in-itself of the work. Such a study, contrary to many misconceptions, would not, as I understand it, correspond with any branch of psychology as at present constituted. Contemporary psychology either refuses to study consciousness on the grounds that it does not exist or, if it does exist, is unstudiable; or else it studies the unconscious mind; or else it studies the structure, not the content, of consciousness. In any case, scientific psychology will not accept description as an end-in-itself, but insists that it is only with explanation and the study of causes that a science is instituted. Existential psychoanalysis does describe individual consciousness as part of its main effort; their work is very close to what I am proposing. Oddly enough, descriptive sociology quite frequently attempts the description of contemporary personal thoughts (whether of single individuals or of average or typical themes among individuals), but it is only a subsiduary part of sociology and is not whole-heartedly valued by the powerful, scientific movement in the discipline. We can, then, envisage a study aiming to report the thoughts of any individuals, whoever they may be. I cannot, I must confess, think of an appropriate name for such study — unless it were called **Humanist Studies!** What would be the aim of such inquiry? First of all, simple curiosity. We are, I think, intrinsically interested to a certain extent in how other people see the world, in what it is like to be in someone else's shoes and to look at things the way they do. If not intrinsic, this interest is certainly very widespread: witness the great popularity of biographies and memoirs, documentary TV programmes with this sort of focus, interviews, etc. But such studies, far from being encouraged academically, are dismissed as journalism. Second, such studies directly serve the moral end of treating other people as ends-in-themselves, with thoughts, feelings, beliefs, equal in importance to our own — our basic moral requirement. We cannot treat other people as equal to ourselves in this way by a decision of the will alone, however: it is only when the moral decision is accompanied by active curiosity that we may discover who other people are. It is only by carefully studying the thoughts of others — whether in a special inquiry or in the ordinary round of life — and it is a hard discipline in

either case to do it sustainedly — that we can be at all responsive to them
in our behaviour. We cannot act humanely without doing, formally or informally,
humanist studies. (There are, of course, certain general rules of common
decency which we can apply in any situation — but they do not take us far
enough without this special effort to understand, begun afresh at each
encounter.)

People, then, have their personal thoughts. But there is also a medium of
ideas in between people, partially expressing and partially obscuring what
they really think. If there is to be one kind of study of the otherwise
unexpressed thoughts of individuals, there needs also to be a rather
separate study of public expressions, of the ideas that do get expressed
openly. We could try to detach the two studies from each other as far as
possible and have them as altogether separate inquiries. If we did so, then
it is this study of public expressions, I suppose, that should be called
Cultural Studies. If we did seek to sever in this way the connections
between the two sorts of inquiry we would have one study, Humanist Studies,
which would deal only with the personal thoughts of individuals; a quite
separate study, Cultural Studies, would deal only with public expressions.
Some members of the Centre for Contemporary Cultural Studies favour such
a programme of separation and Centre practice has by-and-large been confined
to the study of the public medium of ideas. It is one of the main aims of
this essay to argue against such a complete severance. I contend that, while
personal thoughts do indeed differ from public expressions, while the two
things must therefore be studied separately some of the time, the whole
point of the study should be to look in the end at the relations between
the two. **We need, for instance, to be able to compare and contrast what
is thought and experienced in a society with what is openly stated. We should
study personal thoughts and public expressions separately for a time, in
order to look finally at the connections and disconnections between them.
I am arguing, that is, for an integrated study of people and culture.**

A vast amount of theoretical writing in this century has pointed towards
an empirical discipline for the study of culture somewhat separated from the
study of individuals. It is now thirty years since Susanne Langer wrote
of the new key to the understanding of man that had been discovered:

> . . . **symbolism** is the recognised key to mental life which is
> characteristically human and above the level of sheer animality. Symbol
> and meaning make man's world, far more than sensation; Miss Helen Keller,
> bereft of sight and hearing, or even a person like the late Laura Bridgman,
> with the single sense of touch, is capable of living in a wider and richer world
> than a dog or an ape with all his senses intact.

Since that time the argument has gathered even greater force:.it is only
because we are born into a culture, into a world of symbols, of public
meanings, that each of us develops the distinctively human capacity for
thought. Since that book of Susanne Langer, the publication of the later
work of Wittgenstein has added enormous force to the point. A new discipline
for the empirical study of symbols, of culture, is clearly called for and,

equally clearly, has not yet come into being. Such a new discipline would have a great mass of material to study, for there is no existing discipline whose primary aim is the study of the **full** range of expressions in the contemporary world and of the ideas that they express. We are surrounded by ideas all the time — on billboards, on the radio, in letters, in conversations, in interior decoration, in the fashion in clothes. Public ideas mediate all our relationships to each other: people can only get to know each other through the medium of expressions which exists in between them. But where are these public expressions studied? Sociology, sometimes, as a minor method, studies written documents. There are, of course, also mass media studies; but their attention is not usually strongly focused on the ideas expressed in the media. Some art criticism, some architectural criticism, a bit of linguistics, the odd article in *New Society* all touch on the area. But the great mass of public expressions — the cultural air in which we live and which we breathe — receive no study at all. We need, then, a study of public expressions. We also need a study of personal thoughts. Above all, we need a connected study of both, of people **and** culture.

■ **A descriptive study.** Before pressing on, there is a point that ought to be made, in parenthesis. At various times so far I have said that the aim of the study of ideas, in either of its two forms, is to describe ideas, or to report ideas, or to interpret them. These terms obviously require some clarification. First, I would argue, the study of people's ideas should aim to be descriptive, in the sense of not aiming to be explanatory in the scientific manner, not formulating laws of behaviour, not proving cause and effect. The primary interest of the student in this field should not be to seek to explain why people think or say the things they do, he will rather want to concentrate on describing what their thoughts and expressions actually are. That may seem to the reader an oddly limited ambition. Surely explanation is a much worthier end than description? I feel the need to emphasise the importance of 'mere' description because the merits and benefits of explanation in all fields of study are so often and so exclusively insisted upon that the very real merits of description become largely ignored. First of all, description is a necessary preliminary to any explanation. We can only explain what we have first described adequately. The bane of a great deal of social science and psychology is too great a passion for explanatory theories and too little respect for careful, empirical, real-life description. Second, valid explanations are, in any case, very hard to come by; they are not to be had simply by wishing. We cannot explain **in any strict sense** nine tenths of what people do around us all the time. If we cannot explain in a causal way why someone is doing what he is doing, we can always improve our description of what he is doing and what his accompanying thoughts and feelings are. Third, there is a powerful argument (which may well be true) that because men possess **some** free will we will never be able to explain their actions fully: we will always be left in the end describing but unable to explain. Fourth, suppose on the contrary we do not possess free will. The correct explanation of some piece of behaviour might turn out to be biological or chemical. We might discover conclusively, for instance, that some kinds of emotional disturbance are due to a specific chemical imbalance and that a drug therapy will cure them. Nevertheless, while we treat a patient as a body in this way, we should also go on treating him as a person at the same time. Even if his consciousness of the world is only epiphenomenal, even if his feelings and thoughts and fantasies are caused and not causing, it is still *his* consciousness. He may have an objective illness which should and can be cured, but he also lives that illness subjectively. He not only has a body which suffers illness, treatment and cure, he also inevitably tries by himself to make sense of what has been happening to him and to imagine what might happen next. And though it might turn out to be a diseased understanding, it is still *his* understanding. A humane response should respect both elements. A man is a product of factors and also a person who lives for himself there at the end of the causes. Given that we do have a primary curiosity about people, and given also that we have a moral duty to be curious about people, such description is worthwhile as an end in itself.

If our aim is to describe ideas, whether personal thoughts or public expressions, this may be done either by presentation or by interpretation.

To begin with, there is the surface level of actual real world events and things. Of course, I am not using the phrase 'actual real world events and things' here in the way a behaviourist would. Thoughts and feelings are as real as words, or ink and paper — as I see it. By the phrase I mean such things as the actual thoughts of people in their own words; actual intact graffiti; real stuck-on-the-wall posters. One kind of study aims to discover such material and then present it as far as possible; tries to get as close as possible to putting the actuality down on the page — quoting interviews verbatim, for instance, pauses 'ums' 'ahs' 'you knows' and all; printing reproductions of posters and collections of rugby songs. On the other hand, there is the deep level of interpretation, of summary, moving from the real world events to the underlying patterns, essences, themes, ideal types. The aim here is to get as compact as possible a statement of the basic ideas which underly the apparent surface variety of what is thought or expressed. The student, instead of quoting the words of the people he is studying, has to formulate their ideas in his own clearer terms. Both methods apply to both of the types of the study of ideas that I have defined: we can present and interpret personal thoughts and public expressions. Of course, **pure** presentation is not really possible: there must at least be some selection — that should be thoughtful and therefore is, in effect, interpretative. Similarly, unless interpretation is firmly anchored in real world phenomena, it has no point, it becomes mere unattached speculation. In fact, we should always use both methods, moving backwards and forwards between presentation and interpretation. Nevertheless, there is a clear difference between work which tends towards the presentative end of the scale and that which tends towards the interpretative. Both are valuable.

PERSONAL THOUGHT

On the one hand, people's actions follow from their thoughts. People enact what they are thinking. Faced with someone whose behaviour seems strange to us, we only come to understand what he is doing by also understanding his thoughts and feelings, his view of the world, which urges him to act in that way. On the other hand, the relationship between **thought, word** and **deed** is only very rarely straightforward. More often, thought and expression are disconnected from each other to some extent. What people say and do in ordinary social situations does not, normally, clearly reveal what they are thinking. In turn, the things that people say and the things they do often do not neatly coincide with each other. It is because these gaps exist between thought and expression, word and deed, that there is a problem of understanding people, and that there is need of a special effort, a special discipline, of understanding. If everyone, left to themselves, already explained fully what they were doing, what they felt while they were doing it and what they were aiming at, and if we all listened while they were explaining it, there would be no need for a special study to try to uncover and make public their thoughts. The human world would already be clear enough. It is because there are disconnections between what people think and what they say and do, because personal thoughts and public expressions embody somewhat different ideas, that they must be studied, some of the time separately.

The Elements of Consciousness

So far, I have used the word thought to mean everything that takes place in the consciousness of an individual, whether it is openly expressed or not. In this section I will take a closer look at the kinds of thing that go on in people's consciousness and it will become clear that the single word thought is too limiting. My argument will be that any moment of consciousness is always a fusion of four elements:

- **bodily experience**
- **emotion**
- **individual thought**
- **cultural meanings within the individual mind**

Any state of consciousness is always a fusion of all four elements. The sort of study of an individual that I am trying to outline sets out to describe what it is like to be in someone else's shoes — to describe, to take one instance, what it is like to be a skinhead on the day of a Cup tie. On such a day, as on all days, his consciousness will be a mixture of his bodily experience (the sights, smells, sounds and touches of the match), his aroused emotions, his own effort of thinking and the cultural images and ideas that he has in mind. It would be the aim of such a study of the Skinhead's day to describe — in so far as it could, and its attempt will always be very incomplete — all four dimensions of his consciousness through the day. (The question at once arises, how can we know what is in his mind, but is not expressed. Clearly, the task is very difficult. Clearly, it can only ever be done with very partial success. But, also clearly, there are ways of finding out some of what people are thinking, some of what they can smell and what preoccupies their gaze, some of what they are feeling. We can find out bits of what is on someone's mind — bits that they would not express if we were not there making a deliberate effort.)

■   **Bodily experience.** A man is a kind of animal. We are live bodies in a world of things. We are, for instance, mortal and prone to illness; we have many inborn characteristics; we have eyes, ears, nerves, glands, a brain. As live bodies we are described by biology. Our concern here is not that — we begin with the fact that we are live experiencing bodies. Through our senses, our nerves and our brain working together, we get an awareness of the outside world. We see, hear, touch, taste and smell the things all about us. We also sensorily experience our own limbs and some of our insides. We experience the world through our whole bodies. All our senses are continuously active when we are awake and conscious, registering and responding to the world about us. Any human action is always the action of such a whole experiencing body: in a fight, for instance, we are engaged, bodily quickened and alive in all our senses; we see and hear, we touch, smell and taste; we are balanced; we can feel all the time, without having to look and without having to think about it, where our arms, legs, fists, head and chest are and we move them thoughtlessly; we feel our tendons; we feel pain; we feel in our stomach, in the throat and in the mouth; we may feel we are suffocating; we feel our bladder distending. All these are not just bodily **responses:** they are bodily **experiences.** Much more than what I have described is going on in the body during a fight, but we are not aware of it, we do not experience it. Only what we are aware of, what we experience, concerns us here.

■   **Emotion.** Feeling is much more extensive than we generally realise or allow. A few of the stronger feelings have acquired names and have been greatly celebrated. As they are the ones we can most easily speak about, we tend to assume that these are all there are. Fear, love, hate, regret, despair, contentment — these and a few others are what we usually think of in connection with the term feeling. We tend to think that an expression of feeling would be an overpowering (and very embarrassing) statement of one of these — 'Oh, it is all too awful! I despair!' In reality, feelings consist of a continuum, a never-ending stream flowing through all our experience. with thousands of appearing and vanishing components. We notice the stronger feelings, because they have a name and because they have an apparent cause and because it may seem to us to be those feelings which impel us to action. We do not recognise much of the rest of the continuously present stream of feeling. Such nuances of feeling always accompany and colour sense impressions. Travelling home from a football match, as evening falls, through the varying areas of the city, some known and some unknown, we see many different kinds of houses, streets and buildings, and the light is gradually changing. We are not neutrally perceiving all this time. Responding to the sense impressions, seeming inseparable from them, will be subtle feelings, perhaps pleasant, perhaps unpleasant, and perhaps so weak and vague as to defy expression, but feelings nevertheless. These emotions do not impel us to action; they merely give a tone to all our experience. Feelings are made of vapour and are hard to describe, they are constantly shifting and often on the borderline of consciousness. But there is a distinct feeling leaving the football ground on a cold winter later afternoon amidst a solid crowd after a middling home win; another feeling when the crowd has begun to thin out and go in different directions, and you are back on the pavement, walking among the rather seedy factories surrounding the ground; another feeling arriving off the bus in the neon-lit, plastic and glass city centre, everyone now separated in ones or twos, other people going home after shopping, going to the pictures after a shopping outing or going out to the pictures, or whatever, making for their various private evenings; another feeling travelling on the train in the dark past the suburban back gardens, looking in at the tellies and armchairs and lounges; another feeling arriving back in the familiar, well-known side streets and then home. Feelings make a continuous and subtle commentary all the time on our bodily experience. The sensations by themselves are clear and definite, they could be described, given time, coldly and neutrally in great detail. But that is not the way we normally experience the world; such a description does not capture the way that sensations and feelings are thoroughly mixed. Our usual language for describing such feelings is very thin — lovely, nice, interesting, beautiful, pretty (or their hip equivalents). The tendency is to describe feelings as either pleasant or unpleasant and to let it go at that. At times, feelings startle us with their forcefulness; but normally they seem to disappear from our attention.

■   **Thought** Through our senses we become aware of the world about us. This can be thought of as a wholly inactive, receiving of experience. Things in the world simply present themselves and are seen or heard or touched. Their impressions flood into us and we cannot control their entry. Through our senses we are made to experience the world as it is. This idea has much to commend it. We cannot by thought and will alone create a sensuous world different from the one that we do occupy. When we (or the skinhead) open our eyes, we cannot help seeing things and our sight is always much fuller and more detailed than any preconception about the scene that we had. At the same time, by our thought, we do also partly shape the world we see. Our minds are active in sensual experience, attending, neglecting, patterning, shaping, making some sense of it all. What is seen depends not only on what is there, but also on who is looking and what he is looking for. We look upon the world selectively, looking for the things that matter to us or interest us, and not noticing things that are not important. What we pay attention to, we shape. Thus, each of us may experience the same thing in different ways, from different aspects. We need (and it is very rare) a balanced view here: our sensuous experience of the world is always formed and shaped by our preoccupied, attending, interpreting mind, but experience is never wholly submissive and obedient, taken captive. Though we do generally see what we pretty well knew was there already, and pay no attention to at least nine tenths of what is around us, we still do sometimes see what we did not intend to, what we did not want to, what we had thought could never be there. We are sometimes overtaken by sights and feelings. Occasionally the senses and the emotions do take us beyond the mind's ability to understand — though never quite beyond the mind's effort to understand. We do not simply passively experience the world; nor do we dream it all up out of our heads. Instead, we do both at once: experience and interpreting ideas are always thoroughly intermixed.

■   **Individual thought.** The interpreting mind which works over all our experience is in turn, a compound of the individual effort at thought and culturally
received ideas and images. The individual effort at thought can be shown in
an illustration — it will be clear from this, I hope, that the effort involved is not always very great and the thought not always of a specially
high quality. Consider a man sitting in a deck chair in his garden on a
summer afternoon. He has been preoccupied with thinking about work, and then
his chain of thought comes to an end and he notices the scent from a nearby
rose bush. He lingers on the scent because it pleases him. Then his thoughts
begin to work again and he remembers the effort he has put into planning and
growing those roses over the years. He remembers the strain of moving big
stones in the wheelbarrow. He feels a sense of achievement and self-satisfac-
tion: he always wanted a garden of a certain sort and atmosphere and it seems,
on afternoons like this, that he has got it and he can enjoy it now. He
thinks to himself that he's a pretty contented man, all round. The day also
means something to him because it is his wife's birthday — he has cut some
roses for the occasion and they are now in a vase on the table in the lounge,
which he can see by turning his head and looking through the window behind
him. He sees his wife entering the room. She has just had flu and he watches
her, anxiously, moving about, opening the sideboard, getting the tea things
ready. The experience of that fictional man in a brief segment of his life
is being continuously surrounded and framed by his thoughts. Now, clearly,
mean thoughts here in an extended sense — it includes hopes, memories, re-
solutions, concerns, judgements, decisions and the odd fantasy. There is no
thought here in the logical, rational, objective, deductive sense. The mind
wanders and ambles about. It is all thought penetrated by emotion. Perceptions arouse thoughts; thoughts evoke moods and emotions which colour the
perception; feeling prompts resolution. The mind, it might be said, is merely
drifting here, merely idling. Yet it is also doing its work: the man in the
garden is forming out of these various odd bits and pieces a view of his life
and its elements, an idea of himself and his condition. This is not the
detached thought of science — the thought that a few people sometimes practice.
It is the subjective thought that we all live by. In this kind of thought, ideas,
judgements, moods, desires, and acts of will are thoroughly interwoven in the
mind with sensuous experience, and there are many nuances, merging into
each other.

■   **Cultural meanings in the mind.** Much of the contents of the mind
in such a situation do not derive just from the individual activity of thought
and the unique individual biography. People's minds are also stuffed full
with culturally derived images and ideas. These also frame the experience.
A friend at the Centre commented on the illustration I have just offered and
extended it in this direction. He writes, 'The scent of roses is of course
natural: but the fact that a man has the scent growing in his garden, available to him there, is not 'natural' and is not his unique idea either. There
are many rose gardens. And the associations of roses derive even more from
where he has been, what he has read and seen. The scent of the roses is
natural, but the poignancy has been celebrated from Ronsard to Burns to Tamla
Motown. His contact with and response to them will be part of his consciousness of the rose, the pure olfactory sensation.' Someone else then remarked

that the scent of roses is, in any case, only ambiguously 'natural' these days; the rose as we know it is the product of several centuries of man deliberately working on nature, transforming the given rose into the cultivated rose. Both comments are true and emphasise how much of our 'personal' thought is second-hand; we repeat even in our secret day-dreams, the images and ideas with which we are supplied by others. It is inevitable that this should be so: we can only develop the capacity for individual thought because we are first given thoughts by others. And yet, our ideas are never completely the products of others; the experience of that man in his garden, and his thoughts, are not entirely a product of the rose manufacturers' advertising and publicity departments. Sensuous experience, individual thought and culturally derived images and ideas are always intimately mixed.

The aim in this kind of study is, as far as we can, to stand in other people's shoes, to think their thoughts, see the world with their eyes, discover what the world is like for them. An individual's world is always a compound of four elements — sensuous experience, feelings, individual thoughts and culturally derived images and ideas. I have tried to emphasise the interconnection of these parts of the mind: thought does not normally exist separate from feeling or feeling separate from experience; on the contrary, the four elements of the mind are constantly at work on each other and are not readily separable from their mutual relationships. I wish to resist a study of someone's ideas separate from their feelings, of their feelings separate from their experience, of their culturally received ideas apart from their individual effort of thought turned onto those received ideas. It would be the main task, in a study of the rose-grower of the kind that I am envisaging, to describe as much as it could of all this. (I do not suggest that such a study could transcribe more than a fraction of his inner world, and it could only do that with his sustained assistance.)

The Degrees of Consciousness

Experiences and thoughts and feelings are tangled together in the mind and any few minutes of consciousness always contains very complicated sequences and mixtures of moods, images, perceptions and thoughts. But a person's mind is not altogether a random muddle, for our thoughts have a certain dominance over the other elements in the mind. By thought we seek to order what would otherwise be an incoherent jumble and to make some steady sense of our experience. Our thought turns on our varied experience in the attempt to make an adequate map of plan of it. Our thought is turned in our experience and makes some sense of it, but yet we never reach a finalised, definitive mapping. Our experience is never completely made sense of — sorted, labelled and put into place — by our clarifying thought: there is always some incompleteness in our understanding of our experience of things. Within each man, thought turned on experience, and yet thought falling short of experience — that is what is being human. If thought fully mastered experience, then nothing would surprise us, our lives would unroll before us like an old movie we had seen many times before. If thought entirely failed in its effort to order, then we would be incessantly surprised: nothing could ever be expected, and nothing that arrived could ever be compared with what was already known. In

the next few pages I will try to identify four distinct degrees to which
thought may master experience. I call the four degrees:

■ common sense thought
■ articulate thought
■ flow of consciousness
■ power of the senses

■ **Common sense thought.** To begin with, the mind does not normally work in
an exposed fashion as it shapes and forms sensuous experience. We normally make
sense of the world in a routine, habitual way, without noticing what we are
doing, without making a special effort at interpretation. Habitually, we sort
things into place. We are not normally aware of our interpretations as interpretations; we are not aware that nine-tenths of our surroundings have gone
by unnoticed; we think we are merely passively registering what is indisputably
there. That is, we have many subjective interpretations which we do not
notice are subjective; we have many beliefs which we do not regard as beliefs,
but simply as obvious visible facts, common sense, what any reasonable sane
man would recognise as such. This kind of interpretation, below the threshold of consciousness, has been called by Alfred Schutz 'common sense thought'.
It can be uncovered and revealed (with difficulty, by peculiar methods) as
a closely organised collection of beliefs, assumptions, rules and methods.
The individual sees it as being, without question, true and shared by everyone normal. Everyday, practical concerns are especially dominated by this
mode of thought: the individual gets the things done that he has to and
readily makes sense of his ordinary day-to-day experiences. This is our
normal mode of thought. We live most of our time immersed in practicalities.

■ **Articulate thought.** No one lives all his life as a thing of
habit and routine. Sometimes, self-consciously and deliberately, we take
thought about our situation. I call this kind of deliberate thought
'articulate' because I think it is always thought in words. It is what some
writers call 'inner speech'. In such thinking we may be said to be talking
to ourselves. In this way we form projects for the future, we think out our
alternatives, we puzzle about a recurrent trait in our character, try to
remember more examples of it, think about possible explanations. Such thinking is very conscious of ideals and of how the individual stands in relation
to them. It is predominantly, though not entirely turned inwards; it is concerned to develop a theory about the individual's being in the world. At the
same time, it is somewhat detached and self-conscious; some times it seems
to be we who are thinking, at other times it is like a rather critical,
ironic stanger watching us and criticising. This kind of thought could
also be called subjective or autobiographical. It is not, I think, the
province of the intellectual alone: it is part of the life of everyone.

Everyone makes up an interpretation of his own life, for himself: we all tell
ourselves, on occasion, the story of our own life. It deals centrally with
personal meanings, those beliefs, plans, ideals, ideas, remembered experiences, which the individual sees as central to the understanding of his own
life. Because it is articulate, even if it is never openly communicated to

anyone but is kept private and secret, it is nevertheless capable of being communicated.

■   **The flow of consciousness.** Everyone has moments when they are not doing anything in particular, when they are neither performing some routine task nor deliberately thinking. We may just day-dream, letting the mind wander. We often occupy a world of struggling, wandering thoughts, wandering into past and future and fantasy. This is, above all, that mental life in which ideas, moods, emotions, experiences, memories, desires are all interwoven. Our primary, sensuous experience of the world is not only constantly dominated and reduced to plan by our interpreting thoughts, it is also often surrounded and played with by a freer, speculating, imagining, remembering, meandering consciousness — mind not tied to immediate percep- tion or practicality or too much sense. And it is here that the mind is, in some ways, most exposed in its peculiar, intimate play with the stuff of the senses. Somewhere near here, I think, we should locate the formation of our ideals. When strong feelings (and not external reality) are in the saddle and they ride our thoughts, then fantasies are generated — images of worlds dominated by single emotions: a perfectly secure, warm nourishing world: or an unendurably stagnant, fetid quagmire; or a world of incessant, tearing, raging, punishing violence. These fantastic images, perhaps, are the source of the real energy behind our ideals. They are formed by the free unrealistic play of the mind on emtions.

■   **The power of the senses.** I have been discussing the power of thought to define experience. Perhaps most of the time, the mind sorts experience into place in a routine programmed way. Sometimes, we deliberately strive to make sense of things by an effort of thought. On other occasions, our thoughts unpredictably and intricately wander and flow. In these ways, thought exercises its usual dominion in the mind. And yet the power of thought is incomplete; it is always short of full domination. We must be- ware, in a discussion such as this, of seeming to dissolve our sensuous experience entirely into our thoughts, of reducing experience to conscious- ness. Therefore, we must twist round here and insist on the force of our primary sense impressions. The present, as distinct from memory and fantasy, is precisely where consciousness is filled up, flooded by the senses. In contrast to what has been and what may yet be, only in the present is their real fullness of life. This is the sharp, present world, coloured and sounding and smelly sometimes insisting on itself against our preoccupa- tions. We collide against it, we grasp it, it can hurt us. A dull drizzly day in Manchester is a cultural image, a comforting idea to hold in the mind and perhaps laugh about. It can also be a wet reality. This is the character of real experience. This is the character of the world that touches us, is opened to us in its limitlessness, when we are not wholly taken up with our routines, our day dreams or our serious thinking.

We may, then, find ourselves suddenly shaken in body by experiences that we cannot easily assimilate to our normal map of thought. I am unsure of my ground here, but I think that such unassimilated experiences press on us for definition. At least, they press on us for a time until we have become far enough removed to turn our back and walk away. I think that it is perhaps here that differences in talent, differences among kinds of developed intelligence, may be important. By effort, art and intelligence we may learn to encounter more exactly our unassimilated experiences and so attempt to describe them in their very rawness. In that way, we can sometimes communicate something of our primary experience. For example, a man describes the experience of being near to a stabbing:

> No, I know it wasn't Micky Davies. I was right there in that fight, all the time, I was never more than a yard or two away from him. And he didn't have a knife. If he had had a knife, I'd have known. I'll tell you this too. When you've got a knife and you've cut somebody, you know about it. It's like — well, I suppose to someone like you it'd be like when you stepped off the pavement. You know it's happened, you are tensed up, your heart's going bang. It's like that when you've cut someone. You know — and because you know, you know when other people have done it too, it shows, if you're experienced in that sort of thing. And I'll tell you straight: Davies was no boy for the knives, and if he'd just used one I would have known. And he hadn't. He was a bit puffed, and bit out of breath, because he's been doing what he said he'd been doing — having a punch-up. But he'd never been using a knife, I can tell you that, and I was there all the time with him and afterwards too.

There, I suggest, the words are near to touching the experience. Through the words we can sense the moment itself. Alternatively, we may turn away from the effort to put experience into words, we may turn back from such moments to the routine as soon as possible. And so our thought may fail to seize possible grips on our real world, it may lose some of what control it has, become more detached and accustomed to its distance from us, of less real power.

I have been trying, in this whole part of the paper, to define the tasks of a descriptive study of individuals and their personal ideas. The aim is to be able to report the thoughts of other people, whoever they may be. We cannot understand the ideas of individuals in the way that we understand ideas in books of philosophy. Our personal thinking too much exists in its relation to our experience and is not readily detachable from it. There is not just a separate room in the mind, the study, where all the serious thinking is done in proper intellectual isolation. We should, that is, try to describe, not ideas in isolation, but ideas at work on experience. A varying, many-sided inner life is lived by everyone — skinhead, rose-grower and intellectual. (I have been accused of describing only a certain kind of fairly passive, daydreaming, liberal intellectual, tending his roses, whereas most people live hard, even brutal, lives without the time for self-contemplation and fine smells. That seems to me untrue.) All the elements of consciousness, in their characteristic mixtures, in all men and women — that is the subject-matter for this kind of study.

The argument that I have been putting forward as to what is involved in the study of a person's thoughts has special point in relation to an important school of sociology. These sociologists stress the important part played by people's consciousness in the genesis of their actions. They invoke a person's inner thoughts as a part of the explanation of his outer actions. They stress, for instance, the 'subjective meaning' of the action to the actor, or his 'definition of the situation' or his 'opinions' or his 'attitudes'. It will, I think, be clear that this is the kind of sociology to which I owe most allegiance. My effort in this essay has been to insist on some of the complexities of the mental life referred to by those phrases. A person's definition of his situation is a complicated, many-layered thing. It follows that the proper method for this sort of study is something other than the standard questionnaire; there is more in our minds than can be declared in response to one or two direct questions.

■ **How is it done?** It would take a great deal of space to discuss this question adequately and much more needs saying than I am about to say here. But two questions of method seem to insist on asking themselves at this stage in the argument. I will try to deal with these in a preliminary way and then press on. The problems begin when we recognise that we cannot take the lid off someone's mind and look at his thoughts and experiences and feelings inside, in the way that we can take the top off his head and get to work with probes and knives on the grey brains. We can only know thoughts through the medium of expressions: we can only come to know the inward life that individuals will reveal to us. Two problems of method follow from this recognition that we can never study thoughts directly, that we must always work with expressions, that we must always reconstruct the hidden thoughts from the revealed expressions.

First, are we not, after a long digression about a separate study of personal thoughts, now in fact arriving at the conclusion that that study is impossible? That we can only ever study public expressions? That we can only every study what people say, and what they think is, in consequence, forever hidden. I will be looking at this charge more fully in the next part of the essay, in the section on expressions. I can, however, say here in an interim way that we can and frequently do distinguish some expressions which explicitly aim to state a personal view of the world from others that do not. Some expressions aim to be anonymous and impersonal — income tax forms, mathematical papers, traffic signs, for instance — and we do not look to them to find our their authors' personal thoughts. Other expressions, many of which may never be published in any way, do clearly aim to reveal their authors' inner life — diaries, private letters, secret autobiographical writing are all instances. It is also the case that in extended interviews, people who would not otherwise reveal their personal thoughts may do so to a sympathetic inquirer. The study of personal thoughts is not, then, just equivalent to the study of the dominant public expressions.

Secondly: if we are relying in our studies on what people openly tell us, does that not mean that we can only ever get to know the level of articulate thought, because it is the only deliberate thought, the only thought a person is fully aware of, the only thought that is in words? Now, by definition, a man cannot 'frankly declare' his common sense thinking, for it is in such thinking that his experience is habitually placed into moulds of thought **without his being aware of it.** If he becomes aware of what he was hitherto taking for granted, it ceases to be common sense thought — it has become articulate. However, though he does not openly declare his routine assumptions, he may nevertheless reveal them in everything he does and says and makes — reveal them, that is, to someone who is himself sufficiently outside them to notice them. So, an acute observer who looks sustainedly between the lines for what is assumed, taken for granted, implied but never said, may be able to unfathom some of a man's common sense thinking. With articulate thought, such detective work is not necessary. Here we are dealing with the conscious, worked-out thought of people. We need sympathy and tact to discover it much more than forensic skill. We can only come to know some-one's autobiographical thoughts if he will openly tell them to us. We can only study such thoughts with the subject's cooperation.

But what of the other depths of the mind? What of the meandering flow of con-sciousness, the continuous patterns of mood and feeling and what of sensuous experience? Are they not still, despite what has been said, hidden from us? There is, indeed, in the end, a limit here. We are entirely reliant on other people's power to put things into words. It thus becomes a matter of great importance for us that people vary in their power to describe experiences. In some people, articulate wordy thought will be relatively detached from the rest of their consciousness, from their emotional and sensuous experience, from day dreams and fantasies. When such people explain themselves, they will tend to state opinions and beliefs and theories all the time and will not try to render in words much of the fullness or variety of their intricate inner life. If we want to know what it is like to be in someone else's skin, in the full sense that I have been trying to outline, we become straightaway heavily reliant on those individuals who succeed in putting more of their experience and consciousness into words (or pictures, or sound, of course).

So, if we wish to study people's individual inner lives we have to work with their expressions. There is no direct access to the mind. We will have to sort among expressions to uncover those which are aimed to express personal thought and we will have to encourage people to make new expressions especially for us. Furthermore, we will have to sort among those expres-sions to uncover the ones that most fully succeed in expressing a com-plicated mixture of thought and experience together. If we wish to know what it is like to be a skinhead on the day of a cuptie, what he sees and hears and smells, what his altering feelings are, what he thinks and day-dreams, what cultural images rest in his mind, we are in the end dependent upon his telling us. Our main task is to listen.

PUBLIC CULTURE

Because only some expressions — probably, only a few — clearly reveal genuinely personal thoughts, it follows that a study which confined itself in the way I have been proposing to the thoughts of individuals would leave the great mass of public expressions untouched. Since it is rare for an individual to declare at all fully what his varying thoughts and feelings are, much of the public culture of a society as a result embodies ideas which are not the genuinely personal ideas of the people who live in it. (Is that true in all societies? It is certainly true in this one.) We can take a strong but, I think, clear instance of this: the people who are intimately involved in a death, the dying person and the bereaved, are all unquestionably undergoing instense and varied experience; they are deeply

feeling a number of contradictory emotions and are thinking deeply in an
attempt to grasp hold of themselves. Yet little or nothing of all this may
be said or openly expressed in any other way. On the contrary, the
participants may try very hard to maintain a public silence over their
loud private sounds. Meanwhile, they will fit in with the prescribed
hospital routines and all the ordinary politenesses. Later they will follow
the available routines of burial and the forms of mourning. Grief and
mourning — the individual experience and the public expression — do not
readily coincide. As a result, in an adequate inquiry into the culture of
death in our society, there would need to be one study of the grief of
individuals and then a separate study of the public expressions of mourning
available to them. A truly human study, that is, will not be concerned just
with the individual inner lives. Precisely because that is its main concern,
it will also be concerned with this medium of expressions in between people.
For these public expressions embody ideas and definitions and when we maintain our silence, they speak for us.

**The public culture of a people is all the expressions used among them.
It includes their temporary gestures and their enduring monuments.
Expressions are the embodiments of ideas; they are the public form taken by
ideas. In our extended, unremitting conversation with each other — a conversation in which we use many other forms than speech — we give and take and deposit
(that is, we express) a description of the world, a public version of our experience in it, of our ideals for it. A study of the public culture should be
especially interested in uncovering the ordered meanings, the sustained,
frequently present meanings or the powerful meanings in the public conversation of a people. There is, surely, always some order within the publicly
current descriptions of the world. For instance, if we were studying the public
culture of death in this society, we would probably want to note the presence
in our public conversation of two major, differing interpretations of the
world, of life and of death: a religious interpretation and a scientific-
medical interpretation. Such bodies of ideas are not only present among us
when they are openly stated; they are also implicit in many of our practices.
So that when individuals do maintain their silence through the experience of
a death and burial — and which of us ever speaks quite freely? — it is the
religious and medical routines which, above all, speak for us. We are, then,
interested in the public ordered ideas.**

But some order is not the same thing as totalitarian uniformity, and we should
beware of adopting a method of study which systematically exaggerates the
amount of public order that there is. There is not a fully coherent religious
world view, uniformly present and powerful in our society; there are, rather,
fragments of a religious view, variably present, only rarely of great power.
The scientific-medical view is equally incomplete. 'There is not a creed which
is not shaken, nor an accredited dogma which is not shown to be questionable,
not a received tradition which does not threaten to dissolve.' As a consequence,
many of our expressions, being of some length and quite complex, do not
simply state one idea: they may be somewhat ambiguous, they may equivo-
cate, they may reveal a split between two or more opposing ideas. Thus, a

typical conclusion of a study of the ideas embodied in our public culture might be that many of our expressions show that such-and-such a theme is present, but to varying extents, coexisting with opposing views, and with some twists.

■   **The process of communication.** We are, then, considering how a public culture embodying the public ideas, stands in between people. All around this culture, making the expressions and receiving them, are the people, each with their own thoughts. And thus, though we are forced to separate for the sake of presentation a study of personal thoughts from a study of public culture, our real overall interest is not so much in personal thoughts alone, nor just in public expressions alone, but in their connections. That is, we are interested in the whole incomplete, partial process of the movement of thoughts through expressions from one person to another. We are really considering communication.

One important kind of interest in the study of the process of communication could be called 'genetic'. By this I mean an interest in how we come to be able to communicate with each other in the first place. Such an approach would be obliged to stress the inescapable inter-dependence of personal thoughts and public culture. On the one hand, it would emphasise that public culture has arisen only because of individuals' innate capacity to think, and as the sum of the expressions of their thoughts. On the other hand, it would also need to emphasise that we each of us only develop our capacity for personal thought because we are born into a surrounding culture. That is, seen in a long enough time perspective, personal thoughts are formed out of the public culture, and the public culture is formed out of the accumulation of the expressions of personal thoughts. My interest in the process of communication, in this essay, is different from that without in any way contradicting it. Granted that personal thoughts and public culture only develop together, in that interwined way, nevertheless, at any one point in time they do not coincide with each other. What a man thinks very rarely coincides fully with what he says at the time, or with what is said on his behalf nearby. The question that I am asking is not: How have the capacities for personal thought and public culture developed? The question being considered here is: What is the connection at this place and time between these people's inner worlds and the outer expressions that they move amongst?

Individuals can only communicate with each other through the intervening medium of expressions. The process of communication involves, on one side, people making partial expressions — they are partial because they do not say nearly all that the people are thinking. On the other side, it involves other people understanding these expressions — though, again, their understanding will probably always be incomplete. On the one hand, people express themselves to some extent. A public world of ideas is thereby created, available to all; it is a common world, common ground amidst different people. On the other hand, people encounter these expressions and partially understand them.

Individuals with their personal thoughts exist on both sides of the process

of communication. So far, we have been mainly attending to the way people
live with their thoughts before they express themselves and how, by and large,
they only very incompletely express themselves. We are now emphasising that
people also have to live with their thoughts after they have been talked to
by others: they must now respond in their thoughts to the ideas they have
encountered in public. We may think here of a hypothetical, completely social
man who absorbed the public ideas fully. He has responded to them so well that
they have become the thoughts which most intimately frame his own experience
of the world; he would feel his own inner experience fully confirmed outside.
This individual has entered the public ground and he has there been
surrounded by the expressions of others; he has learnt from them the public
ideas; he has identified with those ideas so thoroughly that he is shaped
by them through and through and there is no part of his inner life that has
not passively received their patterning touch; he has drawn the public ideas
into himself and has made them entirely his meanings, and his meanings them.
That straightforward, complete receiving of what we are publicly given happens
to us all, partially. However, a totally socialised individual, one who always
subjectively echoes every available public idea, is not possible. It is certainly not possible in our society if only for the reason that the public
culture is clearly heterogeneous, containing many contradictions: no man can
believe in all available points of view.

The process of communication is always incomplete, from both sides. A man only
partially expresses himself and another man only partially takes his meaning
in. In our reality, the situation is always that many things are being thought
but not expressed; conversely, many things are being expressed that are not the
real thoughts of anybody. and many of the things which are expressed are
variously and incompletely understood and their receivers respond to them
inwardly and do not say what they think.

As a result, we must study the public culture somewhat separately from the
personal thoughts of individuals. Our real, overall interest is in the whole
process of communication, in the movement from thought to expression and
back to thought again: we are interested in the extent to which people make
contact with each other. But precisely in order to study that whole process,
we must study the available public expressions somewhat separately from the
individual personal thoughts — because that is how the public culture exists
in reality, somewhat separately, a third party. We need to be able to study
all the three moments in the jerking movement from thought to expression to
thought. Before we can reconstruct the whole process of communication, we need
first to have described its separate parts. Accordingly, we proceed now to
look more closely at this intervening public moment — the common ground of
expressions between people.

■   **The full range of expressions.** We continue now in the effort to
clarify this (at least partially separated) study of culture. I wish to
establish what an overwhelming amount of culture there is in the world. The
country is crammed full and the seams are bursting with the expressions of
ideas. At the beginning of this essay I wrote (and it was not an idiosyncratic
definition of my own) that culture means 'all the products of a group, all

the thought, speech and writing, actions and artefacts produced by a group.'
In the meantime, I have been proposing somewhat separated studies of personal
thoughts and public expressions — separated for a time in order to bring them
back into truer connection later. That is, I have been saying that we should
take **thoughts** out of that list and put it on one side for the moment: we
are then left with all the **speech** and **writing, actions** and **artefacts**
of a people as their public culture. We are, it should be clear, defining
the public culture here in a very wide sense. It is our argument that culture
is not only what people write and paint or play on the violin: everything that
people make and do is a public expression of ideas. Men and women have a kind
of Midas touch: everything we deliberately handle and work over turns into
an expression. We all make expressions and we are all surrounded by the
expressions of others. Though we may all as individuals keep very quiet, we
are surrounded by a thousand objects which speak for us. **Cultural studies
should be the study of the ideas in all public expressions.**

This broad definition of culture is not idiosyncratic. For instance, writers
in what Raymond Williams has called 'the culture and society tradition' strived
to see all society as a culture, all social life as the enactment of ideas,
ideals, images of the good and bad. In scattered writing throughout the
nineteenth century, that view of social life was sustained in commentary
upon the developing society — the effort was to see the new society, not
as the enactment of necessity, economical or technical, but as the product
of a choice of values. The men who were building factories were not simply
engaged in producing more goods, they were also creating and imposing a limited
idea of human needs and experience, an image of nature, a narrow thwarting
view of life. The very buildings, the machines, the products, the imposed
patterns of life in the factories, all expressed that idea. Whatever the
entrepreneurs may have thought to themselves in their secret heart of hearts,
these were the things that spoke for them in public. And whatever the personal inner life of the workers, this is what they had to listen to all day in public. Again, in this century, T S Eliot stressed the anthropological notion of
culture — I will not quote his well known list. F R Leavis has had a wide
notion of the meaning of culture; he has repeatedly spoken of a 'folk
culture', alongside the literate culture, enacted in patterns of speech,
crafts, manners of living. Richard Hoggart has studied 'working class
culture', embodied in all areas of working class life. In *Uses of Literacy*
he looked at such things as orally transmitted phrases and tags; at *Old
Moore's Almanac;* at the *In Memoriam* columns of newspapers (you generally
choose a message from the selection of printed cards available); the notices
on library walls; men's Masonic type organisations; whist drives; and, inside
the home, '. . . . plastic gewgaws and teapots shaped like country cottages
. . . . lace paper d'oyleys, complicated lace half-curtains, crocheted table
runners, fancy birthday and Christmas cards . . . .' and so on. More
recently, the notion of a 'pop culture' or 'youth culture' has circulated
widely: such a culture is partly enacted in pop songs, but also in clothes,
hair styles, posture and gesture, patterns of speech, styles of relationship
and organisations. We derive, I think, from such sources a firm sense of
the range of expressions, the overwhelming multiplicity and diversity of

the embodiments of ideas that surround us, constituting the atmosphere between us, both joining and separating us.

Recent writers on culture have stressed the contemporary importance of the mass media and it is, of course, quite right that the central place the mass media have in our society should be recognised. Nevertheless, that place can be over-stressed. Important as the mass media are in our lives, people live most of their lives in a world of speech, in buildings of many kinds, amidst traffic signs, notices, instructions, posters, in the live presence of other people who wear clothes and have hair styles, who gesture and talk. This is the primary world of expression. By comparison, we only live a fraction of our lives being addressed by the mass media. It is only by such an extension of our understanding of what our effective public communication is, that we are able to recognise what is perhaps the single most powerful mode of communication in our society. I am thinking, here, of all the expressions of mass administration, whether in words, business letters, duplicated matter, forms, IBM cards, orders, analyses and officialese. It is on communications of this type that all our large-scale organisations depend. It is probably the case in our society that more people communicate more things to more other people in this mode than in any other. These sorts of expressions, I suggest, constitute a very large part of our public culture. A study of the mass media on their own — while it is certainly valuable and it provides a point of entry into the whole field — ought not, I suggest, to be isolated for long from the study of all forms of expression.

Perhaps it will clarify this broad definition of culture, if we distinguish well-known or deliberate forms of expression from less well-known forms of expression. No one doubts, so no one needs to argue, that speaking, writing and blushing are all forms of expression. When we use language, for instance, we intend to express ourselves or to communicate something. Other expressions are not intentional in that way, but are nevertheless well-known. We don't generally intend to blush, for instance, but when we do blush we know that we have 'given ourselves away'. Drawing, painting, making music are also all unmistakably forms of expression. We can go on in this way a little but not much further, naming the forms of expression that are well-known by all their users to be forms of expression or communication and which serve no other clear purpose. However, there are other forms of expression which are not generally recognised to be such, which are often not meant to express ideas, but which are intended to serve other practical ends. On many occasions, when we are going about our business and not thinking of communicating, we are nevertheless unintentionally, unknowingly expressive. All human activity is shaped in its course by the thoughts, feelings and decisions of the actors. Therefore, everything that we make or do, individually and socially, gives some sense of what we have in mind. We communicate far more than we intend to. A woman's gestures, her lined face, her posture, her manners, her clothes, her accent and tone of voice, the type of her house and the way it is decorated inside, the garden, her hobbies, her job and the way she does it, all are expressions: they were not intended to express a state of mind, but they do. Everything that a people does embodies their distinctive public intellectual and imaginative life. The technical expert says of a new bridge that it is a more or less efficient way of getting a specified job done. No, says the student of culture, it is also a way of making a monument to a certain view of the world — and that, let us be clear, is not at all like saying that it is a pretty bridge or an ugly bridge: we are asking, what does the whole conception of the bridge signify? If the reader finds this notion of a bridge signifying something is a strange one, let him think of the various bridges over the Thames in London: all of them are, I trust, efficient — yet what contrasts!

■ **The Complexity of the Public Culture.** In the discussion so far of the notion of 'public culture' I have been making two main points. (1) I have.been trying to convey a sense of the range of expressions in this society, to indicate how massive and varied our public culture is. My point has been to suggest by the broad use of the term 'expression' that there is a great territory here, largely unexplored, full of things to be studied. (2) I have made it clear from the start that my interest in these expressions is in the ideas embodied in them. We can either present or interpret expressions. When we interpret them, we are seeking to lay bare their underlying ideas or themes or values or meanings. If those two points are taken, it will be clear that they inaugurate a whole new field of studies, for the full range of human expressions are nowhere studied today.

I have just defined the field of Cultural Studies in a very wide sense, yet it is not my intention to argue that all expressions are the same as each other, embodying ideas in the same way, all equivalently meaningful. On the contrary, I wish to emphasise the heterogeneity, the variety, the many-layeredness, the complexity of the public culture. Because there is such a great diversity of kinds of expressions in our society — a much greater diversity than in any hitherto existing society — it is possible for a great diversity of ideas to have expression, to achieve some public presence among us. There are, of course, the very powerful mass media. They have not replaced, but exist alongside, all the modes of face-to-face communication that have existed in all societies. In addition to these two basic modes of communication, there are many other new modes of communication, which are dependent on new technologies but which are not mass media. We have, for instance, the phone-call, the snap shot, the home movie, special blue movies and filthy pictures, the fishing club's duplicated monthly new sheet, the parish magazine, ham radio, the tape recording of the family sent to relatives in Australia as a Christmas present, Christmas cards, silk-screen posters advertising a local dance, shop fronts in neon lights, libraries full of books written all over the world in different centuries, prints for the wall from small editions to The Laughing Cavalier, film societies, art cinemas, *Black Dwarf, The Buddhist Weekly,* photographic society exhibitions, underground tapes of Bob Dylan. I contend, then, that the expressions in circulation in our society are of very diverse kinds and the ideas that they express are also very diverse. If the mass media do dominate our communication with each other, it is not a simple domination. If our culture is one-dimensional, it is not a self-evident, straightforward, one-dimensionality. In other words, the order that does exist exists amidst a great variety.

Order does, however, exist amidst variety. If we do not live in a simple autocracy, we do not live in a simple democracy either. It is not the case amongst us that everybody feels free to use a great variety of forms to express whatever is happening inside them. If that were so, the distinction between personal thoughts and the public culture would be abolished. The nature of the limits on full, open communication become clear if we recognise the importance of two distinctions. First, expressions may be more or less public. Second, expressions may be more or less authentic.

First, we need to make more complex the notions of expressions being public. Once an idea is uttered, written down, painted, or in some other way expressed and published, it does not immediately become directly available to every member of the public. Not everything that is public is equally public. It is not all public in the same way. There are different kinds of publicness and there are degrees of publicness. Some ideas are more public than others.

Second, I am concerned with the notion of expression. When dealing with this term it is essential always to bear in mind the essential paradox involved in the movement from thought to expression. On the one hand, I have said that anything that reveals thoughts is an expression: on the other hand, I have said that expressions do not normally fully reveal thoughts. Expressions, I say, embody ideas: but they do not fully embody the ideas of their expressors. Or, to put the same paradox a third way, we can only understand another person's thoughts by means of his expressions: but, at the same time, understanding his expressions is something different from understanding his thoughts. We only resolve this paradox when we get to a distinction between the authentic part of expressions (that part which does reveal an individual's thought accurately) and the inauthentic part (which does not). If all expressions were authentic, there would be perfect communication and all our personal thoughts would be public. If all expressions were inauthentic, there would be no real communication at all and we would be altogether alien things to each other, no different from natural objects. In actuality, we live in between those two states, veering from time to time towards one pole and then back towards the other. The public culture is the mental air between ourselves and others. Sometimes, perhaps most often, that air is all fog: we can see nothing through it, only the thick obscuring medium itself. At other times, the air becomes clarified and we see, at varying distances from us, other people.

What we most need to avoid here are two contradictory over-simplifications. On the one hand, there is a very powerful sociological/anthropological/political spirit abroad which persuades us that the public realm is the only real one. Man is a political animal. We are thoroughly formed, inside and out, by the culture into which we are born. Our inner selves are either entirely products of the public culture, or else they are unstudiable in themselves, or else they are irrelevant or meandering and unstable. (A propos that last point, Max Weber, despite being the sociological theorist of subjective meaning, considered that people's inner thoughts were too changeable, self-contradictory and ambiguous ever to be properly studied: all we could study, in his view, were the thoughts that men acted on, for then you had proof that they believed in them.) According to this sort of perspective on man, all we can ever know, all we can study, all that is of

real importance, is the public life of people. I think I recognise a good
deal of truth in that whole intellectual atmosphere — it was the atmosphere
my mind was reared in. But it is nevertheless the main aim of this whole
paper to argue against what I think has become a characteristic over-
emphasis of the view.

**The sociological perspective on man is not the whole truth. Man is more than
a political animal. Man is, surely, profoundly shaped by his surrounding
culture. Yes, he can only be known by way of his public expressions. Nevertheless, people do also have inner, personal lives — a life of the senses,
feelings, daydreams, half formed hopes. It is true that most individuals
make very little of their inner worlds known to others, but it is possible,
by study and effort, to expand the amount of individual thought and experience that is available in public. So, I wish to counteract what I see as a
now characteristic sociological over-emphasis.**

At the same time, there is an equal and opposite error. The personal may be
seen as the only reality and the public world, the world of action, collective life may be dismissed altogether, without qualification, as entirely
and uniformly inauthentic. If we follow this line of thought, we come to
believe that it is only when we escape inwards, only when we turn entirely
around inside ourselves away from others and the narrow public grooves to
which they confine us that we become truly individual and alive. That kind
of perspective, while it recognises the importance of inner experience,
denies any reality to anything else. I am not proposing that view. I would
argue that in our personal thoughts and experiences we cannot help being
ourselves. We all, inwardly, have the distinct individual lives that we do
have. The question is, do we manifest them? The question that a wholly
sociological perspective or a wholly subjectivist perspective cannot answer
is, what is the connection at this particular time and place between these
people's inner lives and the expressions that they move amongst? The public
world is not equally, uniformly inauthentic. The distinction between
authentic and inauthentic expressions is a distinction between kinds of
public life, kinds of public activity, possible social forms.

■   **Kinds of expressions.** I suggest, then, that we approach the study of the
public culture with the following intentions. (1) We intend to study the full
range of expressions. (2) Our aim is to uncover the ideas embodies in them.
(3) We then want to establish how large a place in the public realm each of
these expressions of ideas occupies. (4) We wish to establish to what extent
each of these ideas corresponds to the real experience of anyone in this society.
I am proposing those as the four main tasks of cultural studies. Within that
framework, I will now proceed with some more distinctions between kinds of
expressions in an attempt to further clarify the extent of the range of expressions and also to clarify the ideas of publicness and of authenticity.

■   **Natural and conventional expressions.** Natural expressions —
such as going white with anger — are instinctual. They occur on the surface
of the body and reveal some of our strong emotions. Natural expressions are
universal among the species. Conventional expressions — speech and writing,
for instance — are all those forms of expression that are not inborn but

are acquired in society and they vary, accordingly, from society to society and from time to time. There are very few entirely natural expressions; even when we weep we usually, but not always, hold in our tears with many acquired restraints. The great bulk of human expressions are conventional. In a study of the public culture, we will nearly always be dealing with conventional expressions. However, many expressions which are predominantly conventional nevertheless contain some element of natural expressivity. When we are in the presence of someone and he is speaking to us, his face by its natural expressivity may unintentionally reveal a subtle, qualifying commentary on the expression that he is making in the conventional medium of words. Our interpretation of what he is clearly saying in words may be modified by what he is less clearly revealing, if we care to look for it, with his hands, his eyes, his face. (The reader should beware in the presence of these terms of the ancient confusion of the conventional with the inauthentic. A man's truest statement, *King Lear,* a traffic signal and a bare-faced lie are all conventional expressions. Some conventional expressions are authentic, others are inauthentic; or, perhaps it would be better to say, some are more authentic than others.)

■   **Making unique expressions and exchanging public counters.**
Consider one of the examples I quoted from *The Uses of Literacy* — that of the *In Memoriam* columns of newspapers, where the individual must choose from among the limited selection of printed cards available at the office. Many conventional expressions are of that type — there is a very restricted set of complete expressions open to us and everyone alike must choose one of the set. This is true, for instance, of anything we buy in a shop — kinds of Christmas cards, kinds of teapot, kinds of motor car — we have to choose from the range displayed. 'I'm afraid that's all we've got in stock, dear!' Some expressions, however, we make for ourselves (whether we use shop bought materials or not). In this case, however poor our invention, there is an infinite range of expressions possible: no two hand-made expressions are exactly alike.

It is now clear that both of these tendencies are deeply built into language. On the one hand, language is so formed that there is no limit to the number of things that can be said in it. (All men could type for ever, not repeat themselves, and not write the works of Shakespeare.) Anyone who knows the language has the capacity to say an infinite number of new things; he has the capacity to make every sentence he uses different from any sentence ever used before. On the other hand, there is a tendency for language to congeal, to become standardised into fixed forms or idioms, so that the individual always uses ready-made sentences for ready-made occasions. 'How are you?' 'Very well, and you?' 'Not too bad.' 'A bit windy, isn't it?' 'Milder than yesterday, though.' Everything has been said before, many times. Language here becomes like the cards in the newspaper office. A great deal of our actual language, spoken and written, consists of fixed routine bits responding in a fixed way to other people's fixed routine bits. At the same time, having acquired this capacity from our society, we also in the same breath acquire the other capacity, to say entirely new things. From a limited stock of public goods, it is nevertheless possible to construct an infinite number of unique new things. What we are given in the speech of others may be mainly inauthentic; but in being given the power of speech by them, we are also given the power to go beyond anything that has been said already. Thus, we all of us, as possessors of language if not in other ways, have some capacity to state a definition of ourselves as ourselves, to go beyond how our world is being labelled by other people and to insist on ourselves, on our own definition of our own experience, in public. Given that power, we may nevertheless settle, in public, for the stock fashions to dress ourselves in, straight off the peg. We may then become used to a state of living where the words we use never really grip our own individual experience, and so can never hold out to others.

■   **Individual expressions and collective expressions.** Some expressions are the work of individuals, however socially influenced they may be, acting on their own: for example, speech, informal writing, gesture, doing your own garden, do-it-yourself interior decoration. Other expressions are the joing interactive work of many people: income-tax forms, the Bull Ring in Birmingham, most movies, political demonstrations, the Royal and Antediluvian Order of Buffaloes. (This distinction should not be confused with the previous one: collective expressions may be every bit as unique as individual expressions. There is a common opposition between individual, unique, natural, personal expressions and collective, conventional, stock, public expressions: it is that simple opposition that I am trying to break down here into various parts. All the distinctions that I am now making are amongst expressions — that is, amongst things in the public realm. Individual and collective expressions, unique and routine expressions, natural and conventional expressions, authentic and inauthentic expressions are all forms of public activity. They are all different ways of being in public.) Collective expressions are influenced in their course by many people — I am not thinking of expressions where one creator uses other people purely as a means to obey his commands absolutely. Of course, some people always exercise a bigger influence than others; very few collective expressions are more than a little democratic. But the essential point is that collective expressions do not express the thoughts of any individual in particular; they express the ideas that have happened between people on some occasion.

■   **Fleeting local expressions, the mass media and artefacts.** One kind of expression – such as gesture, speech, dancing, action — can only exist in the present moment in the immediate presence of the expressor. Other kinds of expression may reach a larger, more distant audience. Some expressions, that is, are more public, available to more people, than others. Basically, this extension beyond the immediate presence may be done in two ways.

First, in modern times, new techniques have made possible the mass communication of expressions to millions of people in a very short period of time. There may be an audience of hundreds of millions for an expression in the very instant of its delivery! At the same time, a great many of the products of the mass media are very perishable; they do not survive beyond the instant of expression.

Second, other kinds of expression — writing, painting, sculpting, building —

result in more-or-less enduring end-products, or artefacts. Once produced, such expressions do not quickly disappear again: they stay, recalcitrant, not to be wished away, perhaps long after the original thoughts and feelings which they expressed have disappeared. Inside his mind, an individual may wander at will: he may hope, wish or remember a multitude of constantly changing things; he can dream of different societies and imagine himself in all sorts of fantastic situations; tomorrow he may think something entirely different from what he thought today. Many of his expressions are just as quickly passing, and therefore changeable: I can take back today a good deal of what I said yesterday. But the objects that people make are much more resistant. Buildings remain, only to be changed with much effort, long after their architects are dead. We are surrounded by expressions that no one any longer means, but which still embody their original meanings. Who now thinks like John Donne? Yet, thankfully, the poems and sermons survive. Who now thinks like the makers of Stonehenge? Yet every one in the country over infancy must have encountered the image, or a reproduction of the image, that they formed. Who now thinks, even, like the designer of the Albert Hall or the rest of our Victorian public buildings? That is, who would now express themselves in that way? And which of us could do so, even if they would? Or, again, many things which are only thought by a few of the people some of the time may be given a massive, monumental enduring form among us all. Does anybody really think the things that the Shell building expresses? And how many think like the Hayward gallery next door? Conversely, much is now thought and experienced by many people that isn't expressed at all. And much that is expressed isn't given a permanent or enduring form. The experience of the time, the thought of a time, the expressions of a time and the artefacts (the monuments) of a time stand in complex relations to each other. There are degrees of publicness. There is not just one public place to which we all bring our thoughts to be made known for ever. There are many public places of varying sizes. What is said in one place may never be said in another.

■ **Situated and unsituated expressions.** Some expressions are responses to particular situations; they refer to some actual event and are meant to cope with it in some way; they are not intended to enter general circulation. Other expressions are not tied to local contexts in that sense, but are meant to be widely applicable, available for common use, truly public property. To illustrate the point of this distinction, we can take the example of suicide. To begin with, there obviously are generally circulating ideas about suicide in our society: for instance, there are probably, across the whole length and breadth of the country, a hundred abstract moral arguments a day about whether suicide is ever justified. There are certain words and phrases which crop up again and again in such arguments and in all public references to suicide — 'despair,' 'unhappiness,' 'life is not worthwhile,' 'escape from harsh realities,' and so on. In such phrases we see the core of a public idea about suicide. When we are detached, not inside a suicidal situation, we feel that because we have these phrases we know the meaning of suicide; we have a vague image of the event, a rough idea of its main theme. It is not very difficult to apply the vague, abstract language to unreal (not necessarily fictional; unreal to us, distanced) situations. In a newspaper book review, recently I read this sentence (it was all that was said on the matter) about the companion of a famous writer: 'She shared his life for sixteen years, killed herself in despair soon after his death'. We read it, the event makes sense to us, it fits into a pattern, we feel we have understood it, 'how awful life is' we say to ourselves: we pass on. It is, however, very difficult to apply this vague, abstract common language of suicide to actual encounters with suicide. The meaning of particular suicides to those closely involved is not given to them by the public, communicated culture. Because of the inadequacy, the incompleteness, of the general public meanings, those involved experience a loss of meaning, a failure of events to make sense, an inability to come to terms with what is happening. The effort to make sense is, in part, a personal, perhaps private one: the individual must come to some terms with the event himself.

That individual work I have dealt with already. But there is also a *social* effort to understand and that is my main concern here: those who are closely involved, however secretive they may be, must reveal something of their response, they must express themselves in some way. Moreover, the participants must come to some terms with the situation that now faces them as a group. So, those closely involved exchange meanings with each other, however covertly, and by this conversation construct a social, *situated* meaning — the meaning that works among them.

■ **Personal and impersonal expressions.** There is an important distinction, often made, between those signs, speeches, writings and drawings which are *expressive* and those which are *objective*. (This distinction, in turn, readily gives way to some of our favourite cultural stereotypes: *emotional, subjective, adolescent, neurotic, feminine* versus *informative, scientific, logical, impersonal, masculine.*) Such a stark opposition between the two modes is, however, unhelpful. We will be misled unless we recognise that the purely expressive and the purely objective are the two end points on a scale that has many intermediate points. A fuller version of the scale would begin by including some of the following types.

There are moments when the primary human emotions (anger, grief, sexual passion . . .) seem to break through to the surface almost unchecked, no longer filtered through the restraints and channelings of the mind. At such moments we lose control. We break down and sob uncontrollably. Or we go white with rage and strike with whatever comes to hand. At such moments we are nearest to being purely *expressive.* We come closest to behaving naturally, pre-culturally.

We are not normally so overwhelmed by major emotions. Rather, all our sensory experience, our thoughts, memories and images, are toned by subtle feelings. This emotional texturing of life, changing and changing from mood to mood, cannot be released by a cry. It can only be expressed by being described. We attempt to *describe our feelings.* That description cannot be completed by sheer, brave self-revelation — though that helps. It requires also a capacity for subtlety, for care and power, in the use of words to match the subtlety of the feelings. Here we are engaged in the very difficult and rare effort to be objective (that is, honest, precise, descriptive) in the public expression of our personal experience.

There is a different kind of mixture of objectivity and feelings. We may set out to describe some situation outside ourselves and yet (intentionally or unintentionally, clearly or unacknowledged) our emotions may flow into the description. We use colourful language and imagery. This is *emotive description.*

Outside the sciences, the effort to erase the individual voice, to rule out all expression of feeling and value, is very common in our civilisation. We are encouraged to adopt the *impersonal voice.* This is the voice of bureaucracy, in particular. It is also the voice of scientism — the attempt to carry the language and stance of science beyond the proper sphere of science into our subjective lives, our acting lives. Value judgements are made but are not stated in an openly evaluative, expressive form: they are stated as the impersonal judgement of an 'exhaustive technical reappraisal'. In *scientific* writing, all that results from individuality and emotionality is systematically erased: not in order to disguise the covert presence of these things, but in order to attain a genuinely impersonal position — the objective truth.

All the points along this scale are expressions, in the sense in which I have been using that term throughout this paper. However, the purely expressive and the purely scientific are on the very margins of the proper concerns of cultural studies. A primary emotion releasing itself from us by its own force, would be pre-cultural: it would still be in the realm of nature. A purely objective truth would be post-cultural: man would have transcended his local or individual, subjective visions and would be returned again to nature, this time reflectively. In the meantime, it is how we express our distinctive subjectivities, and how our activities in the world constantly declare or reveal or partially conceal our subjectivities, that is the central concern of cultural studies.

■   **Conclusion.** I am proposing that the basic task of Cultural Studies should be to uncover the ideas embodied in all the various kinds of expression in our society. Of course, expressions do not just state one idea; they are often ambiguous, equivocating between several varying ideas. As a consequence, interpretations will most often be of the form that such-and-such an idea was present in this expression, but waveringly so, in tension with other opposing views. Having done that, we would next proceed, by using categories of the sort that I have just been proposing, to place this expression of an idea within a complexified notion of the public realm. As we did that, we would be moving beyond the study and interpretation of one isolated expression; we would be placing that expression within the context of the extended, unremitting conversation of expressions among people that is the public realm. We would now be dealing with a number of different expressions, comparing the various ideas embodied in them, assessing the differing presence and permanence they had among the public. Finally, we would look at the extent to which each of these ideas correspond to the real experience and thoughts of anyone in this society. We would, that is, assess the authenticity of these ideas. But this, it should be clear, could only be done by comparing these public expressions with the personal thoughts of the people involved. It is at this point that the two, so far separated, studies of people and culture intersect. That is, we return to the study of the whole process of people communicating with each other. Thought to expression to thought is the circle of culture. It is this full, incomplete, partly succeeding and partly failing, movement of thoughts through expressions from one person to another that I am proposing as a focus study. For the sake of presentation, I had to separate the study of personal thoughts from the study of public culture. In actual study, also, they will have to be undertaken separately a good deal of the time. But as a final aim, I suggest, what is wanted is an interlocked study of people and their culture, of people in a very incomplete way speaking to each other.

I will finish off by offering an illustration of what this might mean. Take the case of Western films on television. If we studied them we might be interested in their treatment of violence. Our question would then be: What idea of violence, or what conflict between ideas, do these films portray? But the culture of violence in our society extends far beyond television films and it exists in very many modes. We get a very inadequate idea of the whole culture of violence if we look at TV alone. That whole culture also includes Horror films, contemporary cinema Westerns, sado-masochistic pornography, *War and Peace,* editorials in *The Times,* letters to *Any Answers,* pulpit pronouncements of many varieties, Judge's summings up, Probation Officers' reports, rugby club male cameraderie, Skinhead folklore — the list could go on a long way, but the idea is clear enough already that very different ideas of violence circulate in many different channels in this society. There is, however, some order among this variety: some expressions about violence are more public than others. We would, then, get a clearer picture of the significance of the idea of violence carried by TV Westerns if we saw them in the context of the whole variegated culture of violence in this society. We would, in other words, be putting the voice of the TV Western in its proper place in our extended, continual conversation with each other about violence. But finally, I suggest, our interest in this diverse culture is that people live in the midst of it. This culture is us talking to each other! In the end, then, it seems to me, our interest should return to include the people living in the culture, to their actual varied experience of violence and their thoughts, at many levels, about it. That is the context in which we should locate the culture of violence when we undertake the study of the whole process of people communicating with each other. With this approach, then, the question that we would end up offering an answer to about violence on television would not be: What is its effect? The question that such a study as I have proposed would end up trying to answer would be: To what extent in these programmes are these people succeeding in talking to each other about what they really think and feel, their real experience, of violence?

References

p. [68] Susanne K. Langer, *Philosophy in a New Key* (Mentor books) p.34.

p. [74] This illustration is not really mine. I found the man contemplating roses in Peter Rickman's introduction to his translations from Dilthey — H P Rickman, *Meaning in History* (Allen and Unwin, 1961) pp. 30 & 31. In the succeeding versions of this essay I have steadily altered the man to fit my argument more exactly. Though he is still recognisably Rickman's man, I have played about with him a bit. I would have made up a different example, but other people had begun to offer comments on this one and it seemed better to keep it. In other ways, too, I am indebted to Rickman's book.

p. [78] Tony Parker, *The Plough Boy* (Arrow books 1969) p.232.

p. [81] Matthew Arnold, 'The Study of Poetry', *Essays in Criticism,* vol. 2

p. [91] I am drawing here on Jack D Douglas *The Social Meanings of Suicide* (Princeton University Press, 1967).

A Note on Sources

I think it may help the reader to follow my argument and to place it if I sketch here what I see as the main strands of thought that I have tried to weave together in this essay. First of all, this essay has been written in the course of an extended, still continuing debate at this Centre about what we should be trying to do here. The Centre is, in my experience, rare among academic institutions in the emphasis it gives to debate about its own first principles. I could not have written such an essay as this without the continuous debate here over a number of years. Moreover, many members of the Centre gave a lot of time to the discussion and criticism of an early draft of this essay. In a number of ways, then, I am very dependent on my colleagues here and I am grateful to them, though they will undoubtedly disagree with much that I am saying.

I was awakened to the existence of such a field of study by reading, as a student, Richard Hoggart's *Uses of Literacy* (Chatto and Windus, 1957) and Raymond Williams' *Culture and Society* (Chatto and Windus, 1958) and *The Long Revolution* (Chatto and Windus, 1961). I first read these books round about 1960 when I belonged to the New Left as was and so the issues of *Universities and Left Review* and the early issues of *New Left Review* and Edward Thompson's *Making of the English Working Class* (Gollancz, 1963) were also very potent, connected influences. Following on from Raymond Williams' book I came to read some of the culture and society tradition and Coleridge in particular. The work now being done, in a sort of continuation of that tradition, on the problems of teaching English literature, especially poetry, in schools seems to me to be of great interest. David Holbrook's *English for Maturity* (Cambridge University Press, 1961) and *English for the Rejected* (Cambridge University Press, 1964) are both very good of this kind; so is James Britton's *Language and Learning* (Allen Lane, The Penguin Press, 1970).

At the time I was reading these books, I was also trying to become a sociologist and I have been influenced a great deal by the two grand masters of sociology, Max Weber and Emil Durkheim. If the reader is not familiar with their work, I think he will find their greatest books, Weber's *The Protestant Ethic and the Spirit of Capitalism* (Allen and Unwin, 1930) and Durkheim's *Elementary Forms of Religious Life* (Allen and Unwin, 1915) very illuminating and in many ways complementary to the insights of the English tradition I have mentioned above. I am also a great admirer of Weber's predecessor Wilhelm Dilthey. I don't read German and little of Dilthey's work has been translated into English, but there is an excellent little collection of extracts called *Pattern & Meaning in History* (Allen and Unwin, 1961) translated and edited by H P Rickman. There is also a book by Rickman, reworking some of these ideas, called *Understanding and the Human Studies* (Heinemann, 1967) though the second half collapses too much into orthodox divisions of the disciplines for my liking. I have also been influenced by a different sociological school, the symbolic interactionist school founded by G H Mead. Howard Becker's *The Outsiders* (Glencoe Free Press, 1963) offers a good introduction to this work. I have also been very influenced by a brand of anthropology, that which is perhaps best represented by Professor Evans-Pritchard and his books *Withcraft, Oracles and Magic among the Azande* (Oxford University Press, 1937) and *The Nuer* (Oxford University Press, 1940). I became very dissatisfied with a purely sociological approach. This dissatisfaction was crystallised by existentialist writers, especially Sartre's *Being and Nothingness* (Methuen, 1969). My interest in the study of people's emotional life was stimulated by Melanie Klein — see, for instance, *Love, Hate and Reparation* (London, 1953) My thinking about what a descriptive study of the thoughts and experiences of particular individuals would be like has been much stimulated by the books of Tony Parker, such as *The Courage of his Convictions* (Hutchinson, 1962) and *The Plough Boy* (Hutchinson, 1965). John Berger's *The Fortunate Man* (Penguin Books, 1969) could also be taken as an instance of the sort of humanist study of individuals that I have tried to define in this essay.

A RESPONSE TO PEOPLE AND CULTURE
Stuart Hall

PEOPLE AND CULTURE is an impressive paper, above all, for the consistency of its
tone and approach. I assent to many of its original formulations. But I radically dissent
from what I take to be its central thrust. This is difficult to pinpoint, since the paper is
so comprehensive. I believe, however, that within the fat and rounded argument, there
is a smaller argument struggling to get out. My aim is to disentangle — and quarrel with—
some central propositions which flow directly from the theoretical heart of the paper.
My comments are therefore less than fair to the paper as a whole. The central area of
disagreement must be formulated in general terms first.

The paper takes up a position within the 'break' with positivistic types of explanation in
the human studies, and makes a decisive stand on the question of meaning and intentional
action. I strongly agree with this point of departure. However, the argument seems now
to have gone clean through to the other side. People and Culture adopts a phenomenological position so radical that for two-thirds of it, virtually everything is bracketted which
cannot be directly referred to individual consciousness. Ideas have not only been restored
to a prominent place in the scheme of things — they seem altogether to have vanquished
the notion of activity, of *praxis,* or of relationship. Individual subjectivity is reaffirmed,
but at the expense of any distinctive notion of *the social.*

I do not believe that the idea of culture can be properly conceptualized from this position. The 'methodological individualism' of the paper recreates all the problems of the
positivistic approach *in reverse.* The paper has abandoned the struggle to clarify those
issues which form the core problematic of cultural studies: the relationship of subject
and object; of culture to society; the reciprocity between meaning and structures; the
problem of history and historical development; the dialectic between consciousness and
social being. Consciousness is given an unproblematic status. The model which links
consciousness to culture is essentially linear. It proceeds from the authentic source, in
"personal thought", via expressions, towards the wider, and on the whole more inauthentic, realm of "public meanings". The movement is one-way: there is no reciprocal determination. Thus the central issue — that men actively make culture and are then in turn
shaped by it — is suppressed.

The perspective adopted in People and Culture is fundamentally idealist — 'Any
human activity . . . is the product of ideas'. Ideas are not embedded in social situations,
in social relationships or experience. They inform situations, but — so to speak — from
outside. The process of having ideas and of expressing them is treated as discrete: 'Men
have ideas and *then* they act on them' (our italics). A radical break is thus affected between the ideas 'he may . . . keep inside his own head' and their public expression.
Throughout subjective meaning is identified with personal thought, and personal though
with 'individual consciousness'. The notion that collective patterns of thought exist and
have as palpable a reality as the ideas that haunt individual minds is never centrally taker
up — not at least until Section 3, when the realm of personal thought has been fully and
separately articulated.

But *where* and *how* does individual consciousness, the self, arise except — as Mead put it — 'in social experience', and through the 'conversation of gestures' with significant others? The way to approach that question is not to invert the positivistic paradigm (society-over-self) into its opposite, since both formulations collapse back into that polarity — individual-versus-society — which has been such a profound blockage to cultural studies. The question is, rather, how subjective meanings and intentions come, under certain determinate conditions, to create and inform the 'structures' of social life? And how, in turn, the structures of social life shape and inform the interior spaces of individual consciousness. As R E Park remarks: 'man is a creature such that when he lives at all, he lives in his imagination, and, through his imagination, in the minds of other men . . . The consequence is that the individual in society lives a more or less public existence'. Park does *not* mean that only the objective facts of social life are real. Rather, as he says:

> All his acts are anticipated, checked, inhibited or modified by the gestures and intentions of his fellows. It is in this social conflict, in which every individual lives more or less in the mind of every other individual, that human nature and the individual may acquire their most characteristic and human traits . . . We come into the world as individuals, achieve character, and become persons. ('Human Nature and Collective Behaviour')

What is 'personal thought', then, outside this interior/exterior reciprocity? A richly phenomenological account is offered in Section 2 of the paper; one far more adequate in its complexity than the usual accounts of 'mind' available to us from traditional psycology. But this account itself seems inadequate, because so rigorously sealed off from 'exterior' influences. Take, for example (Section 2) the treatment of 'common sense thought'. 'Common sense thought', incorporated here into 'personal thought' as one of its aspects or 'layers', is conceived in a manner very similar to the way it is defined by Schutz and Husserl: the informal meaning-structures which govern our routine, 'taken-for-granted', social existence in everyday life. 'Common sense thought' (as Schutz, and Berger and Luckmann have argued, and as the paper achnowledges) is 'a closely organized collection of beliefs, assumptions, rules and methods'. But how do such 'beliefs and assumptions' arise, and in what sense are they best defined as *personal*? They are 'personal' because 'below the threshold of consciousness': but they are also massively 'collective' — interpretations, habits, typifications internalized from and exteriorized in our *most publicly routinized social existence.* Common sense thought, far from being a realm of consciousness intelligible in terms of the individual actor alone, arises essentially in *intersubjective* experience. It is one of the provinces of consciousness most thoroughly penetrated by the social. Schutz indeed describes it as the realm, par excellence, of typification, of sedimented social knowledge. The concept seems to me to have been wrenched free of its position in phenomenology. For Schutz, it was the point from which he began to sketch out a 'phenomenology of the social world'.

Here, and elsewhere, it seems as if crucial but complex ideas, which offer the beginnings of an alternative theory of culture, have been pulled up from their moorings in a whole body of thought, and freely inserted into a much simpler schema. The use made of phenomenological concepts throughout the paper is perhaps the most striking example of this. It seems to have been forgotten that Schutz's work, for example, begins with a radical critique of the Weberean notion of 'subjective meaning'. In the *Phenomenology of the Social World* Schutz writes:

> What concerns us is that Weber reduces all kinds of social relationships and structures, all cultural objectification, all realms of objective mind, to the most elementary forms of individual behaviour . . Never before had the project of reducing the 'world of objective mind' to the behaviour of individuals been so radically carried out.

Schutz recognised that the Weberean perspective made it possible to 'disclose the structure of the social world . . as a structure of intelligible intentional meanings' — but *only*, he argued, if the subjective meaning-complex of action is firmly grounded in the intersubjective world. Otherwise, Schutz argued, Weber could not draw any distinction 'between the meaning of the producer of a cultural object and the meaning of the object produced, between the meaning of my own action and the meaning of another's action, between my own experience and that of someone else, between my self-understanding' and my understanding of another person'. These criticisms seem to me to apply, *tout court,* to **People and Culture.** If the concept of *culture* is to be clarified within the phenomenological perspective, it requires, at the very least, the decisive shift which Schutz accomplished, against Weber, from 'subjective' to 'intersubjective' meaning: and then the further expansion, via the notions of 'reciprocal perspectives' etc. It was these moves which enabled Schutz to deal 'not only with the single meaningful act and the context or configuration of meaning to which it belongs, but the whole social world in its fully differentiated perspectives'.

For myself, I doubt whether the concept of culture is graspable from the phenomeno-logical perspective alone. This perspective does not allow for the intrinsically double-sidedness of culture on which Berger and Pullberg have remarked:

> The human enterprise of producing a world is not comprehensible as an individual project. Rather, it is a social process: men together engage in constructing a world which then becomes their common dwelling . . . Man the world-builder and man the name-giver are possible only as manifestations of man the social being. Every human society can thus be understood as a world-building enterprise, that is, as a world-building activity. The reality of such a world is given neither in itself, nor once and for all. It must be constructed and reconstructed over and over again . . . the world must be confirmed and reconfirmed *by others* . . . Being in the world means, for men, being in the world with others . . . the world is produced by means of a human enter-prise that is social in character. As a product this world possesses expressivity, that is, it manifests the intentionality of those who produced it. Because of this, it is possible for others to understand this world, that is, to understand the intentionality of those engaged in building or having built this world.

> ('Reification and the Sociological Critique
> of Consciousness')

This seems to me a more adequate point from which to approach the idea of culture, while holding firmly to the perspective of human agency. I do not mean that it resolves the issues, but it *poses them correctly.* From this position we begin to see the inadequacy of trying to conceptualise culture in terms of the ideas of the individual actor. Berger and Pullberg, and before them, Hegel and Marx, insist that society and culture *begin* with the reciprocal relation of Self/Others. In **People and Culture** 'Others' form a sort of block to the otherwise free transmission (expression) of meanings from their inner source to the outer world.

It is true that **People and Culture** calls, time and again, for "connected studies', for atten-tion to 'the whole process of communication', for a study of 'the movement from thought to expression and back to thought again'. But the actual thrust of the exposition seems to be moving in a different direction.

The paper treats expressions as the end product of personal thought. But expression is also a form of *praxis,* and praxis is a social not an individual enterprise. It always takes place, not in some ideally free and undistorted realm, but in the real and determinate conditions and quite concrete and specific historical situations. There is no such thing as 'perfectly undistorted, free expresssion'. To express (i.e. to communicate) at all, ideas pass through the mediations of a social praxis. The so-called 'loss of meaning' is not a special condition but the condition, *sui generis,* of all the real communications which compose the real culture which men 'construct' in circumstances which, though man-made, are not wholly of their making. ·One crucial form of expression which is dealt with in the paper is expression through language. But language is, through and through, a social praxis — that specially human activity which the French call *signification* and which Lefebvre calls *poesis.* Language, as Marx observed, begins as 'practical conscious-ness'. In making use of the medium of language, ideas and meanings which appear to have a fundamentally individual root enter a social space, an already-objectivated and un-folding social practice. They enter time, history. They gain a life of their own (objectivation); meanings which, though never separable from the individual project which made them, are no longer reducible to the terms of individual intention. As Sartre suggests:

> Thus significations come from man and from his project, and the significations reveal to us men and relations, but they are inscribed everywhere in things and in the order of things. Everything at every instant is always signifying, and the significations reveal to us men and the relations among men mediated by the structures of our society . . . Our understanding of the Other is never contemplative; it is only a moment of our praxis, a way of living — in conflict or in complicity—the concrete, human relation which unites us to him.

Here, the dialectic of culture is joined: it cannot be torn asunder. The interpreter must not then confuse — as I believe **People and Culture** does — the attempt to recover the praxis behind what appears as a simple process (a project which has to be interpretative because expression is socially mediated, un-transparent) with the dissolution of the mediations. We cannot get round the mediations, as this paper tries to do: nor can we repress them, as both positivism and mechanical marxism, in their different ways, have attempted. We must go through the mediations. But instead of this passage through the mediations **People and Culture** seems to me to erect a simple opposition, counterposing the relative authenticity of individual expressions to the relative inauthenticity of the social world. Expression, not conceived as an activity, is experienced simply as a dehistoricized alienation, attributable to 'the human condition'. The world of culture is thus represented as the sphere of a *general* and permanent impoverishment. Yet this 'loss', this impoverishment, is the medium in which culture is objectivated. Without it culture would not exist.

People and Culture rightly insists that there are radical disjunctures within any 'whole process of communication'. But the paper·locates the disjunctures only at the gap between Self and Others. There is no discussion of the possible disjunctures *within* the self: i e between consciousness and the unconscious (in Freud's sense); or between personal consciousness and 'unconscious structures' (in Levi-Strauss' sense); or between our intention to express and the ruling ideas in which often we are forced to communicate (the problem of ideology and 'false consciousness', in Marx's sense). Expressions have been freed, from the notions of repression ideology or power. The public meanings available to us through the agency of men in history, seem in this paper, separate from human agency: they are never the products of former human practices and projects which, as Sartre says, 'address us through them'. There is a persistent failure to deal with the question of collective ideas and meanings. **People and Culture** is correct when it argues that public definitions are not to be *identified with* the subjective meanings individuals have about their experience. In this respect, both the early Durkheimean perspective and the mechanical version of Marxism which has for so long vitiated cultural analysis, are both inadequate. They lack any conception of the dialectic. That is why the recovery of phenomenology, and with it, the restoration of the subject-object problem at the heart of the field, marks a new departure. But **People and Culture** seems now to desert the ground of dialectic on the opposite front.

To take an example from the opening of Section 3 it is true that the public meanings of grief and mourning available to us from the public culture, are inadequate to the individual experience of death. As Douglas argues in *The Social Meaning of Suicide*, many of our crucial meanings are constructed with others in the concrete and immediate situation of facing death — they are 'situated meanings'. The way this 'inadequacy' in the public culture is experienced by an individual is, of course, a perfectly proper kind of study. I am not certain, however, that I would call a study with *this* emphasis 'cultural studies'. Indeed, some confusion seems to arise here, because of an indiscriminate expansion of the scope of what is to be included in 'cultural studies' — an expansion which identifies the field with the study of virtually everything which is 'distinctively human'. This is a too inclusive — even imperialising — a view of 'cultural studies'. For one thing, history is virtually absent from its perspective — surely part of the domain of the 'distinctively human ? True, the human studies have been·fatally compartmentalised: true the subject matter of the human studies constitutes a single, complex totality. But this totality can and has to be studied from more than one vantage point, without falling into fragmenta-tion. The study of grief and mourning as proposed here is really more a study in what I would call 'existential biography' — not so much psychology as normally understood, but rather what Sartre calls 'improving biography'. This is to approach the problem at the privileged level of the individual life-situation rather than of culture as such. From that perspective, certainly, a 'connected study' would still allow us to see the relation of life-situation to culture   but it would not desert its own special point-of-departure out of some mistaken view that everything can be seen from only one point of view.

The study of 'the *culture* of grief and mourning' (my italics) would approach the same subject matter from a different vantage point. It would be concerned with the socially-situated construction of meanings and definitions adequate to the situation of grief, with how men fill the void between inadequate collective representations and imperfect private meanings. How — through what praxis — do men give definition to such experiences, events, etc, which are imperfectly or problematically defined in the public culture? How — in what terms, on the basis of what possible field of meanings — do men handle mean-ingfully events which seem intrinsically 'meaningless'? Such a study could *not*, by defi-nition, be — as proposed — 'one study of the grief of individuals and then a separate study of the public expressions of mourning' (our italics) but precisely a study which tried to grasp, as a single intelligible phenomenon, the reciprocity between these two poles in the social construction of death as a meaningful human passage in social life.

In general terms, there is a tendency throughout the paper to polarise the problem in terms of a dichotomy between the inadequately given public meanings (. . about death or suicide) on one side, and the 'effort of personal thought' on the other. Douglas, who also uses the notion of situated meanings, and on whom much of the argument at this point in **People and Culture** depends, is pointing to a third, if you like, intermediary stage between these two polar extremes; the level at which the actors, together, construct some defini-tion of suicide or death, more adequate to their experience than is available to them *either* at the wholly public *or* the wholly private level. Situated meanings are indeed recognized in the paper as 'the meaning that works among' the participants to a social situation, but the deeply intersubjective nature of this kind of meaning-construction is not, I think, really sustained.

Douglas is not, in my view, altogether clear on the point. But, as I understand him, he argues that, (a) situated meanings are to be distinguished from both private and abstract-public meanings; and (b) that, though we must study meaning construction 'from the clearly observable concrete phenomena upward', yet shared cultural meanings do provide a sort of rough map of 'the possible or plausible meanings of these phenomena (including criteria of various sorts)', which limit and frame, to a degree, which meanings will be con-structed through the intentional actions of the individuals involved. In the study of all such ill-defined and problematic areas, there must be a sort of 'double-fitting' between meanings which are generally available, and those which are situationally constructed. Situated meanings are therefore, in Douglas' model, neither wholly determined by the public meanings, nor wholly free of their determination. Here we have the beginnings of a dialectical model of social meaning. How men define death or suicide to themselves in our culture will be neither wholly given nor random. Our ideas about such pivotal ex-periences and life-crises in our culture are neither the pure reflexions of the 'dominant ideas' (ideology) of our epoch, nor ever free of their constraining and informing power. The degree of 'closure' is, of course, to be empirically determined in each concrete in-stance — the purpose of such studies being, not to 'dissolve men in a bath of sulphuric acid', but, as Marx once said, 'to rise from the level of the general to the concrete'.

If such a model proves difficult to apply, it remains, nevertheless, the only one which is 'true' to the situation — true, I mean, in the sense of adequate to our experience of the reciprocity of freedom and constraint inside the notion of culture. Edward Thompson, discussing the problem of class-consciousness in 'The Peculiarities of the English', wrote

The problem is to find a model for the social process which allows an autonomy to social consciousness within a context which, in the final analysis, has always been determined by social being. Can any model ecompass the distinctively human dialectic, by which history appears as neither willed nor as fortuitous; and neither lawed (in the sense of being determined by involuntary laws of motion) nor illogical (in the sense that one can observe a *logic* in the social process)?

Sartre, in *The Question of Method,* is suggesting something of the same kind when he speaks of the 'impulse toward objectification' (the individual project) projecting itself 'across a field of possibles, some of which we realize to the exclusion of others'. Such a method, Sartre insists, must always attempt to 'determine the field of possibles, the field of instruments'; it must 'at once place the agent or event back into the historical setting', not in order to repress human agency, or reduce the specificity of the event, but rather, precisely, to reveal, by 'these procedures — regression and cross-reference . . . the profundity of the lived'. Such a progressive-regressive method — 'determining a biography (for example) by examining the period, and the period by studying the biography' — requires, in its turn, a number of concepts which are, on the whole missing from **People and Culture**. The paper, we argue, lacks any true conception of *praxis.* But it also, more surprisingly, lacks any notion of the *project* (in the sense of a surpassing, by intentional action, of all the determinations, the actor 'going beyond his situation . . . by what he succeeds in making of what he has been made'), or of *determinations* (which is different from determinism; Lefebvre's account in *The Sociology of Marx* is brief, but classic).

People and Culture affirms that, 'Thought to expression to thought is the circle of culture'. I think the formulation in Sartre is less elegant but truer:

"The joint necessity of the internalization of the external, and the externalisation of the internal. Praxis is, indeed, a passage from objective to objective through internalization. The project, — the subjective surpassing of objectivity towards objectivity, stretched between the objective conditions of the environment and the objective structures of the field of the possibles, represents in itself the moving unity of subjectivity and objectivity, those cardinal poles of activity. The subjective appears then as a necessary moment in the objective process".

My criticism is that **People and Culture** carries a sort of phenomenological reduction to an illogical extreme. In the process the individual, far from being concretised and particularised, comes through as an inactive subject, an abstract property. Correspondingly, in my comments, I have opened myself to the charge of having repressed the individual aspects of culture and exaggerated the social. I can only reply in Marx's own words:

. . .It is above all necessary to avoid postulating 'society' once more as an abstraction confronting the individual. The individual is a *social being.* The manifestation of his life — even when it does not appear directly in the form of a *social* manifestation, accomplished in association with other men, — is therefore a manifestation and affirmation of *social life.* Individual human life and species-life* are not *different* things, even though the mode of existence of individual life is necessarily a more *particular* or more *general* mode of species-life, or that of species-life a more particular or more general mode of individual life. In his *species-consciousness* man confirms his real *social life,* and reproduces his real existence in thought, while conversely species-being confirms itself in species-consciousness, and exists for itself in its universality as a thinking being. Though man is a *unique* individual — and it is just his particularity which makes him an individual, a really individual social being — he is equally the whole, the ideal whole, the subjective existence of society as thought and experienced. He exists, in reality, as the representation and the real mind of social existence, and as the sum of human manifestation of life.

Thought and being are indeed distinct, but they also form a unity.

Economic and Philosophical Manuscripts

* The term 'species' was used by Marx, following Feuerbach, to refer to man's awareness of his general human qualities, of belonging to the 'human species'.

The Abuses of Literacy
Colin Sparks

from

Working Papers in Cultural Studies, 6, 1974.

Reprinted by permission of the author.

I

THE ABUSES OF LITERACY

Colin Sparks

The Working Class has no golden age in the past;
our golden age is the future.

Harry Wicks.

Most of the current discussion in Cultural Studies concerns the question of methodology. It seems to be generally agreed as to what we are looking at, and all that remains is to settle the way in which we should look at it. The central concern of this paper is to argue that this accepted definition of the object of study takes its fundamental characteristics quite uncritically from much earlier conceptions of the nature of Cultural Studies, and that consequently the bulk of contemporary practise is radically misconceived

In order to argue this case, it will be necessary to return to some of the seminal texts of cultural studies and to look at the ways in which they have been subsequently used. The problem of the relation and mutual determination of methodology and problematic has not, as far as I know, been subject to much investigation, and I cannot here attempt to deal with it in any detail; rather I have tried to illustrate the consequent arbitrary dislocation in the course of the argument about the nature of the problematic itself.

Cultural Studies has had, from its inception, a certain flavour of radical brimstone about it. The writers who may be considered, without too much argument, as the founders of discipline, had and have, by the standards of British academic life, highly developed and eccentric concerns and ideas. In particular, the two leading figures (Richard Hoggart and Raymond Williams) display in the genuinely seminal works of Cultural Studies quite definite and unconcealed political intentions. The case of Williams is self-evident but *The Uses of Literacy* itself has its definite plea for political actions:

> If the active minority continue to allow themselves too exclusively to think of immediate political and economic objectives, the past will be sold, culturally,behind their backs. (1)

The two perspectives are different, but they share important common ground: both writers attempted to re-integrate a huge submerged area of human experience into the study of culture.

It is possible to overstress the importance of biographical factors in the initial impetus towards Cultural Studies. It is possible to locate a number of the central concerns within the more general intellectual climate of the time. I cannot here details the evolution of the period, but some of its salient features can at least be remarked upon. If one recalls on the one hand the complex of ideas which a combination of Cold War and Long Boom generated; the notion of a problem-free post-Keynesian capitalism; the alleged disappearence of the working class; the agonised convulsions of the Labour Party; the bankruptcy of the pretenders to alternative leadership and in particular the steril-ity of the Stalinist version of Marxism; the changing modes of working-class activity and experience, one can see a good part of the forces at work. If we set alongside that the strengths and weaknesses of the powerfully established literary analysis of 'Culture' and the contrary and equally ambivalent sociological studies of 'mass society', then much more is visible. If we examine *The Uses of Literacy* we can see clearly how a number of central definitions emerged.

The dominant impressions which a reading of *The Uses of Literacy* leaves one with are curiously unintellectual: they are nostalgia and self-recognition. These may be to a large part intentional, and they certainly go a long way towards explaining the impact and popularity of the book, but they are also problematic

Nostalgia is built into the whole structure. The warm glow of Hunslet is balanced against the neon and plastic of the 1950's. The world of the 1920's is used as a critical standard against which to judge later developments. It is alleged, quite uncrit-ically, that 'the old forms of class culture are in danger of being replaced by a poorer kind of classless culture, and this is to be regretted' (2).

Regret and nostalgia may be useful and entertaining feelings, but they lead to some very curious conclusions. Speaking of 'Milk Bars', Hoggart says, along with much else of an uncomplimentary nature:

> Compared even with the pub around the corner, this is all
> a peculiarly thin and pallid form of dissipation, a sort of
> spiritual dry-rot amid the odour of boiled milk. Many of
> the customers - their clothes, their hair-styles, their
> facial expressions all indicate - are living to a large extent
> in a myth-world compounded of a few simple elements which they
> take to be those of American life. (3)

It is only too easy to mock this kind of thinking, but to do so
might obscure the substantial point. After a major effort to come
to terms with how one generation of working people saw and defined
their world, and displaying considerable sensitivity to their
modes of self-expression, we are treated to this shabby and cont-
emptuous dismissal of the efforts of a new generation.

Whether intended or not, the intellectual counterpart of this
emotion has entered deeply and cancerously into the concerns of
Cultural Studies. Central to so much of the work which has been
produced is the idea that there was, in the 1920's and 1930's, a
clear and definite working-class culture which was more valuable,
more authentic, more homogenous, more independent...more working-
class, than any subsequent development. This vanished culture
becomes the standard of judgement for later formations, and they
are all found wanting.

I do not wish to quarrel with the idea that there was such a
culture. Much more to the point is how we evaluate it. The
culture was the product of a specific historical experience and
it represented a response to a particular historical conjuncture.
The culture of later decades was a response to a different
historical experience, which included the accretions of the pre-
ceeding experience as well as new elements. It was and is
different, and if we are to judge either it is not by some
nostalgic, inverted teleology of culture. If we accept the
authenticity of one cultural formation, then we must accept the
authenticity of another. How we analyse and compare different
periods in something I wish to deal with later, but we certainly
cannot do so by elevating an arbitrary and particular period to
the status of a proletarian Paradise.

The feeling of recognition adds a further dimension. The figure
of the Scholarship Bay informs the second evaluative crux of the
book. The assumed critical independence which this poor lonely
adolescent has been granted is the vantage point from which the
strengths and limits of two cultures can be assessed. The
limitations of 'high cultural' analysis, and the inappropriate-
ness of the characteristic standards, are forever present. In the
middle of a discussion of very soft pornography we find a passage
like this:

Sanctuary is admittedly an early pot-boiler; yet one can see in it the marks of a serious and disinterested creative writer. A gifted, varied, and complex perception is at work, picking up sights, smells, noises, and weaving them together in a scene of some complexity...(4)

The problem presented by passages like this is: if our critical conceptions and values are those forged by academic English Literature, then we can make judgements on a particular kind of human activity; on the other hand, these methods and values are clearly inadequate to come to terms with the real meanings of the experience and culture of the overwhelming mass of society. Hoggart himself seems never to have solved the problem which his work makes clear. In essays like *Mass Communications in Britain* and *Schools of English in Contemporary Society* he juggles uneasily and agnostically with the difficulties (5). The difficulty, however, resolutely refused to go away.

What occurred in practice was what Stuart Hall later called a 'shift...from the 'aesthetic' to the historical and anthropologic- al conceptions of 'a culture'. This movement was undoubtedly one of the fundamental impetuses in Cultural Studies, and it posed very sharply the need to develop a new theory and a new methodolgy for the study of human experience.

However, like the first impulse, the way in which this second insight was to operate contained, within the impulse itself, pro- found dangers. The internal evolution of Cultural Studies was marked by this impetus. Defining itself in opposition to an avowedly evaluative discipline, it had to create its own values more appropriate to its own material and concerns. If the standards of 'High Culture' were inappropriate to Cultural Stud- ies, so too its own standards were and are inappropriate to 'High Culture'. The values of Cultural Studies have from their origin been rooted in a sentimental myth of past ages, and they do not provide any total vantage point from which to analyse the historical experience of culture.

The difficulty with the value system generated is two-fold. If we erect a critical apparatus which is tailored specifically to the culture of one class, then we are simply in an inverse repetition of the tradition from which we are trying to break. Now, unless independent cultural systems are mutually sealed against each other, then there is only one other alternative: simply to ignore the alternative cultural formation. The problem of the assessment of the 'high cultural' tradition was not subsumed under a new conception, it was consigned, by an approximation to administrat- ive action, to the status of non-existence. The 'high cultural' system of evaluation was the product of a selective reading of a total historical process which was blind to the existence of possible alternatives. What Cultural Studies has done is to erect a different, but equally selective and myopic alternative.

This first objection might be met by arguing along more or less quantitative lines that the new system encompassed the experiences of a far greater number of people than the old, but to answer in that manner is to demonstrate glaringly the second objection to this value system. It is, quite simply, based on a rejection of history. To hypostasize a single, unique development as the calibration-table against which all other developments are to be measured is to reject any notion of the complex historical evolution of social classes in relation to each other. The consequences are quite suprising: much against the conscious intentions of many of the students of Cultural Studies, the argument leads with irresistable logic to a celebration of capitalism in one of its many unpleasant forms. The culture which is chosen as a yard-stick is, it should be remembered, the culture of a subordinate class. If this is the source of our evaluations, then from what point can we criticise the fact of domination?

Cultural Studies thus operated from its inception with a rigid, and thus flawed, notion of social totality. However much it might proclaim its allegience to higher and better things, its failure to give any critical account of itself or what it rejected made it inevitable that it would fail to realise its own potential. This failure leads logically to the third, and in my opinion the most important, legacy of *The Uses of Literacy*. Once again, the Scholarship Boy provides a key to understanding what is going on. A crucial point in the book is the discussion of the antimony of 'Them' and 'Us', and in this chapter, Hoggart has a revealing passage:

> After the age of eleven, when the scholarship boys and girls go off to the grammar-school, the rest look increasingly outward to the real life which will begin at fifteen, to the life with the group of older men and women which, for the first few years after school forms the most powerfully educative force they know. (6)

This is undoubtedly true, but its most telling point is that the scholarship boy has once and for all been out off from that most crucial element in the real life of the working-class work. This is not simply a limitation of biography: it is also a central theoretical absence from the way in which Hoggart approaches his material. A large part of the definition of working-class in this book is geographical, and it is supplemented by a vision throught the lenses of consumption, leisure, and home. One possible definition, which is specifically ruled out through the inclusion of small shop-keepers, is the one which springs most readily to mind: production.

Once again, this perspective had contradictory effects. It opened up a whole new range of topics for analysis and provided a healthy antidote to some dangerous illusions. On the other hand, it seems to me that it produced, in the long run, the most pernicious mis-

analysis that Cultural Studies has suffered from. Consider, for
example, Hoggart's discussion of working-class activists:

> ...I have not referred much to the influence of the 'earnest
> minority' among working-class people, since my chief concern
> has been with attitudes among the majority. Yet I do not
> mean to underestimate the effect the 'earnest minority' has, or
> to imply that this minority has had and may continue to have
> (though this is by no means certain) an influence on their
> group out of all proportion to their number, it is important
> that, something should be said more directly about them. (7)

I do not seek to deny that this minority has been very much of a
minority, but the difficulties inherent in the above formulation
are so many that it is hard to know how to come to terms with them.
If we look at the list of institutions these people supported
(and Hoggart grants them only the ability to *support* we are at
once struck by the fact that one of the most massive and enduring
of them, the Trade Unions, were formed as a direct response to the
central issue of work. The two other most massive ones, the Co-
operative Movement and the Labour Party, have at least strong
links with work. A notable exception from the list is the
Communist Party. Certainly this has always been very small, and
perhaps Gallacher or Hannington were really Russians or at least
middle-class romantics, but it is difficult to see how any
discussion of the working-class activist could possibly ignore
that tragic trajectory. It seems that Hoggart was determined to
ignore that stubborn millenarian ghost clanking its chains
through Conference and Rule Book in so many of those organisations
which spring up from the collective efforts of working people.

Secondly, although it is true that these organisations have very
often depended for their existence and continuation on very small
minorities, it is certainly not true that they were, and are, the
concern solely of those minorities. Take the example of the
Trade Unions these do indeed depend a great deal on a relatively
small number of activists, although that active support is certainly very much larger than is commonly supposed, but the organisations are not the expression of those minorities. They are mass
organisations and they are the expressions of the masses. It is
only in so far as the 'majority' are prepared to organise and to
give their loyalty to their organisations, only in so far as they
are willing to acceed to collective discipline and to suffer
collective hardship, that any Trade Union can even begin to
function.

Thirdly, the concerns of this minority are not the marginal
ephemera of the life of the majority of working people. They
are the crucial determinants of the material and cultural
life of the class as a whole. The culture of the British working
class is not 'affected' by the strengths and weaknesses of its
political and industrial organisations. The relation is one of
mutual determination. The horizons and definitions of the class,

the 'cultural space' within which it operates, are not pre-
given and arbitrary. They are the boundaries set by the successes
and failures of these organisations.

Fourthly, these organisations are not separated off from the
cultural life of the working class in a watertight compartment.
They penetrate and are penetrated through and through the cultural
attitudes which are appropriate even on Hoggart's narrow definition. Take for example the 'Labour Aristocracy'. This formation
entailed far more than membership of a particular exclusive craft
union monopolising the sale of labour power in a particular
skilled trade. It also entailed, and was entailed by, a set of
self-definitions, and definitions of other groups and classes,
which involved dress, housing, leisure, ambition, family...a list
of cultural factors which we could prolong indefinitely. A whole
matrix of cultural patterns of extreme complexity produced and
was reproduced by the structure of occupation and trade union.

Fifthly, the idea that work and the organisations appropriate to
it, form a domain which is radically distinct from that of
culture cannot seriously be maintained if we have any commitment
to understanding the character and meaning of life as a whole.
It may be possible, indeed essential, for conceptual purposes to
divide working-class life into work, home leisure, youth, etc.,
but to ignore the working week simply does not make sense. Even
if we exclude it as an area of study in its own right, how can we
grasp the meaning of external activities without grasping their
relation to work?

Sixthly, there is the complex problem of durability and significance. With regard to significance, the discussion of this, which
relates to earlier arguments, will have to be postponed to the
more positive parts of this paper, but the question of durability
can be dealt with more simply. It is obvious, even on a brief
examination of the history of the British working class, that
formal organisations are immensely durable. This point applies
to a wide range of organisations, including many which I would
evaluate very negatively, but it is true above all of the type of
organisation which Hoggart wishes to ignore. To continue on the
issue of trade unions: these have been continually created and
recreated at great cost and with great effort, and working people
have sacrificed time, money, health, and on occasions liberty, to
maintain them. Clearly, all that blood and sweat was about something important in working-class life, something about the way in
which they saw the world. To ignore them seems at best wrong, at
worst dishonest.

The above considerations are part and parcel of the initial impetus
given to Cultural Studies, and they still remain deeply embedded
in it current practice. It is not that nothing has changed, but
that the transformations of vocabulary and methodology, and even
some of the attempts to negate the Hoggartian framework, remain

trapped within a conception of Cultural Studies which is that
criticised above. As I have stressed, the impetus had enormous
liberative influence, and the negative aspects did not emerge
sharply until later. By mapping out new fields, and discovering
new methods, a great deal of useful work could be done, but the
seeds of sterility were always there, and new concerns sooner or
later gave a bitter withered fruit.

The appropriation of Raymond Williams's work should have opened
up new perspectives, but this too seems to have proved inadequate.
The problem is one of a different order, for the intellectual
superiority of William is self-evident. An indication of the
difference may be seen in the contrasting attitudes to Marxism
displayed by the two writers. There is a movement in Williams's
work from a highly critical engagement with Marxism in *Culture
and Society* towards an attempt to reformulate the theory of
Cultural Studies in explicitly Marxist terms (8). This engagement
had very important consequences in so far as it opened up new
ways of considering problems which Hoggart had explicitly denied,
but in the areas with which I am here concerned it suffered from
crucial weaknesses. The negativity of the following aimed not so
much at Williams's work as the ways in which it has been appropri-
ated.

Many of Williams's major contributions to the theory of Cultural
Studies originate in the period when his thought was highly critical of Marxism or rather, of the Stalinised bastardisation which
passed for Marxism in the bad old days. His famous definition of
culture '...a culture is not only a body of intellectual and
imaginative work; it is also and essentially a whole way of life'
(9), is given in the course of a critique of Marxist notions of
class-culture, but even when the confrontation is at its sharpest
there is a shared sense of matters of importance.

'A whole way of life': certainly in theory at least Williams should
be free of the Grand Remonstrance which can be directed against
Hoggart's ideas. Indeed, in *The Long Revolution* Williams returns
to and spells out exactly the implications of that statement:

> I remember that I surprised many people, in *Culture and Society,*
> by claiming that the institutions of the labour movement - the
> trade unions, the co-operatives, the Labour Party - were a great
> creative achievement of the working people and also the right
> basis for the whole organisation of any good society of the
> future. (10)

However, it is one thing to correctly identify these organisations
as central to any notion of working-class culture, and to acknowledge their theoretical importance. It is another to provide a
theoretical framework for adequately studying them. What is
empirically the case, that the appropriation of Williams's work
did *not* lead to any serious study of these organisations, requires

an explanation, for the theoretical definition is so clear and so evidently central to the whole of his project.

Running through a great deal of Williams's work is a certain linguistic evasiveness, a tendency to circumlocution, which is the counterpart of crucial theoretical obscurities. These are most evident on the narrowly political level with respect to the nature of revolutionary social change, and are clearly related to the ambiguities of certain social and political movements, but a discussion of these issues would at present be diversionary. In the less precise field of cultural theory the problems are less clear, but they can in principle be traced.

Williams counterposed the ideas of the culture of the 'atomic' individual to that if collective development, and located the second of these in the tendency of the institutions of the working class. This is undoubtedly correct, but it is not evident from his discussion whether he is referring, in practise, to the structures themselves or the potential of those structures. Many of those structures have a legacy which is, to say the least, profoundly ambiguous from the point of view of notions of collect- ivity. Williams does not specify in what ways these structures are the bearers of a new society, nor does he specify their relat- ion to Hoggart's 'ordinary people'. The difficulty is compounded by the powerful moralism of the language and thought. This tendency comes over forcefully when Williams discusses developments in the labour movement: he speaks specifically of a 'moral decline' (11). Now I have no objection to morality as such, but it seems to me an inadequate base for a social philosophy, and it provides no point of vantage for a critique of Hoggart. We have once again a picture which relates contemporary developments to a myth of the past, and this clearly confirms the crucial Hoggartian thesis of the fall of working-class man. Without a much more precise and definite analysis of these institutions, their history and their potential, it is difficult to see how they can be re-integrated into Cultural Studies.

The difficulty in analysing social change comes over most strongly in the central concept of 'the organisation of society'. At first glance, this is a conception of social totality which could provide powerful insights, but examined more closely it reveals an evasion of the central problems:

> It is then not a question of relating the art to the society, but of studying all the activities and their interrelations, without any concessions of priority to any one of them we may choose to abstract. If we find, as often, that a particular activity came radically to change the whole organisation, we can still not say that it is to this activity that all the others must be related; we can only study the varying ways in which, within the changing organis-

ation, the particular activities and their interrelations were
affected. (12)

The conception of social totality which is operating here is one
in which the notions of structure and determination are explicity
rejected. What the above amounts to in simple language is this:
everything acts on everything else. With such a theoretical model,
it is inevitable that there can be no coherent conception of
history or social change. Nor can there be a precise analysis of
culture : the discrete levels of ethics, politics, aesthetics, etc.,
cannot be located and specified.

The mention of 'art' in the above introduces my final point about
Williams. We have already seen how the problem of the relation
of 'Culture' to 'culture' was evaded in earlier studies, and once
again Williams dodges the issue. His definition of culture is
wide enough to include 'a body of intellectual and imaginative
work', but the precise ways in which that relates to 'a whole way
of life' is never explored. Indeed, Williams's published work,
perhaps as a consequence of institutional factors, contains far
more analysis of 'Culture' in its concrete form than of 'culture'.
This clearly relates to the failure to specify levels of historical
development: without such specificity it is impossible to locate
an aesthetic level in a social totality.

It is for the above reason that I wish to argue that Williams's
work, however much it may have opened up new ground, did not
provide the basis for resolving problems set by the initial
definitions of Cultural Studies. The plain fact is that the
theoretical recognition of the importance of formal organisations
was not integrated into the practise of Cultural Studies. I
cannot trace that development in any detail, but perhaps the
record can be allowed to speak for itself. In the October 1972
list of *Stencilled Papers, Studies and Collections,* representing
a good chunk of the work done by the Centre for Contemporary
Cultural Studies I can find no reference to a study whose prime
concern is those massive organisations which Hoggart consigned
to the fringes of working-class culture. The same is true of the
Journal published by the Centre. The same is true of current
research interests. The only way in which this experience has
ever been approached is through historical debates, notably the
Anderson/Thompson debate (13). Hoggart had good reason for his
position, but the proclaimed Marxism, or at least Socialism, of
so many of the writers who have contributed to the above
collections makes their lapse indefensible.

Marxism, of course, was the shiny new toy which was to solve the
problems set by Williams. The failure of this solution, I wish
to argue, was the result of isolating the methodology of Marxism
from its proper object and attempting to graft it directly onto
the unreconstructed problematic bequeathed by Hoggart.

What happened in the case of Cultural Studies is that a number of thinkers, of varying degrees of ability, were lifted out of the Marxist tradition and gutted quite unhistorically for the light they could shed on other concerns. With staggering arrogance, the collective experience of millions of working people was tossed away with the label: 'profoundly residual'. The occurence was not an accident. The institutions which have historically been the bearers of this tradition were and are extremely attenuated and most unnatractive to the student of Cultural Studies. The available avenues to Marxist tradition were, with the exception of the old boy himself, via thinkers whose historical importance has been secondary and whose formulations have often been eccentric. The list of reasons could be protracted, but the essential mistakes remain the same. There was not, and never has been, any attempt to come to terms with Marxism as a revolutionary practise, any attempt to critically assimilate the history of that practise, any effort to understand or relate to the organisational expressions of revolutionary practise, any recognition of the historical dynamic of that practise.

Above all the above destruction, I feel obliged to put forward a constructive alternative. It is impossible to elaborate a complete theoretical framework in one half of a short paper, and all that I will attempt is to indicate the major reformulations which follow from my above argument.

In a famous review of *The Long Revolution* (14), E.P. Thompson raised the difficult question of the relation of 'culture' to 'non-culture' which is inherent in the idea of culture as 'a whole way of life'. As we have seen, the basic thrust of Cultural Studies has been to define culture in terms of a whole way of life other than the production and reproduction of material life. This definition is at once too broad and too narrow. From the point of view of the study of a class culture, no definition which excludes the productive relations which constitute the objective definitions of class can really be adequate. On the other hand, if we broaden the definition to include productive relations, it is difficult to differentiate Cultural Studies from History. In the end, we are forced to adopt the latter of the two definitions and recognise Cultural Studies as an aspect of the science of history.

While recognising the inherent totality implied in the concept of history, it is true that, both materially and conceptually, the totality of history is complex, structured and multi-levelled. Cultural Studies is the analysis of one of those levels of articulation with respect to the historical totality itself. Cultural Studies is distinct from, but not divided from, other levels such as economics, politics etc.: it is one of the possible ways of looking at history. If we accept specific levels of articulation, then culture is distinguished from the techniques and organisation of production and from directly productive skills and attributes in so far as they are materially productive. Culture becomes the multitude of beliefs, attitudes, organisations etc., by means of which economically defined classes attempt to define themselves and their relationship to society, and through which they seek to establish a position with respect to other classes.

It is obvious that this view of culture stresses very heavily the primacy of the category of consciousness. The notion of class consciousness is normally used by Marxists in a narrow and specific political context with regard to those activities, ideas and organisations by means of which a particular class establishes its historical identity. This sense it is important to retain within our conception of the domain of culture, although the temptation to reduce culture to the studies of those activities alone should be resisted. What is true is that consciousness, in the sense of identification of historic role, is the crucial determinant of culture in a class society. The values and meanings with which areas of working class life are imbued do not spring out of nowhere: they are part and parcel of the historic self-definitions of that class and are the consequence of its global self-identification.

The practical consequences of this position involve a major redirection of the efforts of Cultural Studies. First of all, we have to be realistic about the specific trajectory of the culture of the class which we spend most of our time studying, the British working class. (I will come to the question of other countries shortly). If we ask the question what is that history?, we too often find the view of the rosy past which was implicit in the Hoggartian model. The truth is very different. The history of the British working class is a history of defeat. It is not a history without great struggles, it is not a history without great gains, but it is a history of failure. The British working class, despite tremendous efforts, remains a subordinate class. It is nonsense to idealise the cultural responses of such a history as working-class culture at its apogee. If we look at the period which figures so prominently in current myth as the finest hour of working-class culture, we find that period is one of tremendous failures. Those failures extended to the great core-values like solidarity, the General Strike was defeated, and victimisation was both normal and successful. In the period when the great myth was being formed, the British working class was forced back from a powerful and aggressive offensive into a long, stubborn and bitter retreat. What are today idealised as the characteristic features of the best of working-class culture were formed in a period of retreat and defeat and they must be understood as attempts to come to terms with that experience. In that black period some of the most massive organisations, most obviously the Labour Party, suffered gigantic fissures, and perhaps our attention should be directed at the remarkable fact of survival rather than accepting such institutions as a minor part of an eternal landscape.

What is required is a recognition of the cultural life of the
British working class as that of a class 'preparing for power';
the fact that it has been a long time doing so may be regrettable,
but there is nothing to be gained by pretending that it is not so.
Our starting point for the critical evaluation of working-class
culture is not the empirical reality of that culture but the
historical role of the class:

> The question is not what goal is *envisaged* for the time
> being by this or that member of the proletariat, or even
> by the proletariat as a whole. The question is *what is the
> proletariat* and what course of action will it be forced
> historically to take in conformity with its own nature. (15)

Proceeding from that as starting point, we can then go on to
analyse the concrete historical experience of culture. The
empirical reality of a culture is a complex of determined factors
made up of profoundly contradictory elements originating in both
the historical and immediate definitions of the class.

Viewed with this perspective, many of the characteristics of the
culture under review take on a different aspect. It is obvious
that the massive organisations of the class take on a central
role. It is not that they should be fallen down before and
worshipped, but that they are revealed as the crucial agents and
expressions of a contradictory experience. The trade unions
provide, once again, an obvious example: these organisations are
at one and the same time organs of working-class self-expression
haggling over control of areas of life, defensive institutions
designed to regulate the sale of labour power, and powerful mediating agencies for the maintenence of a particular form of class
rule.

Secondly, the historical development of a class from a position of
subordination towards a position of hegemony implies not only an
open struggle at the political and cultural level between classes
but also a political and cultural struggle within the subordinate
class, and hence between political and cultural organisations
within that class. In periods when the definitions adopted by
a class limit its horizon to the position of subordination,
enormous amounts of energy and time are poured into a whole
range of activities and organisations: sport, horticulture, drinking, interior decoration etc. A change in the horizon of that
class implies the diversion of time, energy, money, thought and
ingenuity into other channels and organisations: a struggle takes
place over the cultural definitions of working-class life.

If Cultural Studies had ever looked acrosss the English Channel,
it would have seen just that sort of struggle fought out in the
open. Political definitions and cultural life are not mutually
contradictory and exclusive areas. Particular political conceptions and definite organisations of culture are necessary complements. Take the example of Germany: the links between political

party, trade union, sports club, media, drinking establishment, chess club, choir, even armed defence force, were all clearly drawn. In the history of the S.P.D. and the K.P.D. we can see how those cultural and political organisations openly and clearly interacted, and how they produced the tragic destiny of that class. In Britain, the links are much weaker, and may even be submerged beyond recall, but they can in principle be traced. In certain very favourable instances, it is quite a feasible project, and it is high time that tracing these links became a central pre-occupation of our work. It is significant that the only real attempts so far have been made by labour historians (16).

The failure to carry out this task is at the root of many of the current problems. In the first place, the idealisation of a particular subordinate culture leads to mis-evaluation of partic-ular aspects of the field. The writers are full of the best of intentions, but at best they overstress the local, the passive, the quietistic aspects of working-class culture. At its worst, it can lead to the involuntary adulation of genuinely reactionary aspects, racialism, male chauvinism, etc., which are all part of that culture as it stands. What we are faced with is an inverted and perverse form of the ghost of Proletkult. That theory argued that only those cultural manifestations which came directly from the working class (and poor peasantry) were to be encouraged and adulated, and precisely because of their origins. When it was evolved, the theory could at least claim in its defence that the working class was ruling class- the contemporary proponents can make no such claim. They 'fetishize corporateness' in all its ambiguity, and to adulate corporate consciousness is to adulate capitalism.

Even the attempts to break out of this trap by appropriating the vocabulary of Gramsci are prone to pitfalls, which result from the second consequence of the failure to analyse relations within a culture. In accepting the notion of a subordinate class within a hegemonic order laid down by the dominant class, isolated responses to that order are taken as the archetype for potentially hegemonic consciousness. Bits and pieces around the edges of the social totality are held up as potential threats to the hegemonic order without any real analysis of the processes and organisations by which hegemony is maintained.

Hegemony is not some mysterious nerve gas which paralyses the subordinate class and prevents it playing its historic role. It is, much more importantly, a question of organisation and action. Recent developments in Media Studies point quite clearly to this; for example, Stuart Hall's paper *Encoding and Decoding in the Television Discourse* analyses the process of the maintenence of hegemonic definitions both as the construction of hegemonic interpretations and as the communication of such an interpretation in such a form that it is able to resonate with subordinate groups:

> In speaking of *dominant meaning*...we are not simply
> talking about a one-sided process, which governs how
> any event will be signified...it also consists of the
> 'work' required to enforce, win plausibility for and
> command as legitimate a *de-coding* of the event within the
> dominant definition in which it has been connotatively
> signified. (17)

The question of hegemony is thus a two-sided one. The first,
relatively well-explored, is the study of the institutions and
systems which generate and transmit the hegemonic definitions
for the ruling class. The other side leads to the study of those
organisations and systems within the subordinate class which permit
a 'legitimate decoding'. At the ideological level, the process
of the maintence of hegemony implies the convergence at crucial
points of the ideology of the ruling class with that of the subordinate class or classes. At the sociological level, the hegemonic domination of one class over another requires the existence
within the subordinate class of organisations and collective
practices which themselves both command wide support and correspond more or less exactly to the practices defined as legitimate
by the hegemonic order. Common sense is common because it is
commonly practically efficacious.

The focus on those practices and organisations within the dominated class which allow the maintence of hegemony raises a further
issue of great importance. What is usually forgotten is that
discussion of the concept does not refer to some isolated group
of intellectuals taken at random, but to the intellectuals of a
definite class, acting as part of a definite organisation. The
category of 'hegemony' implies the category of *'The Modern Prince'*.
The concept of hegemony implies definite social organisations as
the bearers of hegemonic consciousness. In the case of the
working class, this organisation is specified in considerable
detail by Gramsci, and the crucial relation between its practical
and theoretical role elaborated at length.

There remains one final point regarding the relation of elite and
popular culture. The tendency to dismiss the problem of elite
culture has deep roots in Cultural Studies, but there seems little
basis for continuing in it. The nature of the culture as a sphere
distinct from the narrowly productive allows the consideration of
those activities associated with leisure and the practices of
social groups not narrowly tied to production. There is absolutely
no basis for excluding from the study of culture the initially
rejected aesthetic domain. What has to be recognised is that the
sphere of formal art is one of the aspects of culture. During the
Bourgois Epoch, this activity has been largely restricted to
priveleged members of the fuling class, and it may be the case
that this culture has sunk into decadence as the rule of the
bourgeoisie has become more and more outmoded. But in the sphere

of production the bourgeoisie played an enormously progressive and liberative role; so too in the realm of culture this class opened up a whole new series of human insights. We need in our conception of Cultural Studies to recognise these achievements, to analyse its limits and its one-sidedness. No Marxist has ever argued that we should reject the socialisation of labour and the possibility of a society free from want- on the contrary, we have always argued that these provide the basis for Socialism. Why then should we say that the concomitant cultures is not worthy of consideration? We must be prepared to take that which is beautiful and valuable just as we are prepared to take that which is productive and useful. We can discard the dross of both.

Cultural Studies is nearing its legal majority, and assessments of its childhood and adolescence vary. Perhaps my view is analogous to that of the Stipendary making ready to turn a deviant into a recidivist, but it seems to me that a sentence of three years hard labour history and concurrent retraining in the traditions of Marxism might just do the trick. Unless drastic measures are taken; Cultural Studies will remain a sideshow in the study of society and prove incapable of solving even those problems it currently sets itself.

Notes

1. R. Hoggart *The Uses of Literacy* (Penguin, 1958), p.323.

2. Ibid, p.345.

3. Ibid, p.248.

4. Ibid, p.268.

5. Both are reprinted in the two volumes of *Speaking to Each Other* (Penguin, 1973).

6. *The Uses of Literacy*, p.82.

7. Ibid, p.318.

8. The most explicit Marxist essay is 'Base and Superstructure in Marxist Cultural Theory' printed in *New Left Review*, no. 82 (November-December 1973).

9. R. Williams *Culture and Society* (Penguin, 1963), p.312.

10. R. Williams *The Long Revolution* (Penguin, 1965), p.328.

11. *The Long Revolution*, p.328.

12. Ibid. p.62.

13. When I first drafted this paper, I was able to include the proposed M.A. course in this list. The revised draft focusses heavily on historical questions of this order.

14. This was first published in *New Left Review* of May-June and July-August 1961.

15. I do not have a copy of *The Holy Family,* and my reference is to page 46 of *History and Class Consciousness.*

16. E.P. Thompson is the obvious example.

17. Unpublished paper presented to the Council of Europe Colloquy on 'Training in the Critical Reading of Television Language' Sept. 1972.

Sociology of Popular Culture: The Other Side of a Definition
David F. Gillespie

Originally published in the *Journal of Popular Culture,* vol. 6, 1972, pp 292-299.

Sociology of Popular Culture: The Other Side of a Definition

By David F. Gillespie

One of the first requirements in developing a new discipline, or in setting apart a common area of interest to be studied by a number of disciplines is to specify what is to be known. One of the most difficult and rudimentary steps in this process is the construction of a definition. A definition must identify all the salient aspects comprising a given area, and at the same time differentiate it from other areas. That is, the observation of any given element or event must be unambiguously identifiable as either belonging to the defined area or as not belonging to it. This establishes one common point of reference for scholars studying the phenomena in question. A definition, however, refers primarily to the content of the chosen sphere. Of equal importance, in terms of specifying what is to be known, is an understanding of how this content is being looked at. For example, a book might be seen as an entertainment, wall adornment, conversation piece, status symbol, means of escape, working tool, etc. "The other side of a definition" refers to the viewpoint employed in observing the content of a given field.

The viewpoint or perspective provides the scholar with a consistent means of interpreting the phenomena within a defined space. The various aspects which together make up one's perspective include all of the concepts relating to the area, the relations between these concepts, the assumptions underlying the relations, as well as the rules, methods, and theories guiding the acquisition of knowledge about the phenomena under observation.[1] However, one's perspective is not simply a summation of the various aspects constituting its definition. It is, rather, inextricably bound with the ways in which these various aspects have been used historically. Thus, the perspective is not a rigid inflexible set of blinders; quite the contrary, it represents a way of looking at the world, legitimated by past and present social support, which enables an observer to make sense out of a given phenomenon within a certain arena of focus.

The kind of explanation that results from the observation of any given phenomenon, depends upon the viewpoint that is guiding the observer. The implication is that scholars from the various disciplines observing the same phenomena will each offer different, yet not necessarily conflicting, explanations for the occurrence of some item within a given realm. For example, a psychologist might explain the occurrence of a particular art form as an expression of the artists' emotions; while a sociologist might explain the same art form on the basis of its appeal to a particular segment of the population. Thus, there are two aspects encountered in explaining a given phenomenon: (a) the content definition, and (b) the perspective employed. This distinction is particularly important in considering an interdisciplinary topic, like popular culture.

The significance of this distinction can not be overstressed in an area as rich and diverse in content as popular culture. It suggests that even if "popular culture" were concisely defined,[2] there could be no guarantee that knowledge about popular culture would rapidly accumulate. John G. Cawelti alluded to this problem with his statement that ". . . humanists and social scientists still lack a common conceptual framework through which they can exchange their insights."[3] A clear recognition of the perspective through which an explanation is being presented may go a long way toward facilitating efficient conceptualization of one another's insights. If that is true, then the solution to the problems of interdisciplinary communication may not be quite as forebidding as that suggested by Cawelti, ". . . to find scholars with sufficient competence in several areas . . ."[4] Indeed, there is no reason to suspect that given acceptance of the relatively noncompetitive nature of different explanations (when they are linked to different viewpoints), a solid foundation to the study of popular culture may proceed unhampered from the beginning.

This essay focuses upon the problem of interdisciplinary communication as it is related to the differing viewpoints contributing to explanations of popular culture. A preliminary step in conjunction with a content definition is to ascertain what it is that each contributing discipline can offer in terms of accounting for the various aspects of popular culture. The assumption underlying this contention is that the initial explanations explaining popular culture must be distinguished by reference to the particular perspective employed, otherwise, confusing and contradictory explanations will ensue. The current classificatory confusions characterizing the social sciences in general seem to support this contention. It is being suggested that the study of popular culture can avoid the taxonomical problems plaguing the social sciences by clearly explicating the particular perspectives that are contributing to the explanations of popular culture.

We can look at some *potential* problems in popular culture by examining the confusions that arise whenever a discipline is characterized by explanations deriving from different perspectives. A field closely related to popular culture, the sociology of art, may be used to illustrate the ambiguities and misunderstandings which result from attempts to explain art from two perspectives at the same time.[5] Of course, the following discussion is directed by the perspective of a sociologist.

Vytautas Kavolis states: ". . . [t]hat the main sociological function of artistic *style* is the shaping or emotional re-enforcement of general tendencies to perceive situations of action in certain structured ways, [and] . . . that artistic *content* has the function of helping man to develop an emotional envolvement, [but then] . . . a change in the composition of the art public, in the operations of the art market, or in the amount of artistic consumption by political or religious institutions can be expected to produce modifications in art style . . ."[6] Kavolis has sufficiently transposed the socioligical and psychological perspectives. The reader of these passages may interpret "style" as a determinant of "emotional re-enforcement," or he may consider "style" as an "objectified" equivalent of "emotional re-enforcement." In any case, there can be little doubt that "emotional re-enforcement," "perception," and most probably "style" are the domain of the psychologist.[7] If "content has the function of helping man to develop an emotional involvement," then it too may be best accounted for by a psychologist. However, if "a change in the composition of the art public," [etc.] "produces modifications in art style," then we shall admit the presence of a sociological explanation.

Hugh Dalziel Duncan subsumes his sociology of art under a sociological model of communication. The development of this model follows the perspective of Kenneth Burke. Describing Burke's "Dramatism" Duncan states: ". . . [h]e argues that if we regard man as a symbol-using animal we must stress symbolism *as a motive* in any discussion of social behavior. That is, the kind of symbols we have, who can use them, where, how, and why—these do not 'reflect' motives, they are motives."[8] This is a clearly psychological statement and requires no further comment in terms of the perspective being used here.

However, in an article concerned explicitly with the sociology of art, Duncan maintains that art offers "mankind ways of reducing status tensions to manageable proportions."[9] Here we are again confronted with a split perspective, "status" is an acknowledged sociological concept; while "tensions" would be most generally accounted for in psychological terms. When the two are employed in conuunction, a variety of interpretations becomes possible. We might interpret "status tensions" to mean the difference between spoken statuses and statuses actually acted out; or, "status tensions" might mean divergent action statuses between different social positions; or again, "status tensions" might mean that personality conflicts are reduced through an identification with spoken statuses as represented in various art types; or perhaps the reduction of "status tensions" is referring to art as a kind of therapy. Whatever Duncan's intended meaning, it is clear that the syndactyl application of concepts from different perspectives provides the reader with an "opportunity" to become mislead or confused.

The tendency to employ two or more perspectives in the explanation of a given event may be associated with a hesitation on the part of scholars to recognize the value of an explanation that accounts for something less than the "complete" phenomenon. This tendency may be linked to the antiquated, but still popular large scale historical explanations of the nineteenth century theorists, e.g. Marx, Spencer, Comte, etc. This period was characterized by all encompassing, comprehensive "systems" of explanation. The theorists of this period were economists, historians, psychologists, sociologists, etc. all in one. Explanations of any merit today are characterized by a relative precision and empirical demonstrability, which of necessity narrows one's focus.

The approach towards precision is not provincial, nor does it deny the interdisciplinary nature of the study of popular culture, it only asserts that "inter-disciplinary" must be read as different disciplines contributing to the explanation of a central topic, not as a freeforall, with sociologists becoming pseudo-psychologists, and psychologists becoming pseudo-sociologists. What then is the particular strength of a sociological contribution to the study of popular culture? It should be emphasized that the particular aspects stressed in the following discussion in no way exclude the other aspects as being irrelevant or unimportant, it only acknowledges that the sociologist by his training and perspective is equipped to handle certain features and not others.

The sociological perspective is concerned with elements of popular culture that are social. Behavior is social when it may be said to influence or to be influenced by other persons' behavior.[10] This is an externally observable set of behaviors, which by perspective excludes motivations, intentions, perception, etc., and asserts the primacy of the social environment. The consequence of this perspective is that the primary focal point for a sociological investigation into popular culture places its emphasis upon the popular culture publics.[11] This means that a given feature of popular culture, e.g. a particular kind of painting, humor, music, etc. is viewed as attaining significance as a result of its acceptance by a certain public, and not due to the desires, wishes, or motivations of some major media distributor.

To claim that the media disseminated a particular item because of a profit motive is one kind of explanation; on the other hand, to indicate that this same item became popular due to its status enhancing capacity (there are, of course, many other reasons for acceptance) is quite another thing. Yet, both may be correct, each based upon a different perspective and set of assumptions.

The training of a sociologist includes the use and development of techniques designed to "get at" social behavior. Two techniques of particular relevance for the study of popular culture are the sample survey and the comparative method. The sample survey provides a means of obtaining a descriptive account of large and loosely connected publics, such as those characterizing popular culture. The sample survey is drawn in a mathematically precise manner, which permits the investigator to consider a relatively small and manageable sample of persons as representative of the whole public.[12]

Considering the expansive range of television coverage, magazine distribution, etc. the utility of representative samples describing the particular characteristics of various popular culture publics (or creators, performers, etc.) is clear. That is, rather than having to rely on information volunteered by individuals who for one reason or another are easily accessible, scholars who are supplied with a descriptive account of a "whole public" can seek knowledge about the entire range of persons participating in a certain form of popular culture. For example, the percentage of different occupations, ages, educational levels, etc. represented in the public of a selected cartoon strip would tell us a great deal about the significance attached to that form of popular culture. Further, this type of information provides a foundation for comparative studies.

Comparative studies do exactly what the label implies, they compare the similarities and differences between various publics in terms of some common reference.[13] To illustrate, a comparative study might ask the question: Do the people possessing one characteristic (e.g., certain occupations, geographic location, age, ad infinitum) differ in the meanings that they attribute to a particular cartoon strip as opposed to those who do not possess this characteristic? By comparing these two categories of people in relation to the meanings that each gives to the cartoon strip, we answer the question.

Yet, given a difference between the two categories of people, the answer is generally accompanied by an explanation, i.e., the reasons why such a difference exists. It is this point of explanation where confusion, misunderstandings, and argumentation generally arise. It is the contention of this paper that much of the turmoil surrounding explanations is due to a lack of standardized conceptions in interpreting phenomena. One way to improve this situation is to clearly communicate the perspective that is being used when explaining a given phenomenon.

However, whether or not agreement can be achieved on a given interpretation, the knowledge that different meanings are associated with different attributes of the social structure is still of great value in studying popular culture. That is, the emergence, popularity, and decline of certain elements of popular culture are viewed in a specific context. In brief, it would give us a more "complete picture" of the phenomena subsumed under the rubric of popular culture.[14] On this basis, the problems associated with confused perspectives would become less a matter of polemics and more a matter of empirical demonstrability.

In conclusion, it can be seen that the interests and kinds of predictions that a scholar is interested in determine the way he is going to look at his data. What has been suggested here is that students of popular culture must explicate with well defined precision the way in which they are looking at their data. In this way, confusions that might arise from explanations deriving from different perspectives can be avoided; thus lessening possible interdisciplinary disputes on the one hand, and increasing the power of popular culture explanations on the other. Both of these aspects imply success for the study of popular culture.

NOTES

*I would like to acknowledge the helpful comments and criticism of R. Serge Denisoff, Norman L. Friedman, and Franz Adler to an earlier draft of this paper.

[1]Cf. Garvin McCain and Erwin M. Segal, *The Game of Science* (Belmont, California: Brooks/Cole Publishing Company, 1969).

[2]Cf. John G. Cawelti, *Popular Culture Programs* (Pamphlet distributed by Popular Culture Association, Bowling Green: Bowling Green University Press, 1970), p. 1. Also see Ray B. Browne, "Popular Culture: Notes Toward a Definition," *Popular Culture and Curricula*, Ray B. Browne and Ronald J. Ambrosetti, eds. (Bowling Green: Bowling Green University Popular Press, 1970), p. 11.

[3]Cawelti, *op. cit.*, p. 3.

[4]*Ibid.*, p. 3.

[5]It is perhaps worth noting, that if the sociology of art with an elite nature circumscribing its explanations has been plagued by ambiguity and confusion, then popular culture with its diversified composition must be particularly alerted to this type of problem.

[6]Vytautas Kavolis, *Artistic Expression: A Sociological Analysis* (Ithaca: Cornell University Press, 1968), pp. 5-6.

[7]The question of whether or not "style" is a legitimate concept for the sociologist focuses upon the difficulty of defining "style" in such a way as to ensure that the configurations one has in mind will be identified in the same way by everyone in the population. To my knowledge, no such definition of art "style" has yet been designed; that is, a definition meeting the criteria of mutually exclusive categories.

[8]Hugh Dalziel Duncan, *Communication and Social Order* (London: Oxford University Press, 1968), p. 114.

[9]Hugh Dalziel Duncan, "Sociology of Art, Literature, and Music: Social Contexts of Symbolic Experience," *Modern Sociological Theory in Continuity and Change*, Howard Becker and Alvin Boskoff, eds. (New York: Holt, Rinehart and Winston, 1957), p. 497.

[10]Cf. Franz Adler, "Hacia una Sociologia del Comportanmiento Creador," *Revista Mexicana de Sociologia*, XXVII (Mayo-Agosto, 1965), p. 559.

[11]Franz Adler, "A Unit Concept for Sociology," *The American Journal of Sociology*, LXV (January), p. 360.

[12]Cf. Angus Campbell and George Katona, "The Sample Survey: A Technique for Social Science Research," *Research Methods in the Behavioral Sciences*, Leon Festinger and Daniel Katz, eds. (New York: Holt, Rinehart and Winston, 1953), pp. 15-55, for a detailed discussion on the strengths and weaknesses of this method.

[13]Cf. Hanz Zeisel, *Say It With Figures* (New York: Harper & Row, Publishers, 1947), pp. 175-189.

[14]Cf. R. Serge Denisoff, "The Age of Rock: Sounds of the American Cultural Revolution, etc.," *Journal of Popular Culture*, III (Spring, 1970), p. 858.

The Necessity for an Aesthetics of Popular Culture
David Madden

Originally published in the *Journal of Popular Culture*, vol. 7, 1973, pp 1-13.

THE NECESSITY FOR AN AESTHETICS

OF POPULAR CULTURE

BY DAVID MADDEN

he articulation of a popular culture aesthetics that is at once based on, but that significantly departs from, traditional concepts is, to me, the most difficult and most urgent business before us as students of a new discipline. As we near almost a decade of aggressive study of popular culture, we ought to consider dropping the notion that absolutely anything goes because, as we all know, popular culture, an infant field of study with modest pretentions, is not very well defined. Well, let's *begin* to very well define it. At our conventions, the confusion in the speakers' approaches to their tasks and their performance of those tasks and our responses to those tasks arises because we lack a common aesthetic base for popular culture.

An outside observer, and perhaps some readers of this journal, may regard our efforts to formulate even a tentative aesthetics for popular culture a joke. I know I risk sounding pedantic, and further risk refutation in pedantic terms, but I'm interested enough in the problem and convinced enough of its seriousness to want to try, as a writer working in several literary and performing media, to say a few things about it and start working on it. These are notes on an approach to the awesome task of formulating a basic popular culture aesthetic from which we can venture as far as we wish, and about which we can debate and argue as we will.

I

We who study popular arts, it should be noted at the outset, are schizoid. We must always take this condition into account as we examine the products of popular art, especially when we formulate basic principles, as here in the realm of aesthetics. Schizoid because *The Postman Always Rings Twice,* for instance, was not written primarily for us, nor is it we who respond most fully to its primary elements. On the other hand, in the realm of so-called "high art," those who formulate and evaluate are also those for whom the works examined are primarily produced. In the study of popular art, those who formulate and evaluate are *not* those for whom the work was primarily produced—except in childhood (and so, nostalgia is an active element for *us*, as for the primary consumer: in realms of nostalgia and taste, we share most with the primary consumer). Still the context is larger, richer for us; the experience is conscious for us, unconscious for the ordinary consumer.

We have yet to get in touch with our schizophrenia: as children we were products of popular culture; as adults we were trained, many of us, in high culture, while retaining our affection for and interest in popular culture. Now, we return to popular culture as students and scholars. Consequently, in this transitional stage in the history of popular culture studies, we often speak out of a kind of aesthetic schizophrenia with a forked tongue. Since our own personal and professional interest is in both the popular culture in which we were spontaneously nurtured and the high culture which we willfully acquired, we must, constantly, by deliberate acts of the imagination, look at popular culture from the point of view of makers and consumers (who include our younger selves).

One problem is to determine what concepts and emotions are to be considered in formulating an aesthetics and in what order of importance; what degree of impact can be assigned to each? And should we account for the special experiences of the student or scholar of popular culture in the formulation, and if so, to what degree? Should we attempt to show that there is good art, bad art, and non-art? Should we set out to show that popular art is the same as high art, just not as intense? Or should we discover a new aesthetics for a new sensibility? *Is* there a new sensibility? Or only a new attitude, new superficial characteristics?

"Aesthetics" or "art" is so often used as an honorific term rather than simply as a descriptive term that we shouldn't invite scoffing criticism for a loose appropriation of the term and its precepts. We don't want to seem to be borrowing luster, any more than we want to put ourselves in a position of apologizing. We should neither praise a work the high culture condemns nor support the condemnation itself. Let's strive for a sound, inclusive, though always flexible, *system* of aesthetics.

In the writings of Leslie Fiedler, Kenneth Rexroth, Harry Levin, even René Wellek and T. S. Eliot, one finds scattered comments on the validity of studying popular culture—for social or moral insight into the times. Is popular culture the number 2 brain in the withering tail of the dinosaur? Or the antennae of the race?

In "Aesthetics of Popular Culture," John Cawelti says, "Many scholars and enemies of popular culture share the assumption that a popular work is successful because it embodies or expresses the values of the popular mind in a particularly effective or direct fashion. Thus, social and psychological analysis is the dominant mode of interpretation in dealing with this kind of material. So high art is commonly treated as aesthetic structure or individual vision; the popular arts are studied as social and psychological data" (*Journal of Popular Culture,* Fall, 1971). I agree with Cawelti's contention that this is a pseudo-distinction, for high art too is valued as social and psychological data; and I want to add that popular art is too seldom studied in its aesthetic aspects. Cawelti says, "We ought to ask what psychological process or mechanism makes the expression of commonly held values popular with the public. Is it simply that we find comfort in repetitions of received opinions?" That is, I think, an apt description of what happens in high art, also.

The general assumption is that extrinsic factors are not important in traditional aesthetics. In popular art, however, they may prove to be inseparable from aesthetic concepts. An examination of the forces that produced popular culture originally may suggest concepts for an aesthetics. In his monumental history of American popular culture, *The Unembarrassed Muse,* Russel Nye discusses five main forces that produced and determined the character of popular culture: increased population; mass production; urbanization; universal education; and the electronic revolution. We need to investigate such questions as, How does the economics of distribution affect the popular culture experience aesthetically?

Research into those and other areas can easily be done. The use of statistics is more suitable for popular art than high art. Interviews with consumers about taste and nostalgia as determinants could be conducted. This work would involve the methods of social science. We should examine the environment in which the work is obtained and the *imagined* environment in which the work is made. We should conduct experimental research in the physical energy expended in experiencing a popular culture product. That would involve the biological sciences. Santayana and Dewey based their aesthetics partly on biology. Our emphasis so far has been, as Cawelti observed, mainly social. We must now go very deeply into the psychology of perception (gestalt psychology will probably prove the most useful). The psychology specifically of reading, of movie-going (see Pauline Kael's reviews), of looking at pictures, and of two areas high culture neglects: nostalgia and taste. Research into the psychic energy expended in experiencing a popular art product. The psychological context of a specific work, though not overtly encouraged by the work, comes into play in our experience of popular culture. Let's examine it. And we must study the social, moral, political values involved in the popular culture experience. All these extrinsic factors are important and we should study their effect on the aesthetics of popular art. But these secondary factors now *dominate* our interst in popular art.

Let's look for a moment at some of the insights of a new aesthetician, Susan Sontag: "Interpretation is the revenge of the intellect upon art."/"Interpretation takes the sensory experience of the work of art for granted, and proceeds from there."/"We need an erotics of art."/"In art, 'content' is, as it were, the pretext, the goal, the lure which engages consciousness in essentially formal processes of transformation."/"To speak of style is one way of speaking about the totality of a work of art."/"Transparence is the highest, most liberating value in art. Transparence means experiencing the luminousness of the thing in itself, of things being what they are."/"What is needed is a vocabulary—a descriptive, rather than prescriptive, vocabulary—for forms."/"The function of criticism should be to show how a work of art is what it is, even that it is what it is, rather than to show what it means." (*Against Interpretation*) The aesthetics of popular art ought to deal directly only with those components that may be considered part of the aesthetic experience. The task of other branches of popular culture study is to deal with other aspects: social, political, psychological.

What I am advocating here is that we start from traditional aesthetics as it deals with high art and discover what is unique or different in the popular art aesthetic experience, and then *adapt* to popular culture those traditional concepts that are found to apply. What are the major, basic principles of traditional aesthetics, as well as the new aesthetics? It's difficult to talk about aesthetics because subjective criteria can easily contradict objective criteria in this field so that theories are always partial and tentative. And should be. The literature itself is extremely small, not only in philosophy but in each branch of the arts. About sixty years ago Clive Bell reassured us that the literature is so small aesthetics stands in no danger of being accused of turning out more nonsense than any other field. That's still true.

Before reviewing some of the traditional aestheticians, let's look at a few recent observations.

Although the concept of "camp" always threatens to obscure what we are coming to articulate as popular art, Susan Sontag's famous "Notes on 'Camp' " may be turned around to provide genuine insights into the nature of popular culture. For instance, in her very first note, she makes a claim that popular culture studies should make: "Camp is a certain mode of aestheticism. It is one way of seeing the world as an aesthetic phenomenon."/"Style is everything."/ "The camp sensibility is one that is alive to a double sense in which some things can be taken."/"Camp turns its back on the good-bad axis of ordinary aesthetic judgment."/"One cheats oneself, as a human being, if one has respect only for the style of high culture."/"Camp taste is, above all, a mode of enjoyment, of appreciation—not judgment. . . . Camp taste is a kind of love . . . for human nature. It is neither cynical nor scornful." Well, we need at least as brilliant a set of notes on popular culture aesthetics as Sontag has given us on the camp sensibility.

Sontag's comments on art in general are suggestive for popular culture, too. In "One Culture and the New Sensibility," she attacks the insistence on a division between high and low culture, a distinction "based partly on an evaluation of the difference between unique and mass-produced objects." Recent serious art is "reasserting its existence as 'object' (even as manufactured or mass-produced object, drawing on the popular arts) rather than as 'individual personal expression.' "/"Because the new sensibility demands less 'content' in art, and is more open to the pleasures of 'form' and style, it is also less snobbish, less moralistic—in that it does not demand that pleasure in art necessarily be associated with edification."/"The affection which many younger artist and intellectuals feel for popular arts is not a . . . species of anti-intellectualism. . . . It does not mean the renunciation of all standards. The point is that there are new standards . . . of beauty, style, and taste. The new sensibility is defiantly pluralistic; it is dedicated both to an excruciatin, seriousness and to fun and wit and nostalgia." So, we know, is popular culture studies.

For over twenty years, Leslie Fiedler has been scattering insights into the aesthetics of popular culture throughout his writings. Thirteen years ago, in *Love and Death in the American Novel,* for instance, he said, in the course of a discussion of popular culture elements in the fiction of Nathanael West: "S. J. Perelman has been conducting a strange experiment, whose end is the trans-formation of Surrealist gallows humor into commerical entertainment. . . . The avant-garde images of twenty-five years ago . . . have become now the common property of gift shoppes and greeting-card racks, fall as stereotypes from the lips of hip 12 year olds. . . . In Lenny Bruce, for example, the distance between literature and entertainment, high art and low comedy threatens to disappear." A popular culture aesthetics must account for this close affinity between popular culture and the avant-garde.

Leslie Fiedler could write an aesthetics of popular art if he only would. But I suspect his moral and sociological bias keeps him from sustaining interest in a systematic aesthetic. Meanwhile, as he machine-guns the glass facade of American culture, he will continue to contribute scattered insights into the problem.

The aesthetics of popular culture arises, I think, out of limitations of forms, conventions, tastes, etc., imposed from without by society and audiences upon popular culture artists. Russel Nye, in the introduction to *The Unembar-rassed Muse* (I like to call her the bare-assed muse) says: "The popular artist hopes to do the very best he can within the rigorous limits set by his situation. His accomplishment must be measured by his skill and effectiveness in operating within the boundaries of the majority will and the requirements of the mass media, nor should he be expected to do otherwise. . . . This does not mean that what the popular artist does is not worth doing, or personally unsatisfying, or aesthetically bad, or commercially cheap. . . . With skill and talent alone, sometimes, a popular artist may transmute mediocre material into something much better than it is, or even good; the gradual improvement over the years of standards of performance in the popular arts provides sufficient proof of this. . . . Contemporary popular artists have developed tremendous technical skill, and their sophistication and subtleties of performance are much greater than their predecessors."

Popular art then gets its effects by permissible deviations from limitations. High art gets its effects in tensions between external and internal limitations. I found both in my study of the commedia dell'arte and silent slapstick movies. (*Harlequin's Stick, Charlie's Cane*) Each characteristic of commedia dell'arte and of silent slapstick comedy is an externally imposed or self-imposed limita-tion forcing the actor to develop skills that enable him to control and turn to advantage those limitations. Convention imposed upon the commedia the limitation of the five masks. Technological limitations imposed upon slapstick movies the limitation of silence. The commedia imposed upon itself the task of improvised action and dialogue. Silent slapstick comedy imposed upon itself the limitation of improvised action, which added to the burden of compensating for lack of sound. The freedom of improvisation was exercised within the limitations, externally and internally imposed by a set of stereotyped characters, costumes, acting areas, etc. At every point in a comparison of commedia dell'arte and silent slapstick, we find forceful substantiation of a basic aesthetic principle: that the source of genius is an ability to control externally imposed limitations and recognition of the necessity to risk imposing certain limitations upon oneself in order to realize one's potential. The actor must subordinate himself to the demands of his fellow actors, while giving his own abilities full scope and thrust. Since his character was set, his only freedom is in his art. His task is to control that freedom. We see this principle at work even in the amorphous, rowdy, self-indulgent audience, which helps create, then insists on the observance of, certain confining conventions; but within these conventions, the spectator's imagination is encouraged to range and soar. Because of the film medium's greater visual realism, the movie-goer participates more easily but less imaginatively than the theater-goer.

Neither Russel Nye, Ray Browne, Marshall Fishwick, nor other major popular culture scholars, excepting John Cawelti and Alan Gowans, go deeply into the problem of aesthetics. Pathfinders, they leave map-making to others. *The Journal of Aesthetics and Art Criticism* is a better source for discussions of the aesthetic aspects of popular art than *The Journal of Popular Culture*. I found very few theoretical pieces on aesthetics in the back issues of *JPC*. Several essays have "aesthetics" in the title, but, like the titles of stories in *Secret Confessions*, fail to deliver.

"The Concept of Formula in the Study of Popular Literature" (*JPC*, Winter, 1969) by John Cawelti proves to be an exception to that observation. "Most works of art contain a mixture of convention and invention," says Cawelti. "A formula is a conventional system for structuring cultural products. It can be distinguished from form which is an invented system of organization." (Cawelti's distinction between form and formula is descriptive, not qualitative.) "Formula represents the way in which a culture has embodied both mythical archetypes and its own preoccupations in narrative form."/"Formulas are important because they represent syntheses of several important cultural functions which, in modern cultures have been taken over by popular culture."/"Formula stories seem to be one way in which the individuals in a culture act out certain unconscious or repressed needs."/"To analyze these formulas we must first define them as narrative structures of a certain kind and then investigate how the additional dimensions of ritual, game, and dream have been synthesized into the particular pattern of plot, character, and setting which have been associated with the formula."

More recently, in "Notes Toward an Aesthetic of Popular Culture" (*JPC*, Fall, 1971), Cawelti suggests that we adapt the *auteur* approach to film as one method of analyzing all popular art. "The *auteur* critics, finding artistic value and interest in the Hollywood film, have created a new mode of analysis based on the individual stylistic characteristics and thematic interests of the director as they show up in his collective works."/"The *auteur* is an individual creator who works within a framework of existing materials, conventional structures, and commercial imperatives, but who nonetheless has the imagination, the integrity, and the skill to express his own artistic personality in the way he sets forth the conventional material he works with."/"The artistic dialectic between *auteur* and convention, the drama of how the convention is shaped to manifest the *auteur*'s intention, excites our interest and admiration."

We must take all these approaches into account, treating all as provisional ways of seeing, but striving at the same time for concepts on which a consensus can be reached.

II

"Aesthetics" originally meant "perception," and through *use* became associated with the study of artistic beauty and how it happens. So before we use the term or its precepts in our study of popular art, we must decide whether popular culture products can be termed beautiful. Implicitly, though too seldom explicitly, even high art aestheticians suggest that it can. Susanne Langer cautions, though, that "old words with new meanings are treacherous." I'm not proposing new meanings for old words—rather a putting to new use of old concepts.

I think that even in high art, the purely aesthetic pleasure is rare. I won't contribute to any effort to *merge* high art aesthetics with popular art, to blur lines that ought to remain clear, because an aesthetics should account for all the differences we enjoy between high art and popular art as well as the similarities that clarify the nature of each. We need not only to review, as I recently (too quickly) did, the major principles of Plato, Aristotle, St. Thomas Aquinas, Kant, Schopenhauer, Nietzsche, Croce, Santayana, Dewey, Bosanquet, Clive Bell, Roger Frye, Collingwood, Susanne Langer, the existentialists and the phenomenologists, but to re-experience them, as I hope to do, imaginatively, within the context of popular culture studies. (For a quick review, see *Masterpieces of World Philosophy,* edited by Frank N. Magill.)* Many of the great aestheticians do allude to the problem of the so-called lower degrees of art, and not always disdainfully. I want to call your attention to some of the major principles of the aesthetics of Santayana, Croce, Tolstoy, Bosanquet, and Dewey.

In *The Sense of Beauty* (1896), Santayana says that "nothing in principle can be ruled out as a possible object of beauty." Consider James M. Cain's *The Postman Always Rings Twice.* But not everything is equally beautiful. Consider Camus' *The Stranger* (which Camus claims to have modeled on *The Postman*). Our subjective biases (taste) discriminate degrees of beauty. "Our preferences are ultimately nonrational; things are good because they are preferred."/"Beauty is pleasure objectified; when a spectator regards his pleasure as a quality of the object he sees, he calls the object 'beautiful.' "/"Form pleases when in perception the excitation of the retinal field produces a semblance of motion while the mind synthesizes the elements perceived."/"The aesthetic component 'expression' is the result of the emotional associations excited by contemplation of the aesthetic object."

---

*Quotations that follow are from commentaries in *MWP*.

Tolstoy's *What Is Art?* appeared in the same year as Santayana's book. "Art is the intentional communication of feeling."/"The artist uses colors, sounds, words, or other material to create an object which will provoke in the spectator the feeling the artist himself once had and which he intends to pass on to others." (Art communicates an actual experience.) "True art is not only sincere, but infectious: the more widespread the appeal and effectiveness of the work as a means for communication of feeling, the better the work is as art." (Art and life are not separate, the aesthetic experience is not unique.) "The highest art is that which communicates the feeling of brotherhood and the love for one's neighbor."

Often, it is the more esoteric aesthetician who provides us with clues to the aesthetics of popular culture. Thus, Tolstoy is for me less suggestive than Croce, who said we must "treat works of art not in relation to social history but as each a world in itself, into which from time to time the whole of history is concentrated, transfigured and imaginatively transcended in the individuality of the poetic work, which is a creation, not a reflection, a monument, not a document."

Croce's great work is *Aesthetic* (1901). "Art is intuition and intuition is the expression of impressions."/"A sense impression or image becomes an expression, or intuition, when it is clearly known as an image, and when it is unified by the feeling it represents." (Croce replaces the concept of beauty with expression.) "What gives coherence and unity to the intuition," says Croce, "is feeling," not ideas. Out of pure intuition the artist produces an image that is expressive of feeling. "For Croce intuitive knowledge is the possession of images, but of images clarified by the attention of the spirit, freed of all vagueness in the act of apprehension." Pure lyrical intuition is a work of art, consisting of a "complex of images and a feeling that animates them."/"All true intuition is art." This concept does not exclude popular art. *Only* intuitions are works of art; physical objects are not. Thus, for popular art, we do not concentrate only upon the produced object but the intuitions that occur in the maker and the consumer's spirit. "Works of art exist only in the intuitions that create or recreate them."/"Intuitions are of individuals, not universals."/"The externalization of works of art by the fashioning of physical objects which will serve as stimuli in the reproduction of the intuitions represented is not art."/"Art is not concerned with the useful, the moral, or the intellectual."/"The fanciful combining of images is not art." Art is neither history, nor philosophy, nor natural science, nor the mere play of the imagination, nor feeling in its immediacy, nor instruction, nor rhetoric, nor morality, says Croce. He cautions us not to mistake the intellectual for the artistic, the concept for the intuition. "The theoretical activity of the spirit has two forms: the aesthetic and the logical: the practical activity is composed of the economic and the moral."/"Knowledge has two forms . . . it is productive of either images or concepts."/"The aesthetic values are the beautiful (the expressive) and the ugly: the logical values are the true and the false: the economic values are the useless and the useful: and the moral values are the just and the unjust." The science of art, says Croce, "is the perpetual systematization, always renewed and always growing, of the problems arising from time to time out of reflection upon art.''

Bernard Bosanquet is an English philosopher about whom we seldom hear —the way we hear about Croce and Dewey—but we would do well to rediscover and to study his *Three Lectures on Aesthetics* (1915) closely. "Aesthetic experience is distinguishable from other experience in that it is pleasant, stable, relevant, and common."/"The aesthetic experience is contemplative, not practical; it is organizational, and both personal and general."/"The aesthetic response is a response to form and substance in an appearance, requiring the imagination, and resulting in the pleasant awareness of a feeling embodied in the appearance." Bosanquet stresses the importance of the imagination, which is the mind considering possibilities (similar to Croce's "intuition"?). "The most satisfying aesthetic experience is realized when the artist forms his work in harmony with the character of his medium." Bosanquet was intrigued by the demands of the individual medium. "The properties of the medium lead the artist to do certain things that another medium would not lead him to do." Obviously, this notion applies even more to popular culture's many media than to high culture's. "In its proper sense, beauty is what is common to artistic products insofar as they are excellent; beauty may be easy or difficult; difficult beauty is characterized by intricacy, tension, and width—that is, it is complex, provokes heightened feeling, and demands breadth of interest." Bosanquet argued that easy beauty that is pleasing to everyone—to a wide community—is not to be denigrated; "it can be beauty of the highest type." A single work of art may be difficult to the person with a wide range of interest and easy to the ordinary person. "The aesthetic experience is a response to what is there, to what the object is in itself, and not to some relation the object has to other things or other people." Has Susan Sontag been reading Bosanquet?

John Dewey, reviewing Bosanquet's *History of Aesthetics,* observed: "The entire conception . . . of a fixed distinction between the realm of art and that of commonplace reality seems to me to need a good deal of explanation." To understand the aesthetic, Dewey said, on another occasion, "one must begin with it in the raw." Dewey's *Art as Experience* (1934) synthesizes the best insights of Santayana, Tolstoy, Croce, Bosanquet, and gives them new emphases within the context of Dewey's own revolutionary ideas. The work as a whole is a primer of popular culture aesthetics that not only preserves the most relevant of high art aesthetics but reactivates it in a realm of richer possibilities. "Aesthetic theory should explain how works of art come into existence and how they are enjoyed in experience. How is it that something produced to fulfill a need becomes in addition a source of aesthetic enjoyment? How is it that ordinary activities can yield a particular kind of satisfaction that is aesthetic?" To Dewey, "the most vital arts are popular music, comic strips, newspaper accounts of crime and love, articles on the intimate doings of popular entertainers," and everyday, ordinary activities themselves. Vital art is connected with the actual processes of living. "Any experience that combines memory of the past with anticipation of the future, and is an achievement of the organism in the environment in which it functions, is an aesthetic experience."/

"Art is to be understood as an experience made possible by the organizing and unifying process in which the artist engages; the spectator meets the interest of the artist with an interest of his own in the reciprocal process of going through a similar operation."/"Art supplies mediums of communication, making community of experience possible." Art is an experience of everyday life—the aesthetics of the moment.

To review this review: Santayana: "Beauty = pleasure objectified."/ Tolstoy: "Art = human communication."/Croce: "Intuition = expression" (a charged image in the mind)./Bosanquet: "The aesthetic experience = a feeling of pleasure that is rechargeable, self-sufficient, and common."/Dewey: "Art = an individual experience" (which is the interaction between organism and environment).

Each of these principles can be employed in formulating a popular art aesthetics. How are these principles to be adapted to the different nature of popular art? The popular aesthetic experience, a study of traditional aesthetic theories will reveal, is neither worse than nor the same as the high art aesthetic experience—it is simply different, but not entirely.

We can learn a great deal also from outright enemies of popular culture studies and from high art aestheticians who embark upon slumming expeditions, such as Abraham Kaplan. His essay "The Aesthetics of the Popular Arts" (*Journal of Aesthetics*, 1964) should be required reading for all students of popular culture, especially of its aesthetics. By popular art, he doesn't mean pop art, or camp, or bad art, or merely minor art, but "midbrow" art. "Aesthetics is so largely occupied with the good in art that it has little to say about what is merely better or worse, and especially about what is worse. . . . The priest must become learned in sin. Artistic tastes and understanding might better be served by a museum of horribilia, presented as such. It is from this standpoint that I invite attention to the aesthetics of the popular arts." The context for everything that follows is Kaplan's negative attitude implied in that beginning.

But ponder imaginatively his assertions to see whether they cannot be adapted, not just turned upside down, but *adapted* to make more positive statements about the popular art experience: "My thesis is this: that popular art is not the degradation of taste but its immaturity." (Popular culture can study taste more effectively and with more relevance than high culture can.) "Popular art is never a discovery, only a reaffirmation."/"What popular art schematizes it also abstracts from a fully aesthetic context. . . . Popular art uses formulas, not for analysis but for the experience itself." (Cawelti has given us a workable approach to formula as part of a popular art aesthetic.) "Popular art is doubly derivative: art first becomes academic and then it becomes popular."/"What is unaesthetic about popular art is its formlessness. It does not invite or even permit the sustained effort necessary to the creation of an artistic form. But it provides us with an illusion of achievement while in fact we remain passive."/"Aesthetic perception is replaced by mere recognition."/ "On the psychodynamic level, the aesthetic response is replaced by a mere reaction." (Well, let's formulate an aesthetics of reaction.) "In the taste for popular art there is a marked intolerance of ambiguity." (Popular art creates ambiguity among works in a particular area rather than within a single work.) "Popular art is simple basically in the sense of easy."/"Popular art, far from countering boredom, perpetuates and intensifies it." (Lock me in a room with yet another anti-hero novel and I'll show you how to perpetuate boredom.) "The skill of the artist is not in providing an experience but in providing occasions for reliving one." (Is that what is meant by entertainment? We need to articulate an aesthetics of entertainment—as it also, sometimes, involves elements of instruction.) "Popular art easily becomes dated, as society changes its conventional associations." (Some of it, but not all; just as Bulwer-Lytton *et al*; became dated, but not Dickens.) "Popular art wallows in emotion while art transcends it, giving us understanding and thereby mastery of our feelings as it finds them, formless and immature," and sentimental./"Popular art seeks to escape ugliness, not to transform it."/"Popular art depicts the world, not as it is, nor even as it might be, but as we would have it." (This gets us into the importance of accounting, in our formulations, for the popular artist's assumptions about his audience.) "The self-centeredness of popular art is the measure of our own diminishing."/"There is a time and place even for popular art," Kaplan concludes. He too, we suspect, enjoys the pleasant dreams of popular culture, but can only be grateful when he has awakened.

"Aesthetics of the Popular Arts" is an ironic title, for Kaplan shows, to his own satisfaction, that the popular culture *reaction* is everything the aesthetic *response* is not. Kaplan's half-assed defense, then, turns out to be a full-scale attack, with a reluctant admission that the popular arts deserve study, for non-aesthetic reasons, I suspect. But close examination of his assertions reveals more positive insights into the way a genuine popular aesthetic experience occurs. Kaplan's brilliant attack is the single most effective essay we have to account for in our own aesthetics. None of us has come up with a positive statement of aesthetics as persuasive and well-articulated as his attack.

It is probably in John Dewey's pragmatic analysis of the aesthetic experience that we will find the most powerful refutation of or means of adapting the criticisms of Kaplan and other critics of popular culture. Reading Kaplan and Dewey side by side, we may see the positive face of Kaplan's negative judgments.

Among recent books the one that comes nearest to dealing with Kaplan is Alan Gowans' very well-argued *The Unchanging Art: New Forms for the Traditional Functions of Art in Society* (1971). "To know what art is, you must define what it *does*. You can define art only in terms of function. High art historically grew out of low art, and the functions of low art have remained unchanged throughout history." Although Gowans emphasizes the social and practical functions of art, his book is very suggestive about the nature of popular culture aesthetics.

I may seem to be assuming that everyone who studies some aspect of popular culture is constrained to speak well of it; not at all. From the beginning, simultaneous acceptance and rejection of popular culture has been the double vision of popular culture studies. But effective attack or defense or mere explanation must start with some positive concepts about the subject, not Kaplan's negative prescriptions.

III

Popular culture aesthetics can in turn help to illuminate high art aesthetics. "Bosanquet contends that the aesthetic experience can best be understood by considering simple rather than complex examples." Popular art provides occasions for studying some of the traditional concepts of aesthetics in purer form. In the past few decades, high art has been overwhelmed by non-aesthetic demands on it—psychological, then sociological, now political; a set of extrinsic concerns different from those in popular art has commanded our attention. Perhaps in contemplating a popular culture work which can have no overtly serious "expressive" or secondary associations, we experience the pure whatness of it and can come closer to aesthetic pleasure than we do in serious works— which we approach with expectations of receiving a rich cluster of secondary values: themes, ideas, symbols, etc. Perhaps popular art comes closer than high art to art for art's sake.

What my students and I discovered is that serious and popular novels employ most of the same artistic elements, techniques, devices, and contain many of the same social messages, though with contrasting degrees of complexity and for very different ends. Of course, some elements are experienced only in one and not in the other. But comparisons help to illuminate what makes each a good example of popular culture or high culture fiction.

To test the validity of what I've just said, I went to two of my own books and compared my chapter on Wright Morris' craft with my chapter on James M. Cain's craft and discovered that indeed I had used almost exactly the same aesthetic concepts in discussing the one as I had the other. A few concepts applied only to one and not the other. And each, as individual artists, forced me to create new terms for what each had uniquely done. Morris remains a master high culture writer; Cain a master popular novelist. Elements of high culture are found in the works of Cain, elements of popular culture in the works of Morris. But no blurring of the lines occurs.

Compare Morris' first person description in *Love Among the Cannibals* of the girl called the Greek when Horter the songwriter first sees her in Hollywood with Cain's first-person description in *Serenade* of the Mexican girl when opera singer Sharp first sees her in Mexico. Neither can be fully experienced without a receptivity to both popular culture and high culture aesthetics.

So it's relevant to look at Cain's plots mechanically—in terms of openings, scene building, endings, and general length. In the opening of *The Postman,* so much happens so fast, the reader either immediately rejects what happens or willingly suspends his disbelief and finer instincts and submits to Cain's will. And no bossier, more willful author ever wrote.

Cain's imagination does not process in terms of a conception and thus transform his raw material, as Wright Morris' does; rather, with basic fictional techniques, he expertly manipulates and controls all the elements for calculated effects. So we speak of Cain's inventive powers, his structuring mind—a mind aware of itself and of the reader's mind—rather than the shaping imagination we know in Morris' work.

The Postman Always Rings Twice is neither serious nor popular; it is pure entertainment, an experience in which strong distinctions between one sort of reader and another seem superfluous. My study of Morris's aesthetics made me receptive to Cain's, and as I analyzed Cain's, I came to understand Morris's better. A carefully articulated and soundly based popular aesthetics may well force a revision of high culture aesthetics.

The aesthetic attitude of high culture is effort, of popular culture is receptivity. "The aesthetic attitude is the first requirement for the experience of aesthetic pleasure, and sometimes seemed," says Langer, "even to be the active source of it." This emphasis on attitude describes perfectly the way most people approach a work of popular art. If, when we approach *The Postman,* we lack an aesthetic attitude, we will not experience the novel's aesthetic qualities consciously.

I trust the power of intuition enough to imagine that young students of popular culture who may be ignorant of high art aesthetics of the past are still, in their undisciplined immersion, receptive enough to intuit and imagine concepts that embody, unaware, the major principles of classic aestheticians. Brian Lindsay's "Joe: The Aesthetics of the Obvious" (*JPC*, Spring, 1971) describes and advocates an "experience-oriented criticism," echoing John Dewey, perhaps unaware, and the substitution of "affective perceptions for cognitive perceptions," as a basis for criticism of films. "Impact" becomes a value in determining significance in a film. The "aesthetics of the obvious" is an apt phrase for this approach.

But, somewhere, some one will put us all in her debt, if she is willing to go back to the origins of aesthetics and reassess and repossess and assimilate.

Now it's time we stopped listening to people like me suggest one of several approaches to the task and past time for some of us to get to work on a flexible system of popular culture aesthetics.

Author of many scholarly and creative books, David Madden is Writer in Residence at Louisiana State University.

Against Evaluation: The Role of the Critic of Popular Culture
Roger B. Rollin

Originally published in the *Journal of Popular Culture*, vol. 9, 1975 pp 355/3-365/13.

AGAINST EVALUATION:
THE ROLE OF THE CRITIC OF
POPULAR CULTURE

By Roger B. Rollin

To evaluate is human, to explicate, divine.

The epigraph is *ersatz*, of course, but it will serve to introduce the argument of this essay: that some of Popular Culture's leading authorities, among them John Cawelti, Leslie Fiedler, and David Madden, have inadvertently proposed what is in effect an impossible mission—to devise an aesthetics of Popular Culture which will incorporate a value-theory. Furthermore, they have suggested that not to accept this "mission" must result in the impeding of the growth and development of Popular Culture study.

The most recent to go on record with this view has been David Madden. In "The Necessity for an Aesthetics of Popular Culture,"[1] he makes it clear that serious students of the Popular Arts have a duty to engage, not only in formulation, but in evaluation as well. He refers approvingly (p. 9) to the English philosopher Bosanquet, who is concerned with the "beauty" and "excellence" of aesthetic objects. Madden also refers to Professor Cawelti (pp. 6-7), whose "Notes toward an Aesthetic of Popular Culture" asserts the necessity of developing "a basic core of assumptions about the *nature and value* of artistic work."[2] Admittedly, neither Cawelti nor Madden centers his discussion upon the question of evaluation: their primary concerns are the obviously essential ones of categorizing the intrinsic and extrinsic qualities of Popular Art and suggesting how these are to be explicated by the critic. Yet Madden also claims that we *"must* decide whether Popular Culture works can be termed *beautiful"* (p. 7, italics added). And from both his essay and Cawelti's it can be inferred that their shared conception of the duties and functions of the critic of Popular Art is not so very different from that conception of the duties and functions of the critic of Elite Art that has dominated Western aesthetics for over two thousand years. Yvor Winters has characterized this traditional view with admirable bluntness: "The primary function for criticism is evaluation, and . . . unless criticism succeeds in providing a useful system of evaluation it is worth very little."[3]

No less respected a figure of Elite Art's critical establishment, David Daiches, is similarly direct:

Although literary criticism has acquired many functions in the course of its long history, the function most often demanded of it . . . is judgment, discrimination, the placing of a given work in a scale of values.[4]

And Daiches, of course, believes it to be proper for critics to accede to such demands.

Criticism, like politics, can make for strange bedfellows. Two more radically different scholarly types than David Daiches and Leslie Fiedler are not to be imagined, yet in his remarks at the Popular Culture Association's 1973 meeting (the panel on "Aesthetics and Popular Culture"), Fiedler, like Daiches, seemed to commit himself to the necessity of evaluation, and later defended his stand with the somewhat cryptic observation that evaluation was necessary because it is such a "human" process. At the risk of misconstruing Professor Fiedler, let us consider what might lie behind his assertion.

Evaluation is indeed human, as this essay's epigraph has suggested. Indeed, few encounters in this life, whether they be with other persons or with objects, do not involve evaluation in some form. Certainly encounters with aesthetic objects, Elite or Popular, are no exceptions to this rule. It needs no B. F. Skinner to tell us that stimulus evokes response and that aesthetic objects are *created* to be stimuli. Nor is there any novelty in the notion that a necessary component of the aesthetic response is emotional, or that emotion, however vaguely, will be positive, negative, or mixed.

In truth, it is *impossible* to have *no* emotive reaction to an aesthetic stimulus. Directions on an aspirin bottle can perhaps evoke a neutral or emotion-free response, but a mere television commercial about aspirin, complete with doctor-like actor urging that "Bayer is better," cannot leave the viewer unaffected: even indifference is the next thing to a clearly negative response, for it entails a rejection of the work's basic intentions.

The evaluation of aesthetic objects then is inevitable. *And because it is inevitable it is unnecessary*—unnecessary at least for the serious critic of Popular Culture, and unnecessary to the construction of a critical theory for Popular Culture. *I Love Lucy* will enchant one viewer, merely pass the time for another, and cause a third to experience acute discomfort in his alimentary system, and no theory is likely to alter these patterns of effect significantly.

One qualification, however. I make a distinction here between the scholar-critic of Popular Culture and the commissioned reviewer. *The New York Times's* "Cyclops," Pauline Kael, and the local newspaper's critic of popular fiction undoubtedly have an obligation to accede to the public's reasonable demand that they, the fraternity of channel-switchers, purchasers of movie tickets, and book-buyers, receive some guidance so as to minimize the wastage of their time, money, and energy. But no serious student of Popular Culture can lose time, money, or energy by tuning in on *Rhoda*, paying to see *Jaws*, or skimming through Harold Robbins's latest opus. Because for such students these activities are called "research," and whether they entail pleasure or pain is immaterial. Nor is the *argumentum ad academium* relevant here—the argument that since many of these scholar-critics are teachers or would-be teachers of Popular Culture, they need some standard of Popular Culture values in order to be able to design courses or structure curricula. Questions of aesthetic value are irrelevant to such practical matters. (For a defense of this stand, see Appendix.)

The only possible functions of the teacher and serious student of Popular Culture are *description* and *interpretation*—"illumination," in short. Description, because the field of Popular Culture is so vast and so varied that even its most assiduous students are bound to have *lacunae*. Interpretation, because explaining the dynamics of a work of Popular Culture and of audience-response to that work can reveal that which is lost upon the casual viewer: what happens at the interface between a work's aesthetic form and the desires and anxieties of its audience, and also what extrapolations can be made from that interaction with regard to the society of which the audience is a part.

In rendering this important service to scholarship, (and possibly to society), the scholar-critic's evaluation of the work has no necessary part. The only evaluation which counts is the strictly quantitative one: how large a proportion of the work's potential audience responded to it positively. Did it receive a respectable Nielsen rating? Did *Variety* rate it a box-office success? Did it appear on the best-seller list?

For the only real authority concerning the "beauty" or "excellence" of a work of Popular Culture is the people. "Taste," formal training, teaching experience, publications—all factors which might be construed as validating the "authority" of a critic of Elite Culture—stand for naught when it comes to his or anyone else's evaluation of the "quality" of a Popular Culture work. For, in Popular Culture, the rule is "one person—one vote." However regrettable this may appear to professional students, it is a fact of the discipline. Unless Mr. Nielsen polls me, whether I adore *All in the Family* or detest it is irrelevant. As David Madden has pointed out, works of Popular Art are not primarily produced for the readers of *The Journal of Popular Culture*. For better or for worse (and I am not all that certain it is for worse), Popular Art represents the triumph of a democratic aesthetic—or what is probably the nearest approximation of a democratic aesthetic that is possible within the present capitalistic system.

But there is an equally compelling reason for putting aside the question of "artistic merit" when we set about formulating a unified field theory of Popular Culture aesthetics. Simply stated, it is the truth—which is increasingly, if reluctantly, becoming recognized as a truth—that it is *impossible* to erect a self-consistent, viable set of aesthetic values. Even among scholars of Elite Literature there is a growing awareness that the house of literary criticism, insofar as it is grounded upon evaluation, is a house built upon sand. Those who may doubt that the situation is so desperate should consult an essay entitled "Evaluation and English Studies," by John Fraser.[5] Professor Fraser appears nervous, and his nervousness is understandable. Beginning with his admission that "the idea not only of evaluative criticism but of evaluation itself is under something of a professional cloud" (p. 2), and with the recognition that this cloud has cast its gloomy pall over English scholarship and teaching, Fraser sets for himself the task of renewing the profession's confidence that it is "eminently reasonable *to be paid for specializing in what interests us* and communicating our findings to others . . ." (p. 3, italics added). Yet for all his essay's stout defense of the study of literature as an academic discipline, it does nothing to *demonstrate* the existence of a coherent set of standards of literary value. Indeed, that essay becomes (by omission) an inadvertant argument *against* evaluation. More direct, if no more successful defenses of evaluation are to be found in a book of which Professor Fraser seems to have been unaware, *Problems of Literary Evaluation.*[6]

The traditionalist view of literary evaluation is best represented in this collection by David Daiches' essay (cited above). Rejecting both evaluative absolutism and evaluative relativism, Daiches expends eighteen torturous pages begging the question. Try as he might, he cannot avoid merely asserting what he is attempting to prove, that a hierarchy of literary values exists—except that no one, including Daiches himself, can say where it exists, what it consists of, or how it is to be applied.

Lest it be imagined that professional philosophers are further along in this inquiry, Matthew Lipman offers a corrective:

We seem poised on the threshold of an infinite regress, and it is not surprising that skeptics, relativists, positivists and others have joined forces to cast doubt upon both the possibility and the necessity for the evaluation of works of art.[7]

Professor Daiches' problem, and the problem of all who quest for the one true hierarchy of literary values, can be seen in the broadest historical sense as arising out of the thinking of individuals like Darwin, Freud, Einstein, and A. J. Ayer. Relativism, whether it be among cultures or among psychological, physical, or semantic phenomena, is the main issue. Of primary concern to this paper are psychological and semantic relativism. The problem of semantic relativism is so well summarized by Stephen C. Pepper that it merits quoting at some length:

Recently, due largely to the influence in English-speaking countries of the emotive judgment theory of value supported by the linguistic analytical school of Philosophy, a skeptical view of standards has been in the ascendency. It stemmed originally from G. E. Moore's presentation of the "naturalistic fallacy" in ethics which applied to values generally including the aesthetic. Briefly it stated that "good" could not be identified with pleasure or any other "natural character," for the reason that it always made sense to ask after any such identification whether pleasure was "good." Consequently, Moore argued that "good" could not mean just pleasure or any other substituted character. He argued further that "good" must mean an abstract (sort of Platonic) entity known by an "intellectual intuition." A. J. Ayer, coming after Moore, rejected this last conclusion. He questioned the existence of any such abstract entity or of any peculiar intellectual faculty to intuit it. But he was still impressed with Moore's linguistic argument for the "naturalistic fallacy" and suggested that the reason "good" could not be identified with any natural character was that it did not refer to anything knowable at all. It was simply a term referring to emotional attitudes of approval. And "bad" was reciprocally a term for expressing disapproval. It followed that sentences including "good" and "bad" and their equivalents as grammatical predicates

. . . are not declarative statements of fact . . . but are expressions of emotive attitudes which are neither true nor false nor probable. . . . From this approach it follows that there can be no cognitively justifiable moral or aesthetic standards. . . . This is the most skeptical theory of value ever propounded. For the gist of the argument is that, basically, values are not open to cognitive control in terms of evidence for the truth or falsity of statements expressing them.[8]

A similar skepticism pervades an essay by Northrop Frye, "Contexts of Literary Evaluation,"[9] except that the thrust of his argument is sociological and psychological. "Taste," Frye explains, is the result of acculturation:

The sense of value develops out of the struggle with one's cultural environment, and consists largely of acquiring an instinct for the different conventions of verbal expression. All verbal expression is conventionalized, but we quickly realize that some conventions are more acceptable to our social group than are others. In some societies . . . the different conventions were limited to different social classes, and high and low speech were at least symbolic of the conventions of lord and peasant respectively. Today we still have, despite the linguists, distinctions between standard and substandard speech, and a corresponding distinction, though one quite different in its application, between standard and substandard writing. The critic who fights his way through to some kind of intuitive feeling for what literary conventions are accepted in his society becomes a representative of the good taste of his age. Thus value judgments carry with them, as part of their penumbra, so to speak, a sense of social acceptance.[10]

In the covertly Freudian language that is so characteristic of him, Frye has defined "Taste" as the product of id-ego-superego-external reality interaction, a definition which common experience and Popular Culture history must both validate.

A hypothetical example: an imaginative, aesthetically-oriented child seeks gratification in fictions—any fictions, for initially at least he is indiscriminant. But he finds that superhero comics, which give him so much pleasure, do not win the approval of those whose approval he naturally seeks, such as his parents and teachers. But the tales of Beatrix Potter do. If the child's ego is sufficiently adaptive, he will enjoy his superhero comics in secret, thus gratifying his id and giving him pleasure (if also some guilt) in the process. And he will read (and possibly enjoy) Beatrix Potter in public, thus meeting the demands of his superego. Eventually, grown up to become a well-adjusted college professor (if that is not oxymoronic), that same individual will voice his admiration for Bergman's *Cries and Whispers* at the Dean's cocktail party, but will conceal—perhaps even from himself—the delectation he derived from his out-of-town viewing of *Deep Throat*. Or he will acknowledge his enjoyment of *Deep Throat* or *All in the Family* or Ross MacDonald's latest Lew Archer—whatever current popular works the intellectual establishment has come to allow its members to enjoy without guilt. For our professor's likes and dislikes are not so much an index of the "intrinsic" merits of the works in question as they are a Rorschach of his psychosocial self. As Frye has noted: "When a critic interprets, he is talking about [the artist]; when he evaluates he is talking about himself, or, at most, about himself as a representative of his age" (p. 16). By traditional aesthetic standards, *Cries and Whispers* is an "art" movie—not only "good" but "important." But by

The Test of Time, that flanking movement of the defenders of hierarchical standards, *Deep Throat* (conceivably) might prove to be *more* "important" than *Cries and Whispers* in film history, and possibly even a "better" film in some future aesthetics of the cinema. Mindful of Shakespeare and Dickens, Frye has said:

Every age, left to itself, is incredibly narrow in its cultural range, and the critic, unless he is a greater genius than the world has yet seen, shares that narrowness in proportion to his confidence in his taste (p. 16).

The constant defensiveness of Popular Culture scholarship is not only its most tedious characteristic, but also proof of the correctness of Frye's observations. Trained almost to a man in the conventional aesthetics of the twentieth century, Popular Culturists defend their rebellion against authority by calling for a "new" hierarchy of values to be integrated into the projected Popular Culture aesthetic, even though they have little notion of what shape that aesthetic might assume. That it will be some version of the *auteur* theory—*pace* Professor Cawelti—seems unlikely at best.[11] How practical is it, after all, to try to judge creators of Popular Art by comparing them with themselves? Who could possibly care whether *I, the Jury* is "better" or "worse" than *My Gun Is Quick*? Certainly not Spillane fans, who will read both novels anyway and who care not a whit whether the Popular Culture Association believes they should prefer one to the other. And what validates the *auteur* theory as a method of evaluation of Popular Culture works when most of them have been created by committees—and committees whose memberships are constantly changing, at that?

Neither an *auteur* aesthetic nor any other aesthetic incorporating a system of values will automatically endow Popular Culture study with "legitimacy," with the dignity and respectability so fervently desired by some scholars. Indeed, to attempt to formalize a Popular Culture Standard of Taste will result in entrapment in the same philosophical error that has bedeviled traditional literary scholarship and criticism. Elite Literature has always been to an extent beleaguered and will continue to be so as long as some of its makers (but more of its critics) still insist that it be evaluated and even ranked—but only by that "fit audience though few" who possess Good Taste. And those millions of readers and would-be readers who have in one way or another gotten the message that they lack such taste become resentful and suspicious—and justifiably so. If Popular Culture must make a case for itself that case has to be made—not on the supposed intrinsic aesthetic merits of its subject matter—but upon that subject matter's demonstrable interest and importance. After all, any aesthetic object of the past or present, "good" or "bad," can become what Frye calls "a source of imaginative illumination" (p. 17). How any one individual *feels* about that object is *another* source of *another* kind of illumination. As Professor Frye puts it,

the experience of literature is not criticism, just as religious experience is not theology. . . . In the experience of literature a great many things are felt and can be said, which have no functional role to play in criticism. [Thus,] the attempt to make criticism either begin or end in value judgments turns the subject wrong side out. . . . The value sense is, as the phenomenological people say, pre-predictive (p. 18).

Norman N. Holland seems to have been the first to demonstrate as much. His clinical-type experiments at the Center for the Psychological Study of the Arts (the State University of New York at Buffalo) have confirmed what every student of the arts' experience is likely to suggest—that whether or not an aesthetic object will please cannot be accurately predicted, even though an individual's "tastes" are known, even if (as in the case of Holland's subjects) the individual's psychological "profile" or "identity theme" is known.[12] (I refer here only to an individual's private, "sincere" response, which can of course be different from his public response—in class, in print, etc.—for that public response can, as Frye has indicated, be to varying degrees conditioned without the individual being aware of it.)

How do we evaluate aesthetic objects? All of Holland's investigations lead him to this conclusion: *"we will enjoy and value those literary works from which we can achieve an exciting balance of fantasy and management of fantasy"* (p. 298). Thus my own evaluation of *The Sting*, for example, is based, not primarily upon my conscious, rational, objective, trained analysis of such elements as its script, direction, acting, camerawork, etc., for I will likely be able to find merits in such elements if I enjoyed the movie, defects in them if I did not. Rather, my evaluation will mainly depend upon: (1) the extent to which *The Sting* offered aesthetic materials out of which my mind was able to "shape" a largely unconscious fantasy, thereby "involving" me in the movie; (2) the extent to which my ego was able to cope with, "manage" that fantasy, preventing me from feeling either so threatened or so uninvolved that I walked out of the theatre.

Holland's theoretical model of the complex psychological process which results in such effects is itself complex, but can be generally described as follows:

A reader responds to a literary work by assimilating it to his own psychological processes, that is, to his search for successful solutions within his identity theme to the multiple demands, both inner and outer, on his ego (p. 128).

If I enjoyed *The Sting* and evaluated it as "good"—which is usually, but not always, the same thing, for the ego of the trained critic, especially, can "split" itself—according to Holland at least four processes have been simultaneously involved. 1. I have been able to put the elements of the movie together so that they act out at any given moment my hopes with regard to the work as a whole (p. 114)—for example, my desire to have the heroes get away with their scheme. 2. The movie provides me with materials to create a wish-fulfillment fantasy that is characteristic of my personality (pp. 117-21), for example, my tendency to imagine myself to be a handsome, debonair, rogue-hero. 3. I have been able to synthesize from the movie my characteristic strategies of psychological defense or adaptation (pp. 115-17); for example, the movie afforded me sufficient materials to enable me to "defend against" the anxiety I feel (will Robert Redford escape the assassin?) in the ways that I customarily handle anxiety (ranging from outright repression to my scholar's expectation that *The Sting* is a comic romance). 4. I have been able to "make sense" of the movie, have been able to render the fantasy I have synthesized into some intellectual content that is characteristic of—and pleasing to—me (pp. 121-22), for example, that the very powerful can be brought low by the less powerful.

Thus what my statement that *"The Sting* is a good movie" really means is (to paraphrase Holland, p. 125) this: "My ego was able to use the movie to build from my own unconscious drives through my own patterns of adaptation and defense toward a conscious significance and unity that mattered to me." The fact that this mental process has been replicated by millions of movie goers now improves the odds on predicting whether Jane Doe will evaluate *The Sting* as a "good" movie, but at the time of its release the odds would have been much longer, even were we in possession of Jane's identity theme and had tried to match it up with a psychoanalytical analysis of the depth structure of the Newman-Redford film. Movies *are* in a sense ink blots, but some repressed trauma concerning the era in which *The Sting* is set—or even an over-heated theatre—could alter the response she makes. Thus, even the highly formulaic nature of most Popular Culture works cannot be of much help in predicting how any one individual or even a mass audience will evaluate a movie, television program, or popular novel. What is more important, however, is that by recognizing how aesthetic evaluations arise—out of idiosyncratic unconscious processes at one extreme, out of cultural conditioning at the other extreme—theorists will be given pause when they contemplate attempting to construct standards of aesthetic value for Popular Culture. Not only does the best evidence suggest that such an attempt is philosophically unsound and scientifically ill-founded, but of all people students of Popular Culture should be aware of the ways in which standards of aesthetic value can be transformed into moral imperatives which are then employed to celebrate some human beings and oppress others.

"The attempt of genuine criticism," in Professor Frye's words, "is to bring literature to 'life' by annihilating stock responses, which of course are always value judgments, and which regularly confuse literature with life" (p. 20). Frye's concern here is with Elite Literature but the goal he sets is no less valid for Popular Culture criticism. Serious students of Popular Culture, those who write for other serious students, fulfill their high-minded and useful purpose when they penetrate the stock response to *The Waltons*, for example—as Anne Rolphe has done so well[13]—and describe that series accurately, analyze the psychological, mythic, religious, social, political, economic, and ethical components of its structure and texture, and interpret what the fact that America "likes" *The Waltons* tells us about the character of our society in the 1970s. Such information and insights cannot help but be valuable. Dr. Johnson said that "All truth is valuable . . . ,"[14] but although aestheticians may be loath to admit it, the quantifiable aspect of a truth does count for something. This is so whether it be the number of critics who have pronounced *Lycidas* to be a "great" poem versus the number of those who, like Dr. Johnson, regard Milton's pastoral elegy as a "bad" poem, or whether it is the millions of viewers who turned for solace to that American pastoral, *Bonanza*, every week for fourteen years, versus those comparatively few who watched whatever was being offered on competing networks.

It will be argued, as David Madden implicitly has argued, that social, political, psychological and other aspects of the mass audience's response to works of

Popular Art are not the proper concern of aesthetics, are not to be "considered part of the aesthetic experience."[15] But if the aesthetic experience is not deeply involved with the experiencer's id, ego, superego, and external reality, what is it involved with? As has been said above, the aesthetic experience will entail evaluation, but how is the *ranking* of aesthetic objects to be squared with a thorough understanding of the limitations of criticism as an intellectual activity? As Frye astutely observes, "the more consistently one conceives of criticism as the pursuit of values, the more firmly one becomes attached to that great sect of anti-intellectualism" (p. 20). Or as Professor Lipman has put it, "an eagerness to portray the population of works of art as made up of 'good works of art versus bad works of art' is rather akin to the infantile moralism that reduces the human population to a contrast between 'good guys' and 'bad guys.' "[16]

While my personal approval of *Paradise Lost* is not only "sincere" but public evidence of my "good taste," I have no way of knowing whether the students to whom I teach Milton or the Milton scholars for whom I write are equally well endowed. —Or even whether they can somehow acquire the faculty through exposure to my own "superior" taste. And if they do not or cannot, what does it matter? I can no more read *Paradise Lost* for them than I can force them to like it: all I can do is to try to illuminate Milton's poem for them.

Likewise, my positive response, for example, to *Deep Throat* and my negative response to *The Godfather* finally must say more about me than they do about the aesthetic merits of those two cinema landmarks. That, of the two, *Deep Throat* has more historical importance and *The Godfather* is more obscene, can, I think, be reasonably argued, although the place to do so is not here. Such issues an aesthetic of Popular Culture can confront, but such a confrontation will only result in confusion if the question of "intrinsic" aesthetic merit be introduced. For such questions constitute a trap in which the experience of literature becomes largely divorced from the experience of life. While we may grant that the experience of literature is not infrequently superior to that of life, the two are inextricably linked through the central nervous system, a physiological fact that the practice of criticism ignores at its peril.

Let there be no more judges then—at least among the scholar-critics of Popular Culture. To describe, analyze, and interpret a mass audience's judgment of a work can be a way of knowing one's society; to judge a work of Popular Art can only be a way of knowing oneself, which unlike true criticism is a personal rather than a public *desideratum*. As one of the most ancient communicators to a mass audience has put it: "Judge not lest ye be judged."[17]

NOTES

[1] *Journal of Popular Culture*, 7:1 (Summer 1973), 2.

[2] *Journal of Popular Culture*, 5:2 (Fall 1971), 255 (italics added).

[3] *The Function of Criticism* (Denver: Alan Swallow, 1957), p. 17.

[4] "Literary Evaluation," *Problems of Literary Evaluation*, ed. Joseph Strelka (University Park, Pennsylvania: Pennsylvania State University Press, 1969), 163.

[5] *College English*, 35 (October, 1973), 1-16.

[6] See fn. 4, above.

[7] *Contemporary Aesthetics*, ed. Matthew Lipman (Boston: Allyn and Bacon, 1973), p. 429.

[8]"The Justification of Aesthetic Judgments," *Problems of Literary Evaluation*, pp. 140-41. It should be noted that Professor Pepper rejects the skeptical view and in his essay goes to great lengths to attempt to refute it.

[9]*Problems of Literary Evaluation*, pp. 14-21.

[10]*Ibid.*, p. 15.

[11]"Notes toward an Aesthetic of Popular Culture," *Journal of Popular Culture*, 5:2 (Fall 1971), 255-68.

[12]*Five Readers Reading* (New Haven: Yale University Press, 1975). This work incorporates (with important modifications) ideas advanced by Professor Holland in his seminal study, *The Dynamics of Literary Response* (New York: Oxford University Press, 1968). See also his *Poems in Persons: An Introduction to the Psychoanalysis of Literature* (New York: W. W. Norton & Co., 1973).

[13]"The Waltons," *New York Times Magazine* (Nov. 18, 1973), 40ff.

[14]*The Critical Opinions of Samuel Johnson*, ed., Joseph Epes Brown (Princeton: The University Press, 1926), p. 253.

[15]"The Necessity for an Aesthetics of Popular Culture," *Journal of Popular Culture*, 7:1 (Summer, 1973), 4.

[16]*Contemporary Aesthetics* (Boston: Allyn & Bacon, 1973), p. 429.

[17]The original version of this paper was presented at the 1973 meeting of the Popular Culture Association (Milwaukee, Wisconsin).

APPENDIX: Popular Culture in the Schools

If, as academicians, we can convince insecure colleagues and suspicious deans that it is important to study a phenomenon which engages millions of our fellow citizens—including not only most of our students but most of those same colleagues and deans—then it should be easy enough to satisfy their queries as to the methodology for such a study with the simple answer, "historical." After all, the field of English study, for example, was for much of its little more than a century of existence primarily historical in its methodology. (In certain bastions of academic purity, of course, it still is.) Although Russel Nye and others have made a beginning, the historical study of Popular Culture remains a vast *terra icognita*, whose charting could occupy us permanently, given the expansion rate of contemporary Popular Culture.

But while there can be no easy separation between the critic and the historian of Popular Culture, it could be argued that to study the subject only from the historical point-of-view is in one sense an abdication of responsibility, an avoidance of the problem of Popular Culture aesthetics and the question of evaluation. And I would agree. My only point is that the heavy artillery of history can be employed to defend the study of Popular Culture against tradition-bound academic hostiles. For what it is worth, in my personal opinion any aspect of Popular Culture, like any aspect of history, of elite literature, of physics, can be worth serious study, though what will be worth studying may well be something different for the specialist and for the generalist. But only different, not more or less important. The evolution of the English form of government versus the character of the Rump Parliament, the nature of the Romantic Sensibility versus Keats' conception of the ode, the development of detective fiction versus the style of Ross MacDonald—the places of all these in curricula can be determined only by such extrinsic criteria as faculty expertise and availability, student interests, and technical resources.

To summarize: not all academicians are aware that "the Humanities" need no longer be restricted to the study of "the best that has been thought and said," and some of those academicians who are aware of this development continue, in spite of common sense, logic, and hard data, to resist it. But students of Popular Culture should resist being put in the position of justifying their interests and activities on grounds of aesthetic merit. Not only are those grounds now discovered to be a wonderland—they always have been. And even if it is presumed possible to make meaningful statements about aesthetic values, generic and other aesthetic considerations make plain the bankruptcy of drawing qualitative comparisons between, say, *Crime and Punishment* and *I, the Jury*. "Excellence" and "importance" have never been synonymous.

Roger Rollin recently accepted the position of William James Lemon Professor of Literature at Clemson where, as part of his duties, he is teaching the first course in Popular Culture ever offered at that university.

Indexes

Index to Contributions

Where it might prove helpful, contributions have been entered more than once under leading elements of their titles

BIBLIOGRAPHIES AND REFERENCE SERIES APPENDED TO, OR INCORPORATED WITHIN, CONTRIBUTIONS

Although a considerable number of names contained in footnotes have been indexed, it might be helpful to users of *Literary Taste, Culture and Mass Communication* if they had references to bibliographies, checklists, and reference series appended to, or incorporated within, contributions reprinted.

Listing bibliographies is straightforward but noting where series of references are to be found requires a word or two of explanation. Some contributions review the work done in a particular field. Sometimes the names of scholars only are given in the text, with a reference to their work in a footnote; sometimes there is only a footnote reference and no 'name-key' within the text. Thus, indexing by the name appearing in the text alone represents some articles better than others. The listing here of such systematic surveys (which are, in effect, annotated bibliographies) should enable this imbalance to be redressed. If it is thought that the user might find a reference useful to something which does not fall strictly within this description, it is also included.

The name of the relevant title is given first; this is followed by a description of the kind of list and then by the volume and page numbers.

Index to Names of Persons

This index is to some extent eclectic. It lists references to people mentioned in the texts of articles, whether creative writers, political or public figures, or scholars, ancient and modern. However, where little or no assistance would be given to the user (as in some passing references, names following a stated or implied "e.g.", and in summaries of names — e.g. 1/60, where a succession of thirty or so names is listed) references are not usually included. Authors' names in footnotes and bibliographies are not usually indexed, but those mentioned in Further Reading are. However, the guideline that certain classes should be excluded is not rigorously applied; where it might prove particularly helpful to the reader, names and references from such sources are taken in (as from 2/15-17).

The names of contributors to the series are followed by the title(s) of their contributions and thereafter by references to the contributors.

Crouzet, Francois   5/97
Croy, Homer   10/139
Cuber, John F.   1/145
Cudlipp, Hugh   9/116—17, 128
Culler, Jonathan   7/xii
Culver, Donald *Scrutiny*: a Manifesto
   (with L.C. Knights)   13/63—70
Cunningham, Adrian   13/232—34
Curel, François de   3/36—39, 41, 63
Curran, James   7/xiii; 8/xvii—xviii
Curtis, A.   2/77

Dahrendorf, Ralf   6/9, 17, 19—20
Daiches, David   5/xvii; 6/xvii; 14/212
   214
Dale, Edgar   1/146—47; 6/110; 7/27
Dallas, Karl   8/xviii
Dalrymple, Ian   12/xiii
Dalziel, Margaret   2/284; 10/62; 14/27
Damrosch, Walter   9/277
Daniels, Les   7/xv
Daninos, Pierre   12/239
Dante, Alighieri   11/238, 244; 14/92,
   115
Darwin, Charles   1/95; 6/60; 8/19;
   9/17; 10/164; 12/98; 14/4, 21
Daudet, Alphonse   10/65
Daugherty, William E.   2/13
Daumier, Honoré   12/24
Davenport, Marcia   10/360
David, Jacques-Louis   3/13—14, 25
David, Peter   6/xv
Davidson, Carl   13/247
Davie, Donald   5/ix—x, 84; 10/xiii
Davies, Rev. J. Llewelyn   3/97—98, 204
Davies, W.M.   10/250, 379
Davis, Blevins   9/277
Davis, Clyde Brion   10/361
Davis, H.L.   10/360
Davison, Peter: Afterword to *Songs of the
   British Music Hall*   8/185—95; A
   A Briton True? A Short Account of
   Patriotic Songs and Verse as Popular
   Entertainment   8/263—79; and see
   Introductions: Further Reading;
   8/xii, xvii
Dawson, Christopher   4/225—26;
   13/234
Dawson, Cleo   10/363
Dearmer, Percy   10/376
Deeping, Warwick   10/138
Defoe, Daniel   8/22
Degas, Edgar   12/26
Delmar, Viña   10/138
Deming, Barbara   10/337, 345
Denis, Maurice   4/270
Denney, Reuel   1/143—44

Descartes, René   8/236
Deutscher, Isaac   13/249
Devereux, Edward C.   9/81, 87
Dewey, John   1/30; 9/227; 12/x, xiii,
   8, 17; 14/6, 199, 203, 205, 207
Dibdin, Jr., Charles   8/viii
Dickens, Charles   1/9, 10, 16, 67; 5/222,
   238; 7/5, 98, 101, 113, 129—31, 247,
   338; 8/viii—ix, 108, 124, 189; 10/67,
   74, 205, 213, 368, 380; 11/233, 267;
   12/60, 62, 119; 13/98; 14/205, 216
Dickinson, Emily   10/137
Dickinson, Lowes   11/82—83
Diderot, Denis   12/225, 233
Dilke, Sir Charles   8/194, 266
Dilthey, Wilhelm   14/62, 73, 155
Dimitrov, Georgi   11/96, 119—20, 122
Disher, M. Wilson   8/265
Disney, Walt   2/202; 12/9—10, 15
Disraeli, Benjamin   1/9, 10, 14, 16;
   5/15; 14/72—73
Diver, Maud   10/136
Dixon, Thomas   2/28
Dobrolyubov, Aleksandr M.   3/3—5
Doftman, Ariel   9/xii
Donato, Pietro di   10/361
Donne, John   6/231—32; 7/109, 134;
   8/22, 53, 95; 9/19; 10/72;
   11/90—91, 224; 14/151
Doob, L.W.   2/31
Dornbosh, Sanford   6/7
Doscher, Luelyne   The Significance of
   Audience Measurement in Motion
   Pictures   2/74—80; 2/83
Dostoevsky, Fyodor M.   4/viii, x; 5/99,
   101—02; 6/300, 304; 9/14; 10/151;
   11/233; 13/184
Douglas, J.D.   14/160—61
Douglas, Lloyd   12/38, 95, 127, 129,
   146
Douglas, Norman   10/139
Dowdey, Clifford   10/360
Doyle, Sir Arthur Conan   7/282;
   12/107, 113
Drayton, Michael   7/133—34
Dreiser, Theodore   7/4, 275; 10/151;
   11/45, 191; 12/128
Dryden, John   12/57; 13/99
Duccio di Buoninsegna   3/23
Duck, Donald   9/xii; 12/9
Dudintsev, Vladimir   11/269
Duffus, R.L.   12/45
Dumas fils, Alexandre   3/17—18
Dumazedier, Joffre   12/260
Duncan, Hugh D.   1/142; 6/xviii;
   14/188